SECURITY
SIMPLIFIED

Computer Internet Protection
for Beginners

Arshad Khan

Khan, Arshad
    Security Simplified/Computer Internet Security for Beginners
Arshad Khan. -- 1st ed.
    Includes index.
    ISBN: 0-9772838-6-0
    ISBN-13: 978-0-9772838-6-6

Khan Consulting and Publishing LLC
PO Box 700012
San Jose, CA 95170

www.khanbooks.com

TABLE OF CONTENTS

DISCLAIMER / WARNING

The author does not warrant the accuracy or completeness of the information, text, graphics, links or other items contained within this book. The author shall not be liable for any special, indirect, incidental, or consequential damages, including, without limitation, lost revenues or lost profits which may result from the use of these materials.

Before using any tool listed or described in this book, you must verify its current capabilities because it is common practice for software developers and vendors to periodically add/remove features and functions due to the need for implementing enhancements and bug fixes in reaction to the constantly changing security environment. Hence, before selecting and using such a tool you must verify its latest features, functions, effectiveness, and shortcomings directly from the vendor and/or various reputable review websites or forums. Similarly, before implementing any procedure described in the book, you should verify its applicability to your own computer and browser system.

You should only run tools if they are authorized, especially on networks where the owner's permission must be obtained before installing or running any software. Failure to obtain such permission can cause serious consequences such as termination of employment. You should also be aware that malicious copies of genuine anti-malware software are often available on the Internet and, hence, no software program obtained from an online source can be guaranteed to be safe.

P R E F A C E

Security Simplified: Computer Internet Protection for Beginners is an introductory book for novices and casual computer users with minimal technical knowledge. It targets those who want to protect their computers against malware attacks, prevent identity theft, protect personal and confidential data, increase productivity by reducing spam, secure their home wireless network, buy free security products, use review sources for selecting anti-malware tools, etc.

To follow this book, you are not required to be knowledgeable about or have a background in security. However, since this is a Windows-centric book, you must have the basic skills required for using a Windows-based computer—such as Windows menu and folder navigation, using a mouse, launching applications, web surfing, etc. The operating system primarily referenced in this book is Windows XP, not the earlier versions of Windows (Windows ME, NT, 2000, 9X, etc.). The primary browser covered in this book is Internet Explorer 6 (IE 6), currently the most widely-used browser. You should note that many of the IE 6 functions covered in *Security Simplified* can also be implemented on older IE versions through different menu paths or procedures.

Chapters 2-5 identify and describe various types of Internet-generated security threats including spyware, viruses, worms, adware, Trojan Horses, phishing and spam. Besides identifying their characteristics, they also describe various detection, prevention and removal techniques. Chapters 6-8 cover firewalls and various aspects of wireless networking.

Chapters 9-12 contain step-by-step instructions for securing the Internet Explorer's Internet, Trusted and Restricted security zones. Chapter 13 covers the basics of selecting anti-malware tools. It also provides a summarized list of security tools, including free ones, which can provide a fairly good level of protection. Chapters 14 and 15 identify security tools within various categories such as spyware, viruses and Trojans. Chapter 16 details tips and good practices which are grouped into various categories such as protecting the computer, protecting the browser, downloading, anonymous surfing, and other good habits and practices.

Computer and browser security is a dynamic area in which changes occur every day due to the steady introduction of new parasites that, in many cases, can render a previously effective tool practically useless. Therefore, you should not rely solely on the product information provided in *Security Simplified*, as the effectiveness of any tool cannot be guaranteed over time or against new threats.

The software product prices listed in *Security Simplified* may or may not reflect current list or street prices, which tend to fluctuate. You should also realize that web addresses (URLs) change over time. Therefore, it is possible that some of the numerous URLs listed in this book, last verified in December 2006, may not be valid when you try to visit them.

Besides using effective tools, it is imperative to keep yourself informed about emerging security threats, how they can be defeated, and new developments in this field. Resources that will help you to continue your education are included in the appendices, which contain listings of malware review sites and useful resources, additional protection tools, terminology, etc.

I would like to take this opportunity to thank the following individuals who reviewed the manuscript and provided invaluable feedback, advice and encouragement: Beth Katz, Roger Grimes, Zeeshan-ul-hassan Usmani, Mel Chua and Chris Anthony.

Arshad Khan

ACKNOWLEDGEMENT

Beth Katz
Roger A. Grimes
Zeeshan-ul-hassan Usmani
Mel Chua
Chris Anthony

Introduction

THE PROBLEM
Background
In the past two decades, the use of computers and the Internet has grown exponentially. The breadth of their application is mind-boggling. Their usage extends from a variety of applications used by individuals to diverse business applications in various industries such as communications, entertainment, retailing, business operations, medical, education, defense, investing, banking, etc. Many applications are mission critical. In such cases, the inability of computers or the Internet to operate as expected can cause severe consequences and losses. While reliability problems and breakdowns are expected during the operation of these and other non-critical tools, a different element is brought into play when they fail or do not operate as expected due to malicious and/or unauthorized acts.

What is malware and badware
Malware, which is synonymous with badware, is the slang term for malicious software. Malware is a generic term for software that, as per one definition, "fundamentally disregards a user's choice over how his or her computer will be used." It is designed with the specific objective of disrupting or damaging a computer system. It covers all types of undesirable applications including spyware, adware, Trojans, software that steals data, pop-up ads, system monitors, browser hijackers, etc. Some malware products are completely hidden, while others have a dual role—providing some overt functionality and also performing covert actions. The specifics of each malware type are described in depth in subsequent chapters.

Stealth mode

A common characteristic of malware is that it operates in stealth mode with little or no indication to the user. It is installed without the user being aware of it and tries to remain hidden in order to avoid detection and removal. While stealth is the preferred mode, some programs like adware, which launch pop-up ads, cannot remain hidden due to the interactive task that they have to perform with the user. A program is not bad just because it operates in stealth mode; many good and desirable programs perform in that mode. However, what can make such programs unacceptable is their operation without the user's consent.

Malware characteristics

Malware is characterized by deception, malicious intent and practices, annoying practices, and interference with the ability to uninstall the unwanted application. It often performs its actions, which can include transmission of personal information, drive-by downloading (software installation without permission), bombardment with pop-up ads, exposure to pornographic material, etc., without obtaining user consent.

Legitimate good software, whose features are described in Appendix C, avoids all the characteristics of bad software. It avoids prohibited content and behavior. It is clear and forthright about disclosures and obtains user consent. It enables easy deactivation, avoids bundling with other applications, and does not operate surreptitiously. It does not contain prohibited content like viruses, worms, unauthorized system monitors, etc.

Legitimate, useful software sometimes crosses the demarcation line between good and bad software. This can happen when it comes along with badware or malware, typically through bundling.

Classifying intruders

In general, intruders can be classified into four groups. The first group tries to break into a computer for non-destructive reasons which can include publicity, showing off hacking abilities and demonstrating computer or software vulnerabilities, etc. The second group is driven by the desire to reap financial benefits and tries to access or control the computer(s) in order to steal IDs and passwords, steal a user's identity (identity theft), monitor a user's activities, steal confidential data, perform fraud, obtain confidential information about an organization (corporate espionage), etc. The third group is driven by malice and destructive reasons. They prefer to take over a computer and then use it to execute certain actions on their behalf such as launching a concerted attack by a number of hijacked computers on a chosen target, performing illegal activities, disabling a computer or website, blackmailing, interrupting business operations, etc. The fourth group is driven by other motives such as monitoring spouses, suspected loved ones, etc.

Unexpected intruders

Malware is usually associated with shady organizations and crackers. However, even reputable household name companies have been associated with malware, such as Sony's BMG music division (*www.informationweek.com*, December 29, 2005). In 2005, it shipped music CDs that included XCP rootkit software. A rootkit is malicious software that is used to hack into a PC and gain administrative level access, which allows it to modify operating system functions. It can be used to monitor traffic and keystrokes, attack other computers, modify log files, etc. In the Sony case, a CD would operate normally when played on a standard CD player. However, when it was inserted in a computer, it surreptitiously installed software, which limited the number of copies that could be created and also prevented the transfer of music to music players like the iPod.

Sony's rootkit was not intentionally designed to be malware. However, it added additional vulnerabilities to the PCs on which it was installed and could be synergistically used by other malware programs with more evil intent. Sony was sued, fined and publicly embarrassed. The Sony rootkit incident ended up providing a warning and lesson to corporate America—not to install programs that the end-users did not know about or approve.

Malware motivation

The primary motivation for the creation and distribution of malware is financial gain. This can be manifested in different ways, including the following:

- Stealing of confidential and financial data (credit card numbers, bank account numbers, passwords, etc.)
- Access to valuable financial or marketing and sales data (such as sales, revenues, marketing lists, customer lists, etc.)
- Ad-based revenue and ads
- Revenue generation from redirecting users to websites
- Software bundling
- Pay-per-install revenue (where income is generated for each software download)

Any target, including individual users and businesses, that promises a potential direct or indirect financial benefit can expect to be targeted by malware. The financial gains for those who benefit from the installation of malware can be significant. The biggest beneficiaries are marketing companies, which can profit by collecting and selling personal data, displaying ads, tracking the browsing activities of users, and channeling/directing users to websites. The higher the number of computers installed with malware, the higher the profit its installer can generate. According to one estimate, malware business amounts to over $2 billion per year.

Seriousness of the problem

The problem has become more serious and widespread over the years. Recent virus and worm attacks have impacted millions of computers within a few days. In the past, the objective of most security breachers was to make some sort of a statement or tout their hacking skills. However, over time the motives have changed and they are now far more sinister and destructive. The methods employed, which are described in detail in subsequent chapters, have also expanded to include a variety of techniques and technologies. The problem is serious and cannot be ignored or taken lightly, even though some security companies have overblown some incidents and threats in order to create fear and serve their own benefit. However, prevention is not difficult if a few basic techniques, which are described in subsequent sections of this chapter, are implemented.

Experts, security vendors, operating system and browser vendors, anti-spyware forums, educational institutions, government agencies, concerned individuals and consumer groups are addressing the malware problem. However, so far the attempts to combat malware have not been systematic or concerted.

Role of the Internet

Before the Internet became popular, most infections were transmitted via floppy disks that were shared across computers by friends and/or co-workers. CDs, though they have also been a means of transmission, have never been a major or primary source of infections. Nowadays, the Internet has become the source of most computer security issues due to file sharing, music downloads, sneaky websites, online communications and collaboration (e-mail, chats, etc.), moving of applications from the desktop to the Internet, and networking.

A common misconception is that security is compromised only by inbound Internet traffic—data received from external sources via the Internet. However, security can also be compromised by outbound Internet traffic, also known as client-side attack. A computer user can send data to various Internet sites through file uploads, e-mails, filling out online forms, instant messages, etc. A stealth program installed by an intruder can also transmit data from the computer to the Internet. Therefore, even though the risk from external sources is considerably higher in most cases, appropriate measures are required to ensure adequate protection from both inbound and outbound traffic.

Despite the vulnerabilities and security issues, Internet access has become essential and indispensable for many users and its benefits far outweigh the risks. Therefore, the only realistic option for most users is to continue using the Internet, become aware of the risks, implement protective measures, and know what to do if their computers are compromised.

WHAT MALWARE CAN DO AND ITS WARNING SIGNS

Malware can be very obvious and it can also operate in stealth, which keeps the user in the dark. However, malware can be recognized through a number of common symptoms described in the following sections.

Interferes with user experience

Malware can annoy users in a number of ways. These include significantly impacting their ability to execute applications as expected, surf and enjoy what the Internet has to offer by bombarding them with pop-up ads, causing computer reliability problems, and also creating uncertainty and fear. It can also degrade user productivity.

Degrades computer and browser performance

Malware infection can cause degraded or sluggish computer or network performance. It can cause computer performance to degrade due to heavy consumption of resources (bandwidth, memory, CPU, and disk space). Malware can cause tasks to take longer to perform or complete, drain computer resources, and make the PC slower due to its need to hog resources for loading the bad software, displaying ads, tracking user actions, transmitting information (like user activity, screenshots, data, keystroke logs) and receiving information (like pop-ups), etc. It can also lead to sluggish browser performance and slow Internet access.

Monitors users and applications

Malware can monitor a computer's usage, applications, configuration and settings, vulnerabilities, stored data, etc. It can also monitor, record, and transmit users' online as well as offline activities to those controlling the program, its developers, installers, third-parties, and other computers or locations. The malware can record keystrokes and capture screenshots. It can transmit a wide variety of data including confidential and financial data (such as passwords, user IDs, bank and credit card numbers), individual files and documents, web surfing habits, and shopping preferences. The consequences can vary considerably, with annoying pop-ups at one extreme. At the other extreme, consequences can include identity theft and exposure to financial risk. For businesses, corporate assets can be compromised and trade secrets can be lost.

Invades privacy

Violating the privacy of a user or an organization is one of the worst characteristics of malware. The data captured and transmitted by an invading program without the expressed consent of the owner or user can range from simple browsing habits to confidential and sensitive data. Such programs should be differentiated from legitimately installed programs and cookies that monitor a user only after permission has been granted.

Generates pop-ups

The appearance of pop-up ads if they were previously absent, or an increase, is a good indicator of malware. An even stronger indicator is the sudden appearance of multiple pop-ups across multiple websites that did not previously load pop-up ads. Pop-ups ads can appear when a hyperlink, button, or graphic is clicked. Such ads can be legitimate if the user previously provided consent and, hence, cannot be considered malware. However, if a user tries to leave a website or quit/start an application and is bombarded by unsolicited ads, it indicates malware is at work. An even stronger indication of malware infection is when pop-ups start to appear when the computer is not even connected to the Internet or they address the user by name.

Hijacks browser home page

Malware infection is indicated if the browser's default home page is hijacked, i.e., it changes without any input from the user. Even if the user changes the home page back to its original state, it reverts back to the home page set by the malware. A browser home page is hijacked in order to direct the user to a particular website that stands to benefit from user visits. Visitors to such sites may be exposed to ads and induced to buy certain products, reveal personal information, etc.

Malware is also indicated if the user changes the home page to a particular website and it inexplicably changes itself to another website. It is also indicated if the browser preferences are modified without the user's knowledge or permission. In some cases, the browser settings/preferences are modified in such a way that the user is unable to restore the default settings.

Adds a new browser toolbar

If the existing browser toolbar does not work as expected or a new/different toolbar appears on the browser, even though it was not requested, it can be assumed that malware infection has occurred. Many of these toolbars hijack search results and direct the user to pay-per-click sites or other sites that install spyware via drive-by downloads. Typically, attempts to remove such toolbars fail or, if they are successful, the toolbars get re-installed after they are removed.

Redirects browser

Another malware sign is the redirecting of the web browser to a website that was not requested by the user. For example, if a user types *www.yahoo.com* in the browser's address line, an unfamiliar website is displayed instead of the Yahoo website. Typically, such websites attempt to handle the search function, which they manipulate in order to direct users to specific websites. Another sign is when a requested URL is not found and a different error page is displayed by the error page hijacker.

Adds unfamiliar website to favorites

If an unfamiliar website address is added to the list of browser favorites without any input from the user, it is another sign that malware has been installed. Often new items are added, especially those associated with gambling and porn sites. In some cases, even after they are deleted, these URLs are added back to the favorites by the malware.

Changes configuration

Malware often modifies computer and/or browser configuration without user input or permission. In many cases, the changed settings cannot be reversed.

Changes directories and/or system files

It is possible for an installation program to deliberately hide folders using undisplayable characters, such as the key combination ALT 255, which produces a new folder with a "blank" name. Such folders can be difficult to spot. The appearance of new directories, folders and/or files on the computer should be a warning sign. Such changes are normal when some software application is installed on the system. However, if no new software has been installed and such changes are observed, they should be immediately investigated.

Generates unexpected messages

The appearance of strange and unexpected messages is another sign that malware may be at work. However, it is possible that some messages may be generated by legitimately-installed software.

Skyrockets phone bills

If the phone bill skyrockets due to calls to unfamiliar numbers at very high rates, it could indicate that a special type of malware called a dialer has been installed. A dialer is a program which uses a computer modem to access services or make calls by changing the dial-up settings without the user's knowledge. The connections are typically made to 900, long-distance, or international numbers at outrageous rates, which lead to extremely high phone bills.

Causes modem to become busy unexpectedly

If the user is working offline and the send/receive lights on the modem (dial-up, cable or DSL) flash rapidly, which typically occurs during web surfing and downloading, it could indicate that malware is receiving/transmitting information. Another similar warning sign is the rapid flashing of the system tray modem icon when the user is not connected to the Internet.

Deactivates anti-malware software

In some cases, malware interferes with anti-spyware or anti-virus software. Actions it can take include turning it off, making it malfunction, or prevent it from working as expected.

Changes equipment behavior

Malware can lead to loss of user control, changed computer behavior, computer or system instability, frequent or unexplained computer crashes (shutdown), and the mouse moving and selecting items without the user's input or control. The instability can last even after the malware is removed.

Resists removal

Malware programs often resist removal. Some programs either resist removal or re-install themselves after they are removed. Some programs, like Newdotnet, disable a PC or its network access if the user tries to remove it. The programs that are determined to stay on typically lack an uninstall feature or do not register with the *Windows Add/Remove Programs* list. Some programs can be easily removed using the Windows uninstall program, while others need to be removed via the relatively more tedious manual method using the Windows Control Panel.

Causes memory or disc space problems

If the computer experiences memory problems or it runs out of disk space, there is a good chance that malware may not be responsible. For example, these problems can be caused due to the loading of a memory-intensive application, which can also consume disk space. For many computers, the heavy memory resource requirement may not be as issue. However, for some computers running at their resource limits before the installation, the newly-installed software can cause problems. In such cases, upgrading the memory or disk capacity can solve the problem.

Attacks websites

Some types of malware can initiate a coordinated attack on a computer or website with the objective of incapacitating it. The technique, called denial-of-service (DoS), involves initiating a simultaneous attack using thousands of hijacked computers (called zombies). The target is unable to handle the huge volume of data requests that it has to deal with in such cases and, consequently, is made ineffective and useless.

Acts silently and provides no clues

Successful malware will show no signs of infection at all. On a system that exhibits no symptoms of malware, everything appears to be normal. However, such malware is the most dangerous as it works in stealth mode and transmits data without the user having any idea about what is going on. Hence, the user on such a computer is complacent and takes no action while the damage is being inflicted. In such cases, the damage can continue for lengthy periods with associated financial and other consequences.

MALWARE INSTALLATION

Malware is installed through a variety of methods, typically without the user being aware of it. The following sections describe the most commonly-used methods for installing malware.

ActiveX controls

ActiveX is a programming framework, not a programming language, which was developed to basically allow any other program written in nearly any other language to be distributed over the Internet using Internet Explorer (IE). ActiveX programs are called ActiveX controls. They provide a useful function that makes surfing more versatile and enjoyable. ActiveX enables software to be run directly within the web browser. Malware can be transmitted through ActiveX controls conveyed over pop-up windows. This is one of the most popular methods for spyware installation.

Accepting an EULA

The End User License Agreement (EULA) is an agreement, a legally binding contract, between the software developer/vendor and the user, which specifies the parameters and conditions under which the application can be used. Malware is downloaded or activated when a user accepts an EULA for software that is linked to a spyware source, without being aware of the association.

Web browsing

When a user visits an unscrupulous website, it downloads malware using drive-by download or some other technique, without the user's knowledge or permission. Even a single click on such a website can be sufficient to trigger the malware installation.

Downloading

Malware can be installed when freeware and/or shareware applications such as music and games are downloaded. When a user downloads a file or program, an additional undesirable and bundled program is also downloaded without the user's knowledge or permission.

Hacking

Crackers and hackers break into the computer and install the malware program(s).

Peer-to-peer file sharing

Sharing or swapping music, photos, and other types of files using peer-to-peer (P2P) applications such as Napster and Kazaa is one of the most common methods for the installation of malware.

Bundling

When a program is installed, it can be packaged or bundled with other programs whose existence may be disclosed somewhere in the EULA and, hence, the user may be unaware of it. Adware is frequently installed using this method.

Pop-up ads

To exit and close an annoying pop-up, users try a few techniques, depending on what is displayed on the window. Any technique, such as clicking on the *No* button or "x" (exit/close) can be sufficient to download and install malware.

e-mail or e-mail attachments

Simply opening an e-mail can cause malware to be installed. Opening an e-mail attachment can install various types of malware including viruses and spyware.

Deception

Deception, which can manifest in various ways, is often used to install malware. Some applications pretend to be anti-malware prevention or removal tools, even though they are malware themselves. Some companies use deceptive practices, such as initially hijacking web browsers and changing computer settings, and subsequently scare consumers into buying their products. Some anti-malware products have been known to "detect" malware even when it did not exist on the computer.

Other methods

These include clicking on embedded hyperlinks or downloading attached files during instant messaging (IM) chats, other computer users whose behavior is more risky, and a stealth method used by hackers and crackers that utilizes the Back Orifice Resource Kit rootkit program. More information about this program, which has not been commonly used in the past three years or so, can be obtained from the Anti-Hackers Toolkit. A recent addition to the common sources of malware is the interaction that takes place between MySpace users.

TYPES OF MALWARE THREATS

Computer and Internet users face a wide variety of threats. The nature of these threats, their operating mode, and potential impact on systems and users vary considerably. Therefore, every user needs to be aware of them, know how to take preventive steps, and also know how to deal with infections when they occur.

Most widespread threats

The following is a listing of the most common and serious threats. Each of these five threats is described comprehensively in subsequent chapters:

- Spyware: Spyware is a covert software program. It scans or monitors activities on an online or offline computer or system and, subsequently, transmits the gathered information to other computers or locations on the Internet.
- Viruses: A computer virus is a program that spreads itself by infecting executable files and/or computer system areas and, subsequently, replicates (makes copies of itself).

- Worms: A worm is a computer program, similar to a virus, which self-replicates. In contrast to a virus, which requires an infected host file to spread it, a worm does not need other programs or documents in order to spread.
- Adware: Adware is an advertising-supported software application, the most common form of malware, which displays advertisements on a computer.
- Trojan Horses: A Trojan Horse program is a non-replicating malicious computer program, which appears harmless but can perform a number of harmful actions.

Other common threats

Nuisance or joke programs

These are relatively harmless, though annoying, programs that do not attempt to gather or transmit information. Instead, they tend to modify the behavior of the computer or application through distraction or nuisance. For example, a program will re-open a window repeatedly when an attempt is made to close it. In some cases, a pop-up will repeatedly ask the same question like "Do you really want to quit?" In such cases, the user is frequently forced to reboot the computer. Many of these programs are based on jokes.

Hacking tools

These programs are used by crackers, hackers and unauthorized users to gain access and control of a computer or network, using various techniques for bypassing the computer and/or network security. After a computer is compromised, the intrusion tool transmits information from the hacked machine to other computer(s) managed by the hacker. In some cases, crackers use such computers to implement coordinated attacks on other computers or networks.

Denial-of-service (DoS)

The objective of a denial-of-service attack is to target a computer or website with data requests in a concerted effort in order to make it non-operational. A single computer can be used to implement a DoS attack. In a distributed denial-of-service (DDoS) attack, multiple distributed computers are used to launch the attack. These attacks make the target computer so busy that it becomes practically incapable of usage by its genuine user. For this purpose, crackers typically pre-install a spying agent, a Trojan Horse program, on a large number of computers. Based on a triggering instruction from the cracker, all the compromised computers launch a simultaneous attack on the target, which is overwhelmed by the data it has to receive/send to thousands of computers.

Trackware programs

Trackware programs monitor the activities of the user and the system. The information collected, such as websites visited by the user, is then transmitted to third-parties. Many of these programs, such as tracking cookies, are installed with the consent of the users. They are often packaged and installed along with other software. These programs are passive and typically do not collect personally identifiable or confidential information.

Data miner

In contrast to passive trackware programs, data miners actively collect information about the user, such as consumer behavior, which is typically transmitted to the program installer. This is increasingly being used by market research agencies and for targeted marketing. While data collection can be a legitimate activity, it should be disclosed to the user through a clearly stated privacy policy.

System monitor

A system monitor is a tracking program that monitors computer activity such as computer usage, keystrokes, user names, passwords, instant messages, e-mails, chats, websites visited, personal information, etc. Based on the information transmitted to the program installer, ads or other information may be sent back to the user.

Keylogger

A keylogger is a program that surreptitiously records a user's individual keystrokes and then transmits them to the installer. It has the ability to record e-mails, login IDs, passwords, chats, instant messages, etc. Using keyloggers, the program installer can access confidential data and information. A new type of "keylogger," that records mouse clicks, has been developed.

Home page hijacker

Browser hijackers change the browser's settings without the user's authorization. They are capable of changing the default home page, modifying browser settings, redirecting web searches (to pay-per-search websites), redirecting to a non-default error page when an incorrect/non-existent URL is typed, etc.

Mobile code

Browsers execute mobile code (Java/JavaScript/ActiveX), which are programming languages/framework used by web developers. The code has the potential to be used for gathering information, such as websites visited, or executing malicious code. Java, JavaScript and ActiveX can be disabled by modifying browser settings, which are described in a subsequent chapter. However, most users do not know how to modify these settings.

Browser Helper Object

A Browser Helper Object (BHO) is a plug-in for the Internet Explorer browser, which is designed to provide added functionality. It can be used to search pages viewed in the browser, replace banner ads with targeted advertisements, add a toolbar, monitor user actions, change home pages, etc.

Remote Access Trojan

A Remote Access Trojan (RAT) program provides a cracker control over a compromised computer, just like the genuine user, which can then be used for practically any purpose.

Bots

Derived from the word "robot," this is a type of malware. Bots are automated software programs that operate as an agent and can execute certain commands when they receive a specific input. The Bots attacker can use it to gain complete control over the affected computers, which can then be used to execute DoS attacks against websites, send spam, etc.

Specific actions of some malware applications

Malware applications perform a wide range of actions. Some of these are indicated in the following sections, which describe the features of some recent and widespread malware applications.

CoolWebSearch

CoolWebSearch is an infamous browser hijacker that comes in many variants. The variants redirect users to coolwebsearch.com and associated websites. They are also capable of modifying the browser's home page and Internet Explorer settings, as well as hijacking web searches. They are known to install by exploiting security flaws as well as malicious HTML applications.

GAIN

Gator Advertising Information Network (GAIN) is an adware that downloads and displays advertisements. It specializes in targeted advertising, based on a user's web surfing habits, in return for free services. The software tracks every website visited by the user, based upon which it starts to pop-up ads. It is usually bundled with many free software programs, including Kazaa, the well-known file-sharing program. The program has many versions, which are covered by different privacy policies. It also has spyware characteristics including drive-by downloading, which causes an ActiveX dialog to pop-up that starts the installation process if "Yes" is clicked. Applications from GAIN include eWallet, WeatherScope, and DataManager.

ISTbar / Aupdate

ISTbar is an Internet Explorer toolbar that is installed through drive-by downloads, using ActiveX. This is a direct-marketing adware application that often comes bundled with another program. It is also known as DownloadPlus and SearchBarCash-Hijacker. The adware component, besides installing the IE toolbar, also hijacks home page and Internet searches. The toolbar has links to various pornographic websites. It is used for searching pornographic websites and displaying pop-up ads. The IST.XXX Toolbar is a variant based around pornography. A variant of this malware is known to initiate an error and an ActiveX download. If permission is refused, it continues to re-try.

NetOptimizer

NetOptimizer is an adware application that downloads and displays advertisements. It hijacks the browser error page and redirects users to its own server. It uses pop-up windows to display ads from its own network sites and is also known to update itself.

TIBS

TIBS is a dialer program that can hijack a modem and surreptitiously change the dialup connection settings. Consequently, instead of the ISP being dialed, the computer ends up calling a 900, international, or long-distance number, which leads a very inflated phone bill. Most of the sites called by such methods are access-paid adult pornographic websites.

BlazeFind

BlazeFind is an adware program that redirects search queries and displays ads. It also changes default home pages to its own website, *www.blazefind.com*, as well as other Internet Explorer settings. It is installed as a Browser Help Object.

180Search Assistant

180Search Assistant is an adware program, often bundled, which pops-up targeted ads. It monitors the content of active web browser windows. Based on its monitoring results (search keywords, shopping windows, etc.), it opens up related web pages of associated websites in separate browser windows. The program transmits logs of the websites that a user visits. Since the program is often installed with other adware, it can cause computer performance issues.

Advanced Keylogger

Advanced Keylogger is spyware program designed to monitor the activity of computer users. It has the ability to monitor and record keyboard keystrokes and clipboard contents. It can capture screenshots, passwords and login IDs. The information monitored is saved in the form of a log, which is then transmitted to the program installer. Due to it being sold as a commercial product, many anti-virus software products cannot detect it.

myDoom

myDoom is a mass-mailing worm that spread from computer to computer, via e-mails and other means, by replicating (copying) itself onto a targeted computer. It used a deceptive technique, spoofing (faking) the sender name in its messages, which fooled most users and consequently led to its widespread propagation that wreaked havoc across the Internet. It also spread through the Kazaa file-sharing program. The myDoom program provided remote users with the ability to access and manipulate infected computers, through a backdoor component, by opening ports 3127 to 3198.

Acropolis

Acropolis is a Trojan horse program that permits an infected computer to be controlled remotely by opening a network connection for ports 32791 and 45673.

ComputerSpy

ComputerSpy is a monitoring program that records every keystroke on a computer where it has been installed. The information captured is discreetly transmitted to the installer on a pre-determined schedule, via the Internet, to a server where it can be accessed from any computer at any time.

Malware listings

Appendix E provides a few examples of malware products in various categories. For a very comprehensive list of malware, visit the SpywareGuide.com website (*www.spyware-guide.com/product_list_full.php*). This site, besides providing a comprehensive inventory of over 2,000 malware products, also lists the removal tools that can be used to combat those parasites. Symantec also provides a list of the latest malware threats, along with their risk rating and removal tools, on its website *(http://securityresponse.symantec.com/avcenter/vinfodb.html)*. PC Tools is another source that maintains a comprehensive database of malware products *(www.pctools.com/mrc/infections/)*.

DAMAGE AND RISK ASSESSMENT
Differentiating and rating security risks

The impact of malware varies considerably as it ranges from nuisance, exemplified by irritating pop-up ads that interfere with user experience, to serious security issues like identity theft and computer hijacking. While one can live with interruptions caused by pop-ups, there is no choice except to take immediate action when sensitive and confidential data is involved. Therefore, a distinction needs to be made between serious and non-serious risks, because the urgency with which a problem is addressed should depend on the risk level involved.

Risks should be classified based on the threat's potential impact on the computer and/or user. The impact can be in the area of performance, privacy, stealth, and ease of removal. Due to their security risk, some programs such as spyware should be removed as soon as they are discovered. Others can be tackled as non-critical tasks. By categorizing various threats based on their ability to cause damage, more resources and efforts can be used to neutralize the most dangerous ones.

To determine the risk level of a known security threat, some companies have developed classification systems. For example, Symantec's risk classification system for rating adware and related applications can help decide which applications should be retained or removed from the computer *(www.symantec.com)*. Its classifications include high, medium, and low. Depending on the risk rating, a specific recommendation is provided on how to handle the threat. Another example of the quantification of the risk level associated with a threat is the SG Index *(www.spywareguide.com)*. It uses a scale of 1-10, where level 1 is a minor annoyance and level 10 indicates that the threat is extremely dangerous.

Damage that malware can inflict

Malware's main targets are software programs as well as associated data. It usually aims to obtain information, which can then be exploited in a number of ways, or influence user/computer behavior. Some malware also aims to delete certain types of files though this rarely occurs. For example, the Mydoom worm searched for Word, Excel, and graphics files and then deleted them randomly. However, it is very rare for malware to target and damage hardware such as disk drives, monitors, and other types of peripherals.

A malware item unleashed on the Internet can impact millions of computers and wreak havoc. The Melissa virus forced many large companies, including Microsoft, to turn off their e-mail systems until it could be contained. It has been estimated that the Mydoom worm infected about a quarter of a million computers in one day. In recent years, some of the attacks have cost millions of dollars and thousands of man-hours. The loss of productivity can be significant. Some companies have had their operations shut down, causing them to lose valuable revenue. The costs associated with cleanups after an infection can be staggering.

According to informationweek.com, July 10, 2006, the following is a list of the worst ten malware items, along with the damage they caused:

- CIH: $20-80 million
- Melissa: $300-600 million
- ILOVEYOU: $10-15 billion
- Code Red: $2.6 billion
- SQL Slammer: Hit 500,000 servers worldwide and infected 75,000 computers in ten minutes
- Blaster: $2-10 billion
- Sobig.F: $5-10 billion (generated a million copies in the first 24 hours)
- Bagle: Tens of millions of dollars
- myDoom: Slowed global Internet performance by 10% and web load times 50%
- Sasser: Tens of millions of dollars

PREVENTING MALWARE INFECTIONS

Prevention is better than cure and, therefore, you should take protective steps that can reduce the risk of malware infections. You must always avoid the risky behaviors that are described in this section and elsewhere in this book. Keep in mind that the odds of getting infected by malware decrease considerably when multiple precautions are taken. The following are the most effective steps that should be implemented in order to protect your computer and avoid malware infections.

Keep software up-to-date

The Windows operating system should be kept up-to-date and protected with the latest patches that Microsoft provides regularly. The patches, which ensure that bugs and vulnerabilities are fixed, can be downloaded at Microsoft.com (*www.microsoft.com/ downloads*). Since new threats appear regularly, periodically check to ensure that the system protection is up-to-date. It is possible to customize Windows so that automatic updates are turned on. However, this can potentially cause problems as patches are sometimes reissued. Using manual patching provides an opportunity to evaluate the patches before applying them.

The applications on your computer should also be patched if their patches are available. Patch commonly used applications such as MS-Office, Macromedia Flash, Adobe Acrobat Reader, RealPlayer, etc.

Install a firewall

Install a firewall that can protect your computer from intruders and also prevent any personal and confidential data and information from being transmitted from your PC to other computers connected via the Internet.

Install anti-malware software

Install anti-malware software and keep it up-to-date by installing updates and patches regularly. There are primarily two options for providing comprehensive protection. The first option involves installing a comprehensive security suite, which is a single software program that includes many components such as anti-spyware, anti-virus, anti-spam, firewall, etc.

The second option is to use multiple standalone programs. In this case, the programs to be installed can include anti-virus, anti-spyware, anti-spam, firewall, anti-adware, privacy, pop-up filters, etc., depending on the level of desired protection. This option makes it possible to get the best of breed applications, though the overall cost is higher due to the greater number of applications.

Protect the e-mail system

Viruses and worms have frequently exploited the security weaknesses of e-mail clients. Any security vulnerability of the e-mail client should be plugged and any available patches should be applied. Practice safe behavior pertaining to receiving e-mails. Avoid opening e-mails or attachments and do not click on links embedded in e-mails, especially from unknown senders.

Protect your browser

The browser should be kept up-to-date, locked down, and customized to kill pop-up windows. To ensure that the system cannot automatically download and run malicious code, configure the browser so that a prompt is displayed if an application attempts to install itself. The step-by-step procedures for securing browsers are described in Chapters 9-12. As a precaution, when browsing, do not click "OK," "Yes," or "Run This Program" prompts unless their implications are fully understood

Download with care

You should download only from trusted sources. Before downloading, read the EULA and Privacy Policies carefully and understand their implications. Typically, words like third-party or ad-supported software in the EULA should be a warning as they indicate that software from other companies will also be downloaded. Avoid downloads, especially free ones or from unknown sites that you cannot trust.

Learn how to handle attachments

Never double-click an executable attachment, such as those that have an .exe or .com extension, if it is received via e-mail. If such an infected file is executed, it has the potential to create serious problems.

Practice safe online behavior

Be careful and follow good computing safety habits, especially pertaining to online behavior. Avoid risky behavior such as visiting untrustworthy websites, downloading shareware and freeware, clicking on embedded hyperlinks in IMs, visiting websites in response to phishing e-mails, etc.

Use strong passwords

Use strong passwords, preferably eight characters or longer, which contain characters and numbers. Do not share passwords between websites or with others. Change your passwords at regular intervals.

Learn how to handle pop-ups

Do not click on links within pop-up ads. When closing a pop-up window, use the "x" on the window title bar, not the "Close" link or button. Avoid clicking on "Yes" when dialog windows pop-up and ask for permission to initiate some action (especially a download).

Enable macro virus protection

The macro virus protection of all Microsoft applications should be enabled. Do not permit macros to run if prompted to run them, unless their purpose and function is known. In MS-Word, to access the macro virus protection feature, navigate via the Tools menu option.

Educate yourself

Keep yourself informed about current threats, tricks and techniques used by malware pushers, and new developments in this field. For this purpose, you can use the resources listed in the Appendices. Share your knowledge with others.

Use an alternative OS and/or browser

If you are too worried about the safety of the Windows operating system, the alternatives include Unix and Linux. The problem with these operating systems is that they may be unable to support all the Windows software applications that are currently being used or may be needed. Also, despite the commonly-held belief, these systems are not hacker-proof. Their vulnerability can also increase if they are not patched.

A browser replacement option is Firefox. An even better option is to use the Vista operating system, which includes Internet Explorer 7—a far more secure browser than its predecessor (Internet Explorer 6).

REMOVING MALWARE
Removal methods

The range of actions implemented by malware varies significantly. In Windows alone, there are over a hundred locations where malware can hide and launch from. The listing of these locations, compiled by Roger Grimes, is available at:

http://weblog.infoworld.com/securityadviser/archives/2006/05/where_windows_m.html

In extreme cases, malware can make changes that can effectively prevent the user from reversing the changes or controlling his own computer. Consequently, the changes required to undo the effects of malware vary significantly. For example, malware can be removed using a variety of techniques including the following well-known methods:

- Using an anti-malware program (such as anti-spyware or anti-virus program)
- Using an application's uninstall program
- Performing a manual uninstall using the Windows Control Panel (*Windows > Settings > Control Panel > Add/Remove Programs*)
- Deleting files or folders manually
- Reversing the browser options
- Editing the Windows registry
- Reformatting the hard disk
- Other actions that only an experienced computer professional can perform

More details about how to prevent and remove specific malware, such as spyware and viruses, are covered in subsequent chapters.

Anti-malware software tools
The challenge

Software may or may not be classified malware, depending on who is pronouncing judgment. For example, specific pop-up ads may or may not be considered malware. The user may consider it malware but the adware developer may not because the user agreed to it when accepting the EULA. Also, software acceptable at home may be unacceptable at work or in a networked environment. Similarly, software objectionable to some users, such as adult content, may be acceptable to others. Hence, any software developed to fight and block malware has to be flexible enough to meet diverse and conflicting demands.

Therefore, the challenge is to provide a flexible malware control mechanism, in an extremely diverse environment, that can prevents malware from being disruptive and yet does not prevent users from doing what they want to do. Anti-malware software should enable users to make an informed choice that is suitable and secure for themselves, their family, their employers, and society.

Tools required

Many anti-malware tools are available for fighting different types of threats. Some tools target specific threats, while others are broader in their approach and aim to neutralize many types of malware. A combination of tools may be needed to prevent and/or remove different types of malware, which are installed and propagated using different methods and techniques. For example, spyware tries to remain hidden while adware is very intrusive and obvious. While an anti-spyware program may be effective against spyware, an anti-virus tool may be ineffective in detecting, preventing or removing spyware.

Ineffective and fake anti-malware tools

There are two issues with anti-malware software packages. First, some of them are of inferior quality and do not provide the necessary protection, which can mislead the user into complacency and a false sense of security. Second, some products labeled as anti-spyware or anti-virus software programs are phony and very dangerous because they actually install malware on the computer. Therefore, be careful when picking a product for protection.

A valuable source for virus product information is the Virus Bulletin (*www.virusbtn.com/vb100/index*), which carries out independent comparative testing of anti-virus products. Its VB100% award is given to a product that detects all *in the wild* viruses (uncontained viruses that continue to infect computers) during both on-demand and on-access scanning. Such a tool should also generate no false positives when scanning a set of clean files.

USER INVOLVEMENT
Malware education

Computer users need to be proactive in protecting themselves from malware and share their knowledge with others. Despite the fact that efforts to educate computer users have been limited and non-systematic, users interested in learning about malware can draw from a wide variety of very informative and useful sources. They need to be informed and educated about various threats and security risks so that they can prevent the installation of malware and also be in a position to take effective steps when prevention fails. They should constantly update their knowledge.

Two good starting points for malware education are *www.stopbadware.org* and CERT (*www.cert.org*). Stopbadware.org is a non-profit organization whose aim is to fight malware. It provides reliable and objective information about the malware threat to consumers. CERT is an Internet security expertise center, a federally-funded R&D center operated by Carnegie Mellon University. A number of resources are listed in the Appendices, which can be used to educate users about existing and new threats, preventing and/or removing infections, comparing and selecting protection tools, etc.

How users can help

Combating malware in order to stop its spread on the Internet requires cooperation by consumers, who can help in a number of ways. Users should educate family members, friends and colleagues about the malware problem. They should visit well-known security sites and become aware of the latest issues and trends. Also, whenever possible, they should share their experiences with Internet sites, anti-spyware forums and sites like *www.spywareinfo.com*, and consumer groups that provide education about this problem.

Consumers should also complain about problems to relevant organizations such as malware monitoring sites like Stopbadware.org and the FTC. The Federal Trade Commission (FTC) handles complaints about deceptive and/or unfair business practices. The filing process is easy and can be initiated at *www.ftc.gov/*. The FTC can also be reached at (877) FTC-HELP or at:

Federal Trade Commission
CRC-240
Washington, D.C. 20580

Complaints against a company located in another country can be filed at
www.econsumer.gov/.

MALWARE AND KIDS
The top targets of spyware

Older children and teenagers, who often surf the Internet for hours and download/
exchange a large number of files, are often the targets of spyware and adware. Many
of the sites they visit seem harmless but are actually quite dangerous due to their
spyware installation practices. In particular, peer-to-peer file sharing services are a common source of infections because teenagers share files very heavily and, hence, spread
infections quickly and widely around the networks they patronize. Most users, and
especially teenagers, cannot resist the attraction offered by free goodies and thus expose
themselves to unscrupulous spyware installing sites.

High-risk sources for children

The risks and the types of infections that children are exposed during web surfing are
the same as those faced by adults. However, the following are the most common sources
of infections for children:

- e-mail attachments and links
- P2P file sharing
- Music and other downloads
- Web browsing
- Instant Messaging (IMs)
- Shareware and freeware
- Responding to free online offers

Among the most common sources of pop-up ads and spyware for children are free
peer-to-peer file sharing software, such as:

- GAIN carriers: Some of the bundled software that it installs includes a search
  engine toolbar, screen saver, weather forecaster, etc. GAIN is often bundled with
  free P2P software.
- Kazaa, Ares, Bearshare, Morpheus, iMesh and other P2P programs
- Zango games: Installs adware with games created by 180Solutions

- Lyric sites: Some lyric sites insist on the download of ActiveX controls, which become the source of unwanted adware, even though it is not required for the music
- Illegal music download sites

Some of these companies disclose the existence of adware in their lengthy EULA, during their installation, which hardly anyone reads completely or understands its implications (when they agree to the terms and conditions). In such cases, even though it creates problems for the users, the installation is legal.

Laws to protect children

According to the law, Children's Online Privacy Protection Act (COPPA), children under 13 are legally treated differently than older children. Such children cannot be asked to disclose any personal information. However, that still leaves a very large percentage of children who use the Internet extensively vulnerable to exploitation by spyware and adware vendors.

Teaching and monitoring kids

The first step should be teaching kids basic rules and how to be responsible. Next, they should be taught how to be cautious and make informed decisions. Children should be taught how to avoid peer pressure that can lead them to actions, such as downloading a popular song or visiting a website, which they will later regret when malware creates problems for them. They should be taught the basic techniques for preventing infections and reducing their vulnerability. However, this should be done in conjunction with steps that you should take yourself to protect their computer, so that their mistakes or irresponsible behavior do not compromise their PC.

Depending on the access level and safety that needs to be provided, based on the child's age and responsible behavior (or lack of), you can place restrictions on the websites that they can visit. For example, you can specify that they can only visit the websites in the favorites list or on the desktop shortcuts. To ensure greater protection and control, install a web-filtering software program that will prevent access to dangerous and/or undesirable websites. Some of the filtering programs that can be used include:

- Net Nanny (*www.netnanny.com*)
- ContentProtect (*www.contentwatch.com/products/contentprotect.php*)
- CYBERSitter (*www.cybersitter.com*)
- Cyber Patrol (*www.cyberpatrol.com*)
- Cyber Sentinel (*www.cybersentinel.com*)

- Cyber Snoop *(www.pearlsw.com/products/cyberSnoop/index.html)*
- FilterPak *(www.familyisafety.com/filters/fiss4f.htm)*
- BSafe *(www.bsafe.com)*
- McAfee Parental Controls *(www.mcafee.com/us)*
- Norton Parental Controls *(www.symantec.com)*

CHAPTER TWO

Spyware

UNDERSTANDING SPYWARE
What is spyware

Spyware, a specific type of malware, is a covert software program that scans or monitors activities on a computer or system, online or offline, and then transmits the gathered information to other computers or locations on the Internet. This information is usually collected and transmitted to third-parties, often with malicious intent, without the user's knowledge or consent. Spyware can also make changes to the computer on which it is installed. Among the various types of malware, spyware is one of the worst offenders.

Spyware, which is a fast-growing menace that is a serious security and privacy risk, is marked by deception, which can be manifest in various ways. Most spyware products are completely hidden and actively attempt to remain hidden. Others have a dual role—providing some overt functionality and also performing covert actions. Spyware is difficult to detect. Some spyware programs are characterized by obvious and easily-recognizable signs, which were listed in Chapter 1. However, others do not exhibit any visible signs of infection. Most computer users do not have the technical skills to remove such infections.

All Internet users are susceptible to spyware infection, though standalone computers can also be infected through non-Internet sources. It has been estimated that the vast majority of computers connected to the Internet are infected by spyware. According to informationweek.com (March 27, 2006):

- Spyware infected 81% of consumer PCs in 2005
- Spyware was reported by 80% of respondents in an FBI survey of 2066 companies
- An average company spends more than $1.5 million per year getting rid of spyware
- Anti-spyware sales were estimated to be $214 million in 2006, with the estimate of spending in 2010 rising to approximately $1.4 billion

Businesses are also impacted by spyware, which is one of their primary security threats. Most corporate computers also have spyware, adware, or other undesirable programs installed on them. For example, according to a recent survey by Forrester Research, 55% of IT executives say they are concerned about spyware as a prime security threat, while the percentage for viruses and worms is 73%. Their concern is justified as spyware can lead to significant financial losses for both individuals and businesses.

What spyware can do

Spyware can collect and transmit a wide variety of information to the attacker controlling the program. It can lead to a number of problems including, but not limited to, those described in Chapter I. A single successful attack can impact millions of users. For example, according to InfoWorld (July 17, 2005), "a hacker was able to access potentially 40 million credit card numbers by infiltrating the network of a company that processed payment data for MasterCard International and other companies."

All spyware programs do not present the same level of danger and risk to the user. At one extreme are benign tracking cookies. The actions of some spyware applications are simply annoying. However, some types of spyware represent a serious financial risk due to their ability to steal personal and confidential information, while others can degrade computer performance by impacting its stability and speed. To determine how dangerous a particular spyware program is, check its ratings at websites such as *www.symantec.com* and *www.spywareguide.com*, which categorize various threats based on their risk.

Is all spyware bad

A commonly-held view is that any software installed without permission is unacceptable. Even if a user has granted permission to install a product, it is not acceptable for the software to do something that is not within that user's understanding. It is also not acceptable for a program to hide its true intent in the middle of boring legalese displayed in a EULA.

Some spyware software that is installed does provide some benefits. For example, a user's online activities can be monitored and used to target ads or steer the user to websites that can provide goods or services that he desires or can benefit from. There is obviously a trade-off that is acceptable provided the user has consented to it. However, it should be noted that once permission is granted, covert software cannot be called spyware.

Will spyware go away

The spyware problem is serious. It is not a fad and is here to stay because it has developed on the foundation of financial benefits for those who develop and use it. It is expected that laws will be promulgated to discourage some types of spyware that cross the limits of legal behavior. Also, we can expect the problem to be addressed more systematically by security vendors, anti-spyware groups, and concerned individuals in order to minimize its installation and impact.

Spyware has the potential to remain a threat for the foreseeable future. However, it does not mean that spyware cannot be tackled and managed effectively. For those who are uninformed and do not take appropriate steps, it is indeed a serious problem whose consequences can be severe. However, for those who educate themselves and take preventive steps in conjunction with practicing safe behavior, the spyware threat will be reduced to a very low level.

How spyware is installed

Computers are infected with spyware from a number of sources, which can use different methods that work in stealth mode. The most common method is via an Internet connection, with every computer connected to it being exposed to potential spyware infection. Many of the malware installation methods described in Chapter I are used to install spyware. The specific delivery methods used include viruses, worms, adware, Trojan horse programs, keyloggers, unscrupulous websites, etc. Typically, the user remains unaware of the installation until some symptom provides an alert to the presence of the undesirable software. In many cases, spyware is installed by parents, spouses, loved ones, and employers to track the activities of their children, spouses, loved ones and employees, respectively.

Spyware finds it ways onto the computers of millions of users, even on the machines of those who are aware of this menace, because of the diverse methods and dirty tricks that are used to install it. Spyware techniques are becoming more devious and ingenious all the time. The following are some of the tricks employed by spyware in order to get installed. A particular spyware may use one or multiple techniques. However, not every spyware uses each of these tricks.

- Hiding inside another program: The spyware hides inside another program. For example, when a P2P program is installed, the hidden program, typically adware or spyware, also gets installed.
- Using confusing legal jargon: The EULA is written in language so that most users cannot comprehend the implications of its acceptance. The wording can be vague or imply subsequent actions that the user has no idea of. Typically, the EULA is so long that hardly anyone reads it completely before signing it, which gives the vendor enough leeway to install spyware legally.
- Being persistent: In some cases, during web surfing, if a window pops-up and the

user declines the offer, the pop-up window does not go away. Instead, it continues to repeat the question, despite being declined again and again, until the user accepts it out of frustration.

- Offering free scanning: Some websites offer free scanning. After running a scan, they present the result, which scares the user. In some cases, the scan result includes items, such as cookies, that are not spyware. Consequently, the user is scared into buying the other component of the program—the removal tool.

SPYWARE PREVENTION AND REMOVAL
Approach

The best spyware remedy is to avoid infections which can be achieved, to a large extent, by always avoiding risky online behavior. Spyware should be addressed using a two-pronged approach: prevention and cure. Just using one approach is insufficient and not advisable as having the expectation that spyware will never get through despite preventive steps is unrealistic. The steps required to protect against malware, described in Chapter 1, can also be used for protection against spyware infections.

Use anti-spyware software
Install anti-spyware program

If it has not already been installed, install an anti-spyware software program, which can either be a standalone dedicated anti-spyware program or a component of a comprehensive security suite. If buying protection via commercial software is not feasible, use a free anti-spyware product. Chapter 15 provides a list of scanners, including free ones. It also lists and describes leading commercial anti-spyware programs and security suites.

Be aware of anti-virus software limitations

Anti-virus programs are not effective against spyware programs because spyware and viruses are different types of infections. A virus loads into a computer system without the user's knowledge. Practically no user will desire any virus to be installed on his computer. Spyware may or may not be loaded with the user's permission. In many cases, even though spyware software is installed on a computer with the user's permission, the user does not realize its implications when the installation is authorized.

An anti-virus software has to determine a program's authenticity and also if it is a virus or spyware. Since spyware can be installed legitimately or illegitimately, the anti-virus program can overlook a program based on its determination of the installed program's status. Another important reason for the limited effectiveness of anti-virus software against spyware is that the anti-virus companies arrived late in the game. Therefore, they have not yet developed the technical expertise required to detect and remove spyware with the same efficiency as the anti-spyware companies.

A common misconception among users is that they are protected because anti-virus software has been installed on their computers. However, anti-virus and anti-spyware software are different even though they share some common protection features. A product providing excellent protection against viruses may not stop spyware and vice versa. Therefore, ensure that the product installed provides good protection against both viruses and spyware. If it does not, then both types of protective applications should be installed.

Beware of spyware-free claims

Some companies advertise their programs as being "spyware-free." Such labeling, especially from unfamiliar vendors, should be viewed with caution. The reason is that some shady software vendors have been known to sell products containing items that can be classified as spyware. One of the most widely-used software packages, a P2P program used for file and music sharing, contains a significant amount of adware even though it claims to contain no spyware.

Some vendors provide two versions of the same product—paid (that the consumer pays for) and free. The free product is bundled with a component that can be considered adware or spyware. These vendors use the paid/free distinction to claim that their product is spyware-free, even though one version does contain the unwanted product. Therefore, you should be careful as a claim of no spyware can sometimes be misleading.

Spyware removal challenges

Spyware removal is a challenge because most users are not even aware that spyware has been installed on their computer. A typical spyware program can contain scores of files which are difficult to remove. These files can be located at different places on the computer including files and folders (existing and new), *Windows Start Menu*, registry, etc. Many such programs avoid complete removal due to their installation at many PC locations. When such files are removed manually, they can have unexpected consequences for the computer or a software application. Usually, a good anti-spyware program will be able to remove such programs efficiently and completely.

In some cases, there are two copies of the spyware program that run together in order to protect each other. Even if spyware presence is detected and the undesirable software program or file is removed, a stealth tickler file can reinstall the program when the computer is rebooted. In some cases, spyware vendors ensure that uninstalling a bundled program will prevent the operation of the primary program.

QUICK REMOVAL PROCESS
Using a scanner

A quick and easy way to check for spyware is to use a free scanner to find and subsequently remove the most common infections. When they are executed, scanners with only an on-demand mode will usually search for infections only. Hence, they will not scan during other times, such as when a download occurs, and monitor any new attempts to install spyware. However, most currently available scanners do perform an on-the-fly scan of any open, newly downloaded, and executed files. Using an outdated downloaded version of the scanner is not advisable as it can be quite ineffective without an update, due to the daily emergence of new threats.

When a scan is run, it can list a very large number of items which can sometimes scare users. The various detected spyware items can be deleted, blocked or retained. Be aware that many listed items, such as browser cookies, are relatively harmless. Although third-party cookies can be used to invade a user's privacy, because they can potentially string together visits to a series of websites, they are not programs and usually are not malicious. They can be easily deleted or even blocked from within the web browser.

Scan and remove process

The fast method for identifying spyware involves the following steps:
1. Install the scanner
2. Implement the prerequisites
3. Execute the scanner (i.e., run the program)
4. Remove the identified infections

1) Install the scanner
Note: You can skip this step if a scanner has already been installed.
- Download the scanner and save it on the hard drive
- Install the scanner:
    - Typically, this requires double-clicking the downloaded file
    - Click *Next* as the installation process proceeds
    - Select the default options that are displayed during the installation

2) Implement the prerequisites
Before starting the scan, close any open applications including the e-mail system and the web browser.

3) Execute the scanner

- If the scanner was installed previously, check for updates and download them, if available
- Disconnect from the Internet
- Start the scanner (typically from the desktop program icon or the Windows menu path: *Windows > Start > All Programs > Program Name*)
- Initiate the scan (typically initiated by selecting the *Scan Now* option)

4) Remove the identified infections

Many scanners automatically remove infections as they are identified during the scan run. In such cases, this step becomes unnecessary and can be skipped. Some scanners only identify spyware infections and do not remove them. In such cases, if available, the removal component of the tool will need to be installed or activated in order to remove the infections and complete the process (step 4a). Alternatively, the identified infections can be removed using a dedicated anti-spyware program (step 4b).

4a) If scanner is to be used for removal

- Install the scanner's removal component (if it is not already installed) or activate it, if required
- Run the program, which will remove the infections

4b) If dedicated anti-spyware program is to be used for removal

If a dedicated anti-spyware program, which can scan as well as disinfect, is to be used, the following steps are required:

- Download the anti-spyware software and save it on the hard drive
- Install the anti-spyware program:
    - Double-click on the downloaded file
    - Click *Next* as the installation process proceeds
    - Select the default options that are displayed during installation
- Check for any updates for the software and, if available, download them
- Run the anti-spyware program.
  Depending on how the tool is configured, the spyware items are removed automatically (by the program) or manually (by the user). In the manual procedure, the user decides which items to delete, retain or quarantine, usually by clicking on the spyware item and selecting the appropriate option (delete/retain/quarantine).

Scan, reboot and scan process

Many spyware programs have the ability re-install themselves. Therefore, an effective removal process should, as a minimum, include the following steps:

- Run the scanning or anti-spyware software
- Remove any infections that are discovered
- Reboot the computer (whether or not the anti-spyware program prompts for a reboot)
- Re-scan to ensure that the spyware has been fully and permanently removed. If the scan indicates that the spyware still exists:
    - Re-run the anti-spyware software to remove the remaining items
    - Reboot the computer
- Run the anti-spyware program the third time

If the spyware remains embedded even after the third scan has been executed, use one of the following options:

- A different anti-spyware program
- Restart Windows in *Safe Mode* (described in the next section)
- Uninstall the spyware program using the Control Panel (described in the next section)
- If all else fails, use a comprehensive process for spyware removal (described in a subsequent section of this chapter)

SAFE MODE AND CONTROL PANEL REMOVAL PROCESSES
Scanning in safe mode

The objective of booting in *Safe Mode* is to avoid loading any spyware when the computer is started. When a computer is booted in this mode, Windows starts most system services, registry keys, and drivers. It does not start most third-party services and drivers. However, what does or does not start is controlled by a simple registry key that is often manipulated by malware. *Safe Mode* booting removes many programs from memory, enabling their removal. If such booting fails to work, an alternative method is to boot to the Windows Recovery Console.

To boot in *Safe Mode*:

- Power up the computer
- Hit the F8 key repeatedly
- Select the *Safe Mode* option when prompted to do so

If the option to select *Safe Mode* is not displayed and, instead, the Windows screen is displayed, power off the computer and re-start the procedure.

Removing spyware using the Control Panel

Most spyware and adware vendors do not provide an uninstall feature with their software. However, some of these programs register their entries in the *Add or Remove Programs* section of the *Windows Control Panel* because they know they are safe from deletion, as most users do not know how to use this tool for removing unwanted programs.

Always use a spyware program's uninstall feature, if available, before executing any scan or deleting any suspected files. The reason is that if the spyware program has an uninstall feature, it will be more effective in removing all the program files as it knows where they are located. It will also be in a better position to undo any modifications that were made to the computer and application settings when the program was installed. Anti-spyware programs, while they can be very effective, can leave behind traces of uninstalled spyware programs.

The *Add or Remove Program* function should only be used if you know the spyware's name or have the ability to identify the malware. To use the *Add or Remove Program* function to remove spyware, adware, and other malware programs, navigate as follows:

- Click on the *Windows Start Menu*
- Select *Control Panel*
- Double-click on *Add or Remove Programs*
- Scroll through the list of programs and select the program that is to be removed. This step must be followed carefully because genuine applications are also listed along with undesirable programs. The list of applications can be sorted by name, size, date last used, or install date.
- Follow the uninstall instructions

COMPREHENSIVE REMOVAL PROCESS
Disabling the system restore

The system *Restore* function of Windows XP and later versions is a helpful tool used to facilitate computer recovery when there is a software or driver failure. During normal computer operations, this function is kept in the "on" mode. However, if the computer is infected with spyware or other malware, it is advisable to disable this feature before the infection is removed. The reason is that the backup might contain infected files and therefore the system might be re-infected if a restore is implemented.

Comprehensive spyware removal steps

If a spyware infection has been identified and your initial removal attempts have failed, investigate and search for specific removal instructions from various online sources, many of which are identified in the appendices. You can use Google search for remedies using the keywords "name of spyware" and "removal" as the starting point for your investigation.

If you want to use a systematic and comprehensive process for removing spyware, implement the following steps:

1. Install the operating system (Windows) updates
2. Install the anti-spyware program and other tools
3. Update the anti-spyware program
4. Run the anti-spyware program
5. Retest

1) Install operating system (Windows) updates

The first step requires installation of updates, especially critical ones, to the Windows operating system. The *Service Pack 2* update provides pop-up blocking for the Internet Explorer as well as spyware protection. To check whether it is installed on your computer:

• Click on the *Windows* and *Pause/Break* keys simultaneously

This will display the following window, Figure 1, where the status is shown (Service Pack 2).

Figure 1

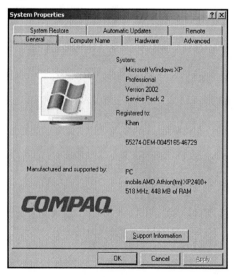

If *Service Pack 2* is not installed, download it from the Microsoft website at *www.microsoft. com/downloads*. The download can also be initiated directly from Internet Explorer by navigating as follows:

- *Tools > Windows Update*

2) *Install the anti-spyware program and other tools*

Install anti-spyware software if it is not already installed on the computer. A number of anti-spyware software tools, some of which are free, are listed in Chapter 14. In this step, other tools, such as those that remove toolbars and cleanup utilities, can also be downloaded and installed. The number of tools required can vary depending on the extent of contamination and level of protection required. The minimum requirement is the installation of one good anti-spyware program.

3) *Update the anti-spyware program*

The anti-spyware software and cleanup products to be used should be the latest versions of the software. Update each software program by following the instructions provided with the appropriate software. Typically, these software programs can be updated by clicking on an updates button that is displayed when the program is launched. Most programs require that the computer be connected to the Internet, from where the updates can be installed.

4) *Run the anti-spyware program*

Launch the anti-spyware program, which can usually be executed from the:

- Program icon placed on the Desktop

or

- Windows menu path: *Windows > Start > All Programs > Program Name*

Now execute these steps:

- Delete any User Accounts that are not to be used in the future *(Start > Control Panel > User Accounts)*
- Turn off the computer
- Reboot the PC in *Safe Mode*

After the computer boots in *Safe Mode:*

- Execute the anti-spyware program (note that some anti-malware programs may not run in *Safe Mode*).
- Run a complete scan

- Delete any infected and unwanted files and programs that are identified
- Reboot in *Safe Mode*
- Re-scan to ensure that no spyware remains

5) Retest
In the final step, reboot Windows in normal mode. If the symptoms and problem persists, an expert professional is required to fix the problem. The last resort solution requires reinstalling the computer's operating system and/or applications.

If the cleanup process is successful and the contaminants are removed, undo the damage that may have been caused by the spyware. This can involve resetting the browser home page (which may have been hijacked), removing websites that may have been added to the browser's Trusted Sites Zone, uninstalling programs that may have been installed (using the *Control Panel's Add/Remove Programs* feature), etc.

FOLLOW-UP STEPS
Remaining protected and continuing the process
Successful disinfection should not be followed by complacency. You should take preventive steps for avoiding potential problems in the future. The most effective protective steps are described in Chapter 1. Implement as many of those steps as you can. At the very least, implement the following steps:
- Install the latest Windows operating system updates
- Patch all applications
- Regularly update the anti-spyware program
- Avoid risky online behavior (visiting porn, gambling, and other untrustworthy websites)

REVERSING SPYWARE CHANGES
Resetting the browser's home page
Many spyware and adware programs change the browser's home page. To change the Internet Explorer's browser's home page:
- Navigate via the menu path: *Internet Explorer > Tools > Internet Options*
- In the address field, enter the desired home page URL, as shown on the following window (Figure 2), where *www.yahoo.com* has been entered

Figure 2

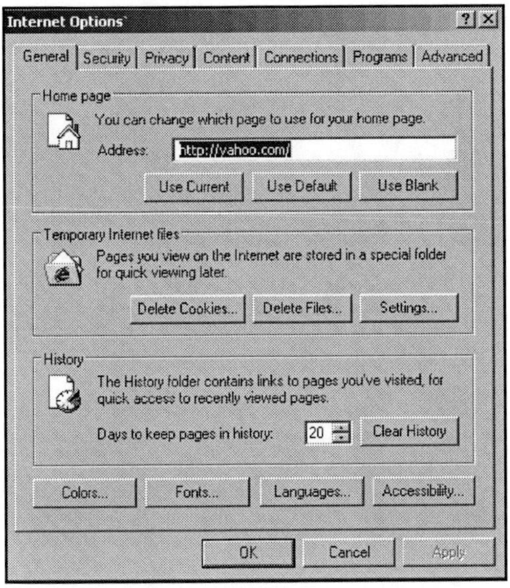

To change the Mozilla Firefox browser's home page:
- Navigate via the menu path: *Tools* > *Options* > *General* > *Home Page*
- In the Location(s) field, enter the desired home page URL

Some malware programs monitor the home page setting. If they detect that the home page has been changed back to its original setting by the user, they change it again. In such a case, a more drastic measure is needed to remove the underlying problem (the spyware), rather than just its effect.

Removing toolbars

To remove unwanted toolbars from the Internet Explorer:
- Launch Internet Explorer
- Navigate via the menu path: *View* > *Toolbars*

This will display the currently-installed toolbars, which are checkmarked as shown on the following window (Figure 3):

Figure 3

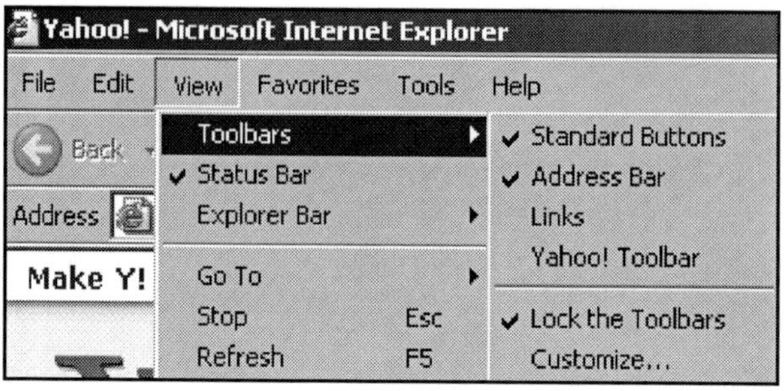

- Click to uncheck the unwanted toolbar(s)

Removing Add-ons

Unwanted Add-ons, which are currently loaded in Internet Explorer, can be viewed and removed using the following steps:

- Launch Internet Explorer
- Navigate as follows: *Tools > Manage Add-ons*

This will launch the *Manage Add-ons* window, which is shown on Figure 4. The items displayed are the Add-ons that are currently loaded in Internet Explorer.

Figure 4

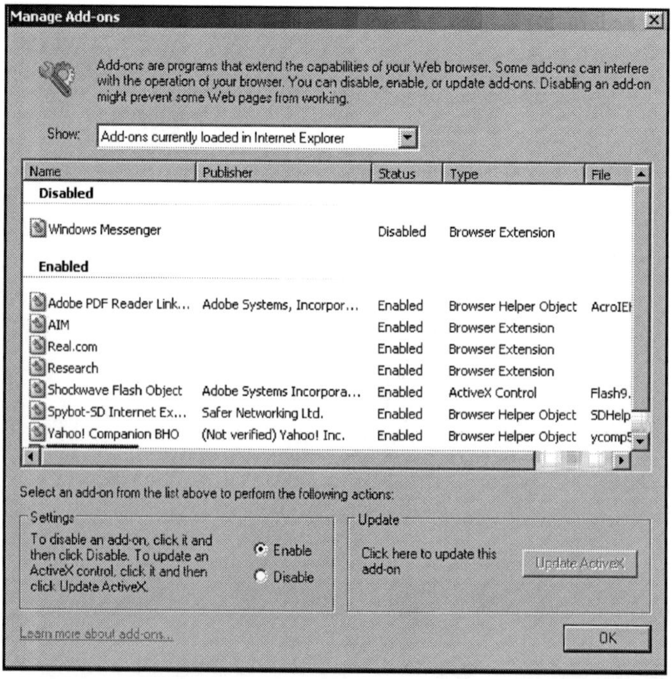

To manually enable or disable an Add-on item:
- Click on the item to be enabled/disabled, such as Real.com

This will highlight the *Enable* and *Disable* radio buttons located at the bottom of the window. To disable the selected item:
- Click the *Disable* radio button
- Click the *OK* button

Additional Adds-ons can be enabled or disabled, as desired. After the changes have been made
- Reboot the computer for the changes to take effect

To display the additional Add-ons which have been used by Internet Explorer:
- Launch the *Manage Add-ons* window (Figure 4)
- Click on the *Show* pull-down menu, which will display the available menu items that can be selected
- Select the item *Add-ons that have been used by Internet Explorer*

This will display the Add-ons that have been used by Internet Explorer, as shown on Figure 5.

Figure 5

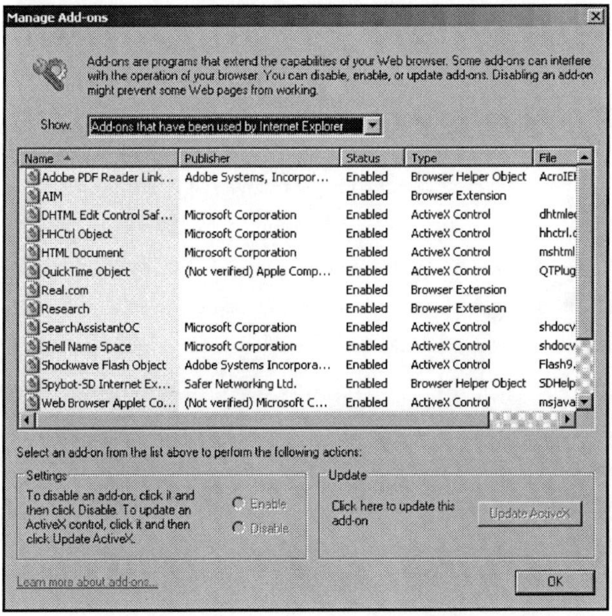

- Click on the item to be disabled, such as AIM

This will highlight the *Enable* and *Disable* radio buttons located at the bottom of the window.
- Click on the *Disable* radio button
- Click the *OK* button
- Reboot the computer for the changes to take effect

ANTI-SPYWARE TOOLS
Scanners
An easy and fast way to determine if spyware is installed on your computer is to use a well-known spyware scanner. Some of the scanners need to be downloaded and then run, while a few online scanners can be run directly from a browser. Scanners provide limited functionality compared to commercial anti-spyware programs. Some scanners are just able to identify malware infections, while many of them are also able to remove them. A list of scanners, including free ones, is provided in Chapter 15.

How anti-spyware programs work
The basic method for detecting spyware and viruses is the same. The anti-spyware program checks for known contaminant files against the databases of known malware programs, which are updated regularly with the definitions of newly-released infections. When the anti-spyware or anti-virus software program is run, it scans the computer and compares the files/folders against the database of known spyware or virus programs. It then lists any suspected files and/or folders. Depending on how the software has been configured, such files/folders can be deleted automatically (by the software) or manually (by the user). Typically, the user is prompted to select the automatic or manual option during the software installation process. The selected option can subsequently be changed.

In the automatic method, after the program is launched, the software removes identified infections without obtaining any user input. In the manual method, the infections are displayed and, subsequently, the user decides whether to delete or retain them by going through the displayed list and taking the appropriate action for each file. Usually, an option is also provided to quarantine such files instead of deleting them.

Since the anti-spyware software often identifies and lists cookies as well, deleting some items can prevent some programs from functioning as expected or prevent desired cookie-generated ads from reaching the computer. Therefore, provided the user is not a novice, it might be a good idea to use the manual process.

ISP products

Some Internet Service Providers (ISPs) provide their own anti-spyware tools, such as AOL's SpyZapper. The ISPs that do not provide their own tool often recommend anti-spyware products, which can usually be procured at a discount by their customers.

Effectiveness of anti-spyware software

Spyware developers are always innovating in order to make their products escape detection by existing anti-spyware programs. Sometimes they succeed and, in such cases, a previously very effective anti-spyware product can suddenly become ineffective. In response to this challenge, anti-spyware vendors are always trying to improve their products and respond to newer threats with better protection techniques. In this cat-and-mouse game, neither side has the upper hand all the time. Therefore, it is unrealistic to expect anti-spyware software to be 100% effective, especially over an extended period.

Keeping the anti-spyware program up-to-date

Anti-spyware programs should be updated regularly after they have been installed. These programs often contain an auto-update feature that enables the software application to be automatically updated with the latest definitions whenever the computer is connected to the Internet. Typically, such programs check the company's website for any updates before they start scanning for spyware. This feature can be disabled. However, it is highly recommended that this feature should be turned on since newer spyware can escape detection if an older version of the anti-spyware software is used.

A non-commercial product user should check how up-to-date the product is, especially if it does not have an auto-update feature. A six- or twelve-month old product is simply too old as newer spyware keeps arriving every day and, therefore, should not be used unless it is first updated.

Selecting an anti-spyware program

Spyware programs become more sophisticated and difficult to remove day-by-day. In response, anti-spyware vendors have started to provide features and functionality in anti-spyware programs that enable users to exert greater control over these tools. Therefore, even the average user finds it challenging to select an anti-spyware tool. Such users, rather than duplicating research that exists elsewhere, should use the reviews posted by trustworthy organizations and online sources that are posted at a number of websites. Be aware that the reviewers include dedicated anti-spyware organizations, professional reviewers, vendors, bloggers, fake review sites, etc.

To make an objective decision, use anti-spyware software comparison charts, which provide a side-by-side comparison of the well-known tools, to determine which tool best meets the desired protection requirements based on functionality, features, cost, and level of protection required. The key is to use charts that are provided by reputable organizations and sites, such as those listed in Appendix A, and stay away from bogus review sites that provide questionable product comparisons.

A review must be considered only if it is provided by a site that is independent, without conflict of interest. It must provide an objective and independent analysis, which should be based on professional testing techniques. A product that is selected based on a questionable review has the potential to cause severe harm. You should also wary of review sites that show up on Google searches, where suspect sites can gain a high-level placement due to a variety of search enhancement placement techniques.

If you decide to choose a relatively unknown product, ensure that it meets the basic requirements of a good anti-spyware product, which are listed in Chapter 13.

Commercial versus free products

Many free anti-spyware products, including some from well-known security vendors, are available for home computer users. Many of the shareware products and free online scanners can identify most of the well-known parasites. However, their effectiveness against the most recent spyware types can be limited. Commercial products are more robust and up-to-date, with updates being applied as soon as a new spyware product has been identified. Many use heuristics, a problem-solving technique that uses intelligent guesswork rather than some pre-established formula, which enables them to identify newly-developed threats.

Misleading anti-spyware software

Rogue anti-spyware programs are questionable and unreliable products that do not provide spyware protection as claimed or expected. Some of them have been known to hijack desktops and also install a large variety of spyware and adware. Some are ineffective and either fail to remove, or only partially remove, any infections. Some of the ineffective products can leave the computer unstable or cause some programs to malfunction. Some products try to mislead by showing the problem to be worse than it actually is. Their objective is to cause fear and force the consumer into buying the product.

Such programs, which may also provide a high proportion of false positives, are often pushed on uninformed or scared users with deceptive and questionable tactics. The listing of rogue anti-spyware programs is available at a number of websites including *www.spywarewarrior.com/rogue_anti-spyware.htm*.

Viruses and Worms

UNDERSTANDING VIRUSES
What is a computer virus

A computer virus is a program that spreads itself by infecting executable files and/or computer system areas and subsequently replicates, without the permission of the user. Computer viruses have traits similar to biological viruses. While a biological virus passes itself from one person to another, a computer virus passes itself on from one computer to another. The definitive characteristic of a virus over any other type of malware is that it must write itself to another host file or code program to spread.

A virus operates by attaching itself to a program (such as an e-mail, spreadsheet, or word processing program), boot sector, or a data file. Whenever the infected program or data file is run, the virus also executes. It then reproduces and attaches itself to other programs or data or performs some destructive act like deleting files and information. The virus can also replace other executable files with a copy of the infected virus file, corrupt data, and spread to other computers and the Internet. These viruses often target documents that support macros or scripting languages.

What a virus can do

Some viruses are relatively harmless, as they only replicate, while others can be damaging. The actual impact depends on how the virus was programmed. While most viruses just propagate, some can damage files and/or directories, erase the hard drive, modify how the computer operates, etc. Even benign viruses can cause problems by degrading computer performance, present annoying messages and pop-ups, cause unpredictable computer behavior, reduce productivity, etc. A virus can directly or indirectly contribute to many of the problems attributed to malware, as described in Chapter 1.

A virus can infect individual computers or networks, replicate very quickly and widely, and bring down entire networks within hours of uncontrolled replication. A serious virus attack can impact millions of computers within a very short period. Such an attack can cause considerable deterioration in Internet access, user productivity, and also impact businesses in a number of ways such as lost revenues, downtime, network failures, etc. The losses due to a virus attack can easily top billions of dollars. An estimate of the losses incurred due to the *ILOVEYOU* virus, which impacted e-mail systems in May 2000, is $10-15 billion.

Differences between viruses and spyware

Both viruses and spyware are malware that are installed without the user's permission. They can be relatively harmless but both have the potential to be destructive. They have many common installation methods such as via websites, downloads, and e-mail attachments. However, their behaviors are different.

Viruses use other host files or code that they add to themselves in order to replicate. In contrast, spyware normally does not replicate. A virus tries to infect a computer with the ultimate aim being to replicate and quickly spread to as many computers as possible. For example, a virus delivered via e-mail will search for the e-mail address book and then send infected e-mails to the address book contacts. Though stealth is a basic requirement for spyware, many viruses are stealth programs that remain hidden from the user.

Viruses are created and installed for a number of reasons, with important ones being the virus creator's desire for fame, demonstration of hacking and virus-creation skills, and malice. Spyware is often driven by monetary gain and is non-destructive as it needs the computer in order to perform its function. Hence, it does not try to cripple a computer, as some viruses tend to do through their actions. Some spyware and virus programs resist removal and, in some cases, can cause the computer to malfunction if removal is incomplete.

There can be some overlap between viruses and spyware, as exemplified by keyloggers and RATs, which can be embedded in both spyware and viruses. Typically, most keyloggers and RATs are Trojans or worms, not viruses.

Misleading symptoms

Computers can exhibit strange behavior for a number of reasons. Do not jump to conclusions and blame viruses for erratic or unpredictable behavior without eliminating some common reasons. Some of the problems that are blamed on viruses but can be attributed to other causes include, but are not limited to, the following:

• Blank screen during computer boot up: This is most likely caused by a hardware problem.

- Hardware problems: Viruses do not cause physical damage to computer hardware such as memory, chips, monitor, motherboards, etc.
- Low memory: It can be caused by too many applications and processes being loaded. Loading of hardware drivers can be a contributing factor.
- Incorrect virus reporting: Two anti-virus programs running simultaneously can lead one to report the other, whose signatures are in memory, as a virus.
- Macros: An application such as MS-Excel or MS-Word can warn that a document being opened contains a macro, which does not necessarily mean that a virus is associated with that document.
- Document fails to open: This can occur due to various reasons including failure to close the document properly, document corruption, etc.

Types of viruses

Viruses can be categorized into five basic types:

- Macro virus: This is the most common type of virus. It infects data files such as MS-Word and MS-Excel documents. Such virus types have the capability to infect by taking advantage of a program's internal programming language (such as Visual Basic). Examples include PayLoad, AAAZAO, W97M Melissa, and WM NiceDay, etc.
- File infector virus: This virus targets program files, such as those with extensions like .exe and .com (which are executable). When a program infected with such a virus is run, it can contaminate other files. Many such viruses reside in memory, whose contamination can lead to the infection of other clean programs when they are executed. Examples include Jerusalem and Cascade.
- Boot sector virus: This type of virus infects the boot record in the system area. The boot record contains a program which is activated when the computer is started. Boot sector viruses can infect hard disks as well as removable disks and floppies. Examples of boot sector viruses are Monkey A, Michelangelo, Stoned, and Disk Killer.
- Master boot record virus: This is similar to the boot sector virus, with the difference being that the virus resides in a different location. Such a virus can prevent a computer from booting. Examples of master boot record infectors are NYB, AntiExe, and Unashamed.A.
- Multi-partite virus: Also known as a polypartite virus, this is a nasty type of virus that targets program files as well as boot records. This creates a removal challenge as both program files and boot records need to be disinfected at the same time. If they are not disinfected simultaneously, cross-infection will occur

(boot record to program files or vice versa). Examples of multi-partite viruses include Natas, Anthrax, One_Half, Emperor, Hare, and Tequilla.

List of the latest viruses

A number of sources provide listings of old and newly-discovered viruses. These sources include anti-virus software vendors, anti-malware organizations, review sites, etc. The following are some sites where the latest viruses are usually identified and listed:

- *www.microsoft.com*
- *www.wildlist.org*
- *http://virusall.com/wormlat.shtml*
- *www.spywareguide.com/*
- *www.symantec.com/enterprise/security_response/threatexplorer/threats.jsp*
- *www.mcafee.com*

What is a worm

A worm is a self-replicating computer program, similar to a virus, which replicates from system to system. It usually exploits security vulnerabilities in a computer's operating system or other installed software. In contrast to a virus, which requires an infected host file to spread it, a worm does not need other programs or documents in order to spread. It is usually spread via e-mails and file transmissions.

Usually, worms do not replace files. They just add themselves as another file on the disk. In contrast, viruses insert themselves in files but do not replace them. Worms are malicious, use computer and/or network resources and bandwidth, and can even cause system shutdown. For example, the nasty Witty worm corrupted the hard drives of infected computers and prevented normal PC operations, which ultimately caused the systems to crash.

A worm often attacks networks where it seeks vulnerable network-attached hosts, which it infects by copying itself. An example of a worm is the Sasser worm, which has many variants such as W32Sasser A. It infected millions of computers. Other examples are the W32.Mydoom and Code Red, which replicated 250,000 times in about 9 hours. Worms such as Nimda and Code Red have targeted servers.

INSTALLATION AND PROPAGATION
Virus activation and infection

Viruses are activated when the computer executes some type of code. Often, the virus remains dormant until something triggers its activation and causes it to spread the infection to other computers. The trigger can be a particular date, a user action, receipt of an e-mail, a clicked hyperlink, etc. In the infection phase, the virus actions can be quite varied and destructive, ranging from simple pop-ups to serious damage.

How viruses are spread

Viruses can be propagated through a variety of methods including P2P file sharing, instant messages, chats, other communication programs, etc. The heavy use of the Internet has become one of the most common sources of virus infections. These days, JavaScript in HTML documents and other types of executable code are a common source of infections. Usually, data files are not the sources of virus infections.

Many viruses are often spread through executable program files such as .exe files. When a program infected with a virus is executed, it can infect other programs and/or computers. They, in turn, can infect other computers and/or programs. Viruses can be spread through shared components like disks, especially if the boot sector is infected with a virus. These boot viruses can infect the system areas of hard drives and disks.

Transmission through e-mails

e-mails are a common transmission medium for viruses and worms, though they are more indicative of the latter. Transmission of an e-mail virus can be via:
- Executable file attachments
- Data files such as a word processing or spreadsheet file containing macros
- Messages that contain embedded executable code (such as JavaScript in an HTML message)

Often the virus replicates by mailing itself to all the contacts in the infected computer's e-mail system. Since an e-mail seems to originate from a familiar address, the users tend to trust such an attachment. Because of this, such a virus spreads very quickly. One of the most-widely spread e-mail viruses was the Melissa virus, which spread in MS-Word documents sent via e-mail. When a Melissa-infected document was downloaded, it triggered the virus, which then sent the document via e-mail to the first fifty contacts in the user's address book. Recipients who opened the attached word document in turn infected another 50 people. Consequently, the virus spread like wildfire.

The *ILOVEYOU* virus was activated when someone double-clicked an infected attachment, which executed the code. It subsequently sent copies of itself to all contacts in the user's address book and also corrupted files on the computer. Other examples of such viruses include W32/Sircam and W32/Goner.

As a safety precaution, a program that is received should not be run unless the source can be trusted. Clicking on embedded hyperlinks in messages should be avoided. Also, programs from unknown sources should not be forwarded to friends and colleagues.

Transmission via boot sector virus

When a computer is powered up, the operating system is launched. One of the first components to be loaded is the boot sector, a small program that instructs the machine on how to load the other parts of the operating system. Boot sector viruses infect this vital component, which ensures that the virus is loaded into memory at machine startup and keeps running in the background.

Viruses and the auto-execute function

The auto-execute feature enables a document to run as soon as it is opened. This feature is available in commonly used MS-Word and MS-Excel documents, which are based on the VBA programming language or VBScript. Viruses like the Melissa virus have used the auto-execute feature, by inserting a program in a document, so that it executes whenever the document is opened. Thus, a Melissa-infected document, when opened, immediately activated the virus, which then performed its programmed tasks.

The auto-execute feature can be disabled for Microsoft applications. The default setting for the *Macro Virus Protection*, which prevents auto-execution, is *High*, which does not run any unsigned macro or script code and presents no warning to the end user. Earlier versions, such as Office 97, allowed users to decide whether to run the macro or not. When a document attempted to auto-execute malicious virus code, a pop-up dialog box warned the user. Since most users were not knowledgeable about macros, they ignored the dialog box and the virus was able to execute.

PREVENTING AND REMOVING VIRUS AND WORM INFECTIONS
Reducing vulnerability through behavior

Due to the widespread use of the Internet, which exposes users to many installation sources, the risk of virus and worm infections cannot be completely eliminated. However, it can be reduced considerably through the use of safe practices and behavior, especially when online, and taking adequate steps to prevent infections. The software protection tools should be used in conjunction with the following behaviors that can reduce vulnerability to viruses and worms:

- Identify: Learn how to identify threats, such as the dangers posed by e-mail attachments, and the types of attachments such as executable files (.exe and .com). Viruses can hide in literally hundreds of different file extensions (for example: cpl, pif, shs, and scr). To aid in this task, enable the viewing of file extensions, which Windows suppresses by default.

- Purpose: Determine if the file received was requested or unsolicited from a known or unknown sender. As a rule, do not open an unsolicited or suspect executable file. Be aware that a file from a known sender can be contaminated and does not guarantee safety. It is also possible that even though the sender may appear to be familiar, the actual sender may be someone else. When in doubt, call or e-mail the sender to confirm the sender's identity.

- Need: If the attached file is not needed, do not open or download it out of curiosity.

- Prefer traditional methods: Purchase software and files from known sources, preferably on CDs. Limit the usage of the Internet for this purpose. To avoid the danger from a boot sector virus, disable floppy disk booting.

Prevention techniques

In order to detect and prevent virus infections and propagation, the basic requirement is the installation of anti-virus software, which can scan and check the computer, e-mail attachments, and documents created by widely-used programs (such as MS-Word and MS-Excel). Such software can also check downloads. The second basic and essential requirement is to install a firewall.

You can also implement the methods and behaviors used to prevent malware infections, described in Chapter I, as they also work against viruses and worms.

Removing viruses and worms

Viruses and worms can be removed. Some are relatively easy to get rid of, while others can be very stubborn and present a real removal challenge—even for experts. Some are designed to reinstall themselves after they have been removed. Viruses and worms can be removed manually or with anti-virus software. Manual removal requires a high computer skill level and should be avoided, especially by novice users.

The manual methods for removing spyware, described in Chapter 2, can also be used to remove viruses and worms. The relevant sections of Chapter 2 pertaining to virus and worm removal are:

- Quick removal process
- Safe Mode and Control Panel removal processes
- Comprehensive removal process

The only difference in implementing these three procedures is that for viruses, an anti-virus tool must be used (instead of the anti-spyware tool that was used for spyware removal).

It is possible for virus removal attempts to fail. A solution that is sometimes recommended in such cases is to backup the data and reformat the hard drive. Users should undertake this drastic step only if they are computer-savvy and understand the behavior of the identified virus. In such serious cases, it is advisable to obtain the services of a professional who has experience in dealing with such a problem.

INSTALLING AND USING ANTI-VIRUS SOFTWARE
What is anti-virus software

Anti-virus software is a program that protects a computer against viruses and worms. Many such programs also protect against other malware types such as spyware, adware, Trojans, etc. Many computers are sold with pre-installed anti-virus software that needs to be activated before use. If anti-virus software is not already installed, it should be procured and installed.

The range of functions available in anti-virus software can be quite varied. Such software can operate and defend in different ways, depending on how the application was implemented and configured. Typically, all anti-virus software programs attempt to determine if a known virus or other contaminants are present. They use virus profiles or signatures that are provided by the vendor. They also attempt to determine if a particular byte pattern, which might be an indicator of a virus, exists in the computer memory or files.

You should be aware that anti-virus software programs have only limited success against newly-developed threats or variations of older threats. According to a Consumer Reports study, the best anti-virus program detection rate for newly modified threats was only 87%, while many of the popular programs were in the 50-70% range.

Configuring the anti-virus software

After an anti-virus software package is installed, it needs to be configured. This can include defining various parameters such as real-time scanning, scanning schedule, full or partial scan, e-mail scanning, etc. Many of the vendor-provided default settings can be retained or changed later as the user becomes more familiar with the software. The real-time scanning option should not be disabled, as it significantly increases vulnerability. This status can be determined from the anti-virus software settings. If it becomes necessary to turn off the anti-virus software due to a requirement to switch it off before installing a new software program, be sure to turn it on after the installation is complete.

Using two anti-virus software applications

It is possible to install a second anti-virus software program even if one is already installed. However, it is not recommended that both be active simultaneously. It is advisable to uninstall the existing program before installing the new application, especially if you plan to use only one program. Retaining two programs can cause them to conflict and interfere with each other.

Keeping anti-virus software up-to-date

An outdated anti-virus program, especially a very old one without installed updates, is a poor tool. Since new viruses are developed every day, a previously-effective anti-virus program may be unable to identify new viruses. Therefore, the anti-virus software must be updated regularly to ensure ongoing protection.

Available updates should be installed as soon as they become available. At the very least, install the latest updates, called virus definition files, every week so that the computer is protected against the latest known viruses. Some vendors provide free updates, though most charge an annual subscription fee. For paid subscriptions, the software is often updated automatically when the computer connects to the Internet. To check whether the installed anti-virus software has the latest updates, open the program, which will typically display a date indicating the effective date of the virus definitions.

Selecting anti-virus software

Anti-virus software programs come in many flavors. Some are standalone applications, while others are bundled with additional products such as firewalls. Some are included in security suites that try to cover every aspect of computer security and, hence, have a very rich feature set. Some applications are free, while others need to be procured. The package selection considerations include desired features, software cost, and the cost of ongoing updates. The desired features of anti-virus software are described in Chapter 13.

Status of an installed anti-virus program

The installed status of an anti-virus program can be determined in a number of ways. These include the list of programs that are displayed when navigating via the Windows menu *(Start > Programs)*. The list of installed programs can also be viewed from the Control Panel *(Control Panel > Add/Remove Programs)*. On some computers, the program may be listed on the system tray. Many PCs are sold with at least a couple of these programs already installed. Be aware that the listing of a program does not mean that the software has been activated. To bring the software into operating mode, it will need to undergo some or all of these steps: launch, activate, configure, update, and run.

Virus education

The virus problem is a dynamic one where new challenges are presented on a daily basis. Every time a new threat is identified, the anti-virus vendors make a determined effort to neutralize the threat. Therefore, users need to be aware of the latest developments and educate themselves, as well as those around them. A number of resources are available for educating users and providing useful information. These include anti-malware vendors, newsgroups, spyware and virus removal forums, blogs, discussion groups, etc. Two useful sites for virus discussions and solutions are *news:alt.comp.virus* and *news:comp.virus*. Well-known forums where information about malware/viruses can be obtained include:

- Aumha *(http://forum.aumha.org/viewforum.php?f=30)*
- Bleeping Computer *(www.bleepingcomputer.com/forums/forum22.html)*
- CastleCops *(www.castlecops.com/forum67.html)*
- Cexx.org *(http://boards.cexx.org/index.php?board=1)*
- Spybot S&D *(http://forums.spybot.info/forumdisplay.php?f=22)*
- Spyware Warrior *(http://spywarewarrior.com/viewforum.php?f=5)*
- SpywareBeware *(http://forums.maddoktor2.com/index.php?showforum=17)*
- SpywareInfo *(http://forums.spywareinfo.com/index.php?showforum=18)*
- Tech Support Guy *(http://forums.techguy.org/f54-s.html)*
- TomCoyote *(http://forums.tomcoyote.org/index.php?showforum=27)*

More information about viruses can be obtained at CERT *(www.cert.org/other_sources/viruses.html)* and ASAP *(Alliance of Security Analysis Professionals)*.

CHAPTER FOUR

Adware and Trojans

UNDERSTANDING ADWARE
What is adware

Adware is an advertising-supported software application, the most common form of malware, which displays advertisements on a computer. Typically, adware is displayed through pop-up windows, which can be generated during either online or offline sessions. Adware can also be generated through banner displays and other forms of displays.

What adware can do

Adware can be annoying and interfere with user experience through bombardment of ads (some of which don't go away), decrease productivity, degrade browser performance, slow or crash the computer, initiate drive-by downloads, generate spam, compromise PC and network security, and impact computer resources (memory, disk space, and bandwidth). Adware is also known to hijack browsers, track the user's web surfing habits, download software programs without the user's knowledge or permission, and transmit information to third-parties. Using such information without the user's knowledge is an invasion of privacy.

How adware works

Adware software runs in the background and monitors the user's activities and behavior, which are logged and used to create a user profile. This information is transmitted to a server which collects and analyzes the relayed information using a number of tools such as data mining. It then determines which subsequent actions are to be implemented, such as causing a specific context-sensitive advertisement to pop-up.

How adware is installed

Adware is often installed via legitimate software whose End User License Agreement allows it to install adware. Strictly speaking, such adware cannot be considered illegal, even though most users who provide the permission via an EULA do not really know what they are agreeing to. The line between adware and ad-supported software is somewhat blurred as there is a conflict between the product's value and the loss of privacy and/or degradation of user experience.

Many adware programs that are downloaded are bundled with other programs whose existence the user may or may not be aware of. Many P2P programs, widely used for downloading music and files, are loaded with bundled programs, which are a very widespread source of adware. Though many programs do indicate in their EULA the existence of the bundled programs, some programs contain adware even though they claim to be adware-free.

Adware is also installed through many of the techniques used to install malware, described in Chapter I. The most common methods are through visiting websites, drive-by downloads, ActiveX controls, downloading, and shareware/freeware.

Benefits of adware

Adware's driving force is financial gain for the software developer or the installer for whom pop-ads can directly or indirectly lead to revenue. Many adware programs also monitor a user's behavior, which can enable targeted advertisements. Adware's benefit for consumers is that they can obtain otherwise unaffordable software at subsidized rates in exchange for being bombarded with ads, loss of privacy, and other potentially negative effects.

Advertising is a part of modern day life. TV programs are interspaced with ads which subsidize the programming. Some adware can be useful and provide benefits to both the user and the companies marketing their products. The difference is that adware can prevent a user from using the computer as desired. While a TV ad can be switched off by changing a channel, adware on a PC can be very annoying as it interferes and also retains control over how the user uses the computer. Also, in extreme cases, it can expose the user to identity theft and financial risk. Adware should be acceptable provided its installer is upfront about its purpose and methods.

POP-UP ADS AND ADWARE
Pop-up ads

Advertisers use pop-up ads that cause a new window to be displayed, in order to get the user's attention. The objective is to steer the user to a website, display an advertisement, provide an enticement to buy or use something, install adware stealthily, etc. Pop-up ads are usually triggered during web surfing, though they can also be generated during offline computer usage. Usually, such ads are able to pop-up because the computer's Internet security settings have been set at "low," which enables many actions to take place without input from the user.

Risks of pop-up ads

Most pop-up ads are annoying and degrade user experience. However, they can be more than a nuisance. They can force a user to repeatedly and unsuccessfully try to shutdown a pop-up window or redirect him to an unwanted website. While pop-ups are primarily installed for displaying ads, they have also been used by spyware to transmit confidential and personal data to third-parties without the user's permission. Deceptive pop-ups can also hijack a browser, initiate a drive-by download, and compromise PC and network security.

Misleading dialog boxes

Many pop-up dialog boxes misleadingly indicate that the computer is infected and offer a free scan. Clicking a button on such windows can generate many actions including drive-by downloads, navigation to a suspicious website, etc. The best way to deal with such pop-ups is to click on the "x" (close) on the top right-hand corner of the window. Sometimes, even clicking the *Cancel* button fails to close the window. When multiple windows pop-up, a useful method is to simultaneously click the CTRL+W keys until all browser windows are closed.

P2P PROGRAMS AND ADWARE
Risk from P2P programs

Peer-to-Peer (P2P) programs such as Kazaa are widely used, primarily by teenagers, to download songs, videos, and other types of files. The risk of being infected due to the installation of P2P software, or from the file downloads, is extremely high. P2P software and downloads are considered to be the leading sources of adware infections. It is estimated that half of P2P packages contain some adware. Some P2P packages have been known to mislead by stating that they are clean and contain no spyware, pop-ups or Trojans. To reduce the risk of contamination from P2P software, it is advisable to stay away from the free versions.

Adware from P2P programs

According to a PC Tools survey in May 2005, the most commonly used P2P programs are, in decreasing order of market share, Kazaa, WinMX, LimeWire, BitTorrent, Ares, Bearshare, Shareaza, eMule, BitTornado, Morpheus and iMesh. The adware or spyware installed through the leading P2P programs include Gator, TopSearch, NavExcel Toolbar, HuntBar Toolbar, and Ezula.

According to an estimate, computers in more than five million homes have Kazaa installed. P2P software can be found on business computers as well, with one survey estimating that 4% of business computers have Kazaa installed on them. Since business computers are usually connected via networks, the contamination of even a single PC can create a serious problem for all computers on the network.

ADWARE PREVENTION AND REMOVAL
Checking for adware
If it is suspected that a computer is infected with adware, based on the symptoms that were identified earlier, perform a scan using a spyware/adware detection tool. A number of these tools are listed in Chapter 14 and Chapter 15.

Preventing adware
Many of the methods and behaviors used to prevent malware infections, described in Chapter 1, can also be used to prevent adware. The important ones include practicing good online behavior, adjusting the browser settings to ensure higher security, installing an anti-spyware/adware package, and using a pop-up blocker to prevent pop-up advertisements that are generated when visiting websites (Windows XP Service Pack 2 contains such a blocker). For downloads, use websites like iTunes that provide adware-free services.

Preventing drive-by downloads
When a window pops-up unexpectedly during web surfing, a user is often presented with some options to proceed (such as accept, decline, etc.). By clicking on any of the presented choices, a drive-by download can be triggered. In other words, a software program can be downloaded without the user's permission or knowledge. On some pop-ups, even if the decline button is clicked, the pop-up window will not disappear until the user accepts what the pop-up window wants it to do. In such a situation, exit by clicking the "x" symbol located on the window's top right-hand corner.

Other methods for preventing this problem include installing Windows XP Professional SP2, Internet Explorer 7, or the Firefox browser.

Removing adware
Adware can be blocked or removed but it may require the host application to be unin-

stalled. In such a case, a user needs to decide whether to keep or remove both applications (host application and the adware). In some cases, adware removal may violate the EULA that the user consented to when downloading the host application (such as Kazaa or eWallet). While some adware can be uninstalled, the problem is that most users do not know and cannot determine which host software is associated with the adware and, hence, do not know which application needs to be uninstalled.

In some cases, adware vendors ensure that deleting or uninstalling a component of the bundled program will either delete the bundled freeware application or prevent the operation of the primary program. They usually dictate how the host and adware software can be de-coupled and uninstalled. Such vendors obviously do not want to provide an application without getting something in return, which the adware provides. In some cases, the computer does not revert back to its original condition after the adware is uninstalled.

Sources for adware-free software

It is possible to avoid adware by downloading online software only from reputable sources. A number of adware-free software applications are available on the Internet. The following are some of the available sites where adware-free software may either be available or recommended:

- *www.cleansoftware.org*
- *www.oldversion.com*
- *www.theopencd.org*
- *http://osswin.sourceforge.net*
- *www.pricelessware.org*

TROJAN HORSE PROGRAMS
What is a Trojan Horse program

A Trojan Horse program, often called a Trojan, is a non-replicating malicious computer program. To a user, such a program appears harmless and, in some cases, useful. However, when executed, such a program performs harmful actions.

What a Trojan Horse program can do

A Trojan Horse program can be installed on a computer with or without the user's knowledge. It tries to run in the background in order to hide its presence. A Trojan lies dormant till a code in the file is executed, which triggers its malicious actions such as the execution of a program file or the opening of a document (such as a spreadsheet or word processing file). It can perform many of the other actions that malware can execute, which were listed in Chapter I.

An example of a Trojan is an apparently harmless game program which may actually be executing a variety of functions unknown to the game player. These can include monitoring and transmitting confidential information to a third-party, manipulating files (deleting, creating, renaming, or transmitting), dialing long distance numbers, erasing the hard disk, e-mailing passwords to others, sending spam, participating in a denial-of-service attack, providing a hacker backdoor access to the computer, installing a virus or other malware, modifying system configuration, etc.

Installation and prevention of Trojan Horse programs

Trojan programs can be installed through the malware installation methods, described in Chapter I. However, the popular methods for their installation include file downloads, executable files, visits to malicious websites, clicking on pop-up windows or e-mail hyperlinks, and opening e-mail attachments. Instant messages also provide a mechanism for installing Trojans. They can cause a Trojan to be installed when a user downloads a file or clicks on an embedded hyperlink. Trojan Horse infections can be prevented by implementing the anti-malware prevention techniques, described in Chapter I.

REMOTE ACCESS TROJANS
What is a Remote Access Trojan

A Remote Access Trojan (RAT) is a malicious software program that enables a computer to be accessed and controlled remotely by an unauthorized user or computer via an Internet connection. A RAT program, once installed, provides information about the computer, such as address and functionality, to a remote host. RATs attempt to hide their presence from the users and also try to cover up any evidence of their malicious actions. Examples of RATs are BackOrifice, Netbus, and SubSeven.

What a RAT can do

A RAT can enable a hacker to execute a variety of actions without the user's knowledge including transmission of confidential data and files, IDs, account numbers, passwords, etc., which can lead to identity theft and financial losses. It can monitor, record, and transmit user keystrokes and/or activities to third-parties. It can also view, delete and/or modify files on the computer.

A RAT can infect other computers on the network or the Internet, attack other computers or participate in a denial-of-service attack, and mislead users into believing that a malicious website is safe and trustworthy. A RAT can execute, abort, or end a program or Internet connection. It can also execute other actions that malware is capable of, which were described in Chapter I.

Installation and prevention of RATs

Remote Access Trojans can be installed through the malware installation methods, described in Chapter I. However, the popular methods for their installation include file downloads, executable files, visits to malicious websites, clicking on pop-up windows or e-mail hyperlinks, opening e-mail attachments and IMs. RAT infections can be prevented by implementing the anti-malware prevention techniques, described in Chapter I.

Spam, Phishing, and IM's

UNDERSTANDING SPAM
What is spam

Spam refers to undesirable and unwanted mass e-mail that is irrelevant and unsolicited. It is also referred to as electronic junk mail. An e-mail is considered unsolicited if the recipient has not provided consent to receive it. Spam should not be considered the same as bulk e-mail. If an e-mail is simultaneously sent to a thousand customers who previously provided affirmative consent to receiving information relevant to their account, as a customer communication, it is classified as bulk e-mail-not spam. Similarly, bulk e-mails sent out to newsletter subscribers, discussion board lists, and customers cannot be considered spam. A message is classified as spam only if it unsolicited as well as bulk. The e-mail content does not matter—if the message is unsolicited and bulk, then it can be classified as spam.

Spam is favored by commercial mass marketers who send out large quantities of e-mail messages, which can number in the millions, as part of their promotional activities. A recent trend has been to send advertisements via text message to cell phones.

Problems due to spam

Spam is a major problem at this time. It has been estimated that spam accounts for about two-thirds of all e-mail, with some surveys indicating a higher percentage. Besides being a nuisance and impacting personal and business productivity, due to the time spent reading and/or deleting such messages, spam also transmits viruses, worms, spyware, Trojans, and other types of malware. Spam is often associated with phishing and other fraudulent schemes, chain letters, pornographic sites, etc.

Spam is cost-shifted advertising. It shifts the costs to Internet Service Providers (ISPs), businesses, as well as users. It consumes Internet users' time. Also, businesses have to handle unwanted huge volumes of e-mails, which puts a strain on network resources and bandwidth and forces them to spend more on hardware and software in order to process and/or keep out spam.

DEALING WITH SPAM
Difficulty in stopping spam

Many businesses and ISPs such as America Online and EarthLink are vigorously fighting spam through the use of anti-spam filtering software. Some laws have also been enacted against spam. However, despite the existence of laws and anti-spam software, spam generators still manage to successfully transmit a huge volume of spam due to a number of reasons. The Internet is open, with easy access to anyone, and spam provides a simple and inexpensive way of reaching a huge audience. Many users exhibit behavior that enables marketers to identify them and subsequently target them. There also exist technical difficulties in filtering spam. If the filters are too strict, genuine messages get lost. If they are not very stringent, a lot of spam manages to get through.

The principle of free speech also prevents the introduction of more stringent, all-encompassing, laws. A number of laws, such as S 877 (CAN SPAM), have been implemented to control spam. These laws have approached the issue in different ways. Consequently, this has caused spam to be viewed differently, which adds to the difficulty of stopping spam.

Opting-out of spam

Many spam messages contain a hyperlink which leads to a website where the e-mail recipient can opt-out of spam. These opt-out offers should be ignored. The reason is that responding to an opt-out e-mail indicates to the sender that the e-mail address is genuine. Therefore, it is likely that such an address will end up receiving even more spam. The key is to determine who to opt-out from. Opting out from legitimate companies will probably ensure better results, while opting out from spammers will be more risky.

Anti-spam tools

An effective way of reducing spam is to practice good e-mail behavior and practices. Avoid circulating your e-mail address, especially at public sites visited during Internet surfing. Limit participation at websites where an e-mail address will be available to a large number of users and organizations such as usenets, discussion boards and groups, sites that provide free products and services, etc. If possible, turn up the e-mail system security setting to high.

In addition to practicing good behavior, use an anti-spam tool. Either use a dedicated anti-spam tool or an anti-malware tool that also provides spam protection. Many of these tools are listed in Chapter 15.

UNDERSTANDING PHISHING
What is phishing

Phishing is a deceptive baiting technique designed to scam the user into providing personal and confidential information. It is a fast growing threat on the Internet that can have serious repercussions for those who fall for it. A user responding to phishing is led to a fraudulent website, which attempts to gather information that can be used for a variety of purposes including identity theft, financial scams, etc.

Phishing is initiated via an e-mail that pretends to be from a legitimate site or someone the user knows. It is based on a combination of social engineering and technical deception. A spoofed e-mail, that appears to originate from a particular source even though it is actually sent from another source, directs the user to a counterfeit website where he is tricked into providing personal and confidential data. Responding to phishing can result in spyware, Trojans, keyloggers, and other malware being installed on the computer.

Phishing-generating e-mails pretend to be from an organization that the user does business with (such as a bank) or from a well-known institution. Typically, these are well-known credit card companies, banks, financial institutions or other types of brand name organizations such as eBay and PayPal. The phishers can collect a variety of data and information, though the most commonly-sought data pertains to account numbers, IDs and passwords, and social security numbers. According to the Anti-Phishing Working Group's report, 154 brands were hijacked by e-mailed phishing campaigns in July 2006, compared to 71 a year earlier.

How phishing works

eBay is a favorite target of phishing scammers. In the typical phishing scam, bulk e-mail is sent to eBay users warning them that their account is about to be suspended unless they update their personal and/or other information. Another common message warns the recipient that his account has been restricted, due to it being compromised. Therefore, in order to lift the restriction, he must provide some verification information. For this purpose, the e-mail recipient is instructed to click on a hyperlink, whose URL description includes some reference to eBay, embedded in the e-mail message.

The URL description is deceptive as it contains the company name (eBay).

However, clicking on the link does not take the user to the eBay website. Instead, it steers the user to the scammer's website, which looks similar to the eBay website (with the company logo, look and feel, etc.). When the user enters authentication information (personal information, user ID, password, credit card number, etc.), the phisher is able to record it and subsequently use it for his unscrupulous objective.

Unsuspecting users often respond to such communications as they are deceived into thinking that such a website is legitimate. Most users cannot even imagine such a type of scam and respond quickly, without verifying the validity of the communication that was received. Millions of users receive such an e-mail. Even if only 1% respond to it, though the typical response rate is higher, the financial benefit to the phisher can be significant.

Example of phishing

The following screenshot, Figure 6, is an example of a phishing scam involving Chase. The e-mail appeared to be authentic with the Chase logo. However, when the cursor was made to hover over the displayed URL (*http://www.chase.com/onlineuser_0475554*), it displayed an unrecognizable URL, which indicated that the e-mail was from a non-Chase company.

Figure 6

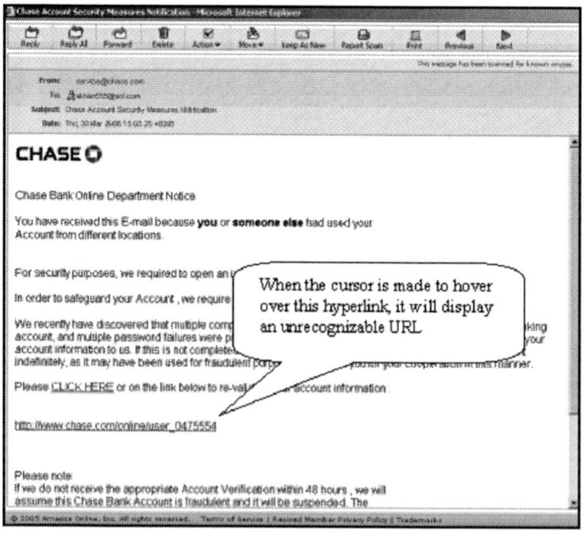

IMPACT OF PHISHING
Phishing trend

The number of phishing attacks is increasing and their sophistication is growing. Phishers use a variety of techniques that exploit both user behavior, lack of knowledge, and operating system vulnerabilities. In addition to e-mail solicitations, phishers now use malware including spyware, keystroke loggers, hijacking tools, etc. They have also started using instant messaging and a new technique called spear phishing, which is a highly targeted phishing attack. Spear phishers send an e-mail that targets employees or members of a particular organization, group, or government agency.

According to the Anti-Phishing Working Group, phishers have attempted to misrepresent almost every major American bank. Most phishing attacks originate in the United States, where most of the targets are also located. However, many are foreign. According to a Gartner estimate, 57 million people have received phishing e-mails. In 2004, the cost to consumers due to phishing was estimated to be over a billion dollars (*www.informationweek.com*, June 24, 2005). A good source for phishing information and reports is *www.antiphishing.org*.

In a new type of attack, called *SMishing*, a cell phone user receives a text message that contains a hyperlink to a website. When the hyperlink is clicked, it leads the user to a website where a Trojan is downloaded. In another method, known as *Vishing* (Voice Phishing), scammers use a VOIP phone number, which enables inexpensive and anonymous Internet calling, to trick users into revealing confidential information like credit card numbers. The Vishing process starts via an e-mail that asks a user to authenticate personal information by calling a phone number, which is attached to a VOIP system.

Laws against phishing

Identity theft, which is the primary aim of phishing attacks, is a federal crime in the US and is covered by the *Identity Theft* and *Assumption Deterrence Act*. The penalty for identity theft can be as high as 15 years in prison. Despite this deterrent, phishing crime flourishes due to the ease with which financial gains can be made. Also, despite the existence of laws, few phishers have been prosecuted.

PHISHING DETECTION AND PREVENTION
Detecting phishing

Phishing can be recognized through a number of signs including:

- Many spelling mistakes in the message
- Grammatical errors

- Forms that require the user to fill in user ID and password, bank or credit card numbers, etc.
- Browser's address field is suspect (URL does not contain the organization's name)
- The hyperlink's text does not match the text that is displayed when the mouse is moved over it; for example, when the mouse is placed over the hyperlink, it does not point to the organization's server, such as eBay.com (if the e-mail pretends to be from eBay)
- Pressure tactics such as threatening to restrict the account if no action is taken within a specified time period
- Warning that a penalty will be levied if action is not taken
- Prompt to change a password
- URL contains an @ symbol (most browsers ignore all characters preceding the @ character)
- Baits such as entry in a competition or selection of some prize

For more information on how to protect against spoofed sites, visit *www.microsoft.com* and read article 833786 as well as other current information on this topic. Two useful sites for obtaining phishing information and how to recognize spoof e-mails are *www. phishtank.com* and *www.millersmiles.co.uk*.

Checking if a displayed URL is genuine

In order to hide their true identities, phishers try to hide their real web addresses and URLs. To determine if the website that you want to visit is genuine, type the address of the website in the browser's address bar. Do not use the embedded link that you may have received via e-mail or some other suspect source. You can also use the Internet Explorer 7 or the Firefox 2.0 anti-phishing utility to verify the link.

If you are an advanced user, you can use the following method to check the real address of a website (URL of the current web page):

- Type the following address in the browser's address bar:
  javascript:alert("Actual URL address: " + location.protocol + "//" + location.hostname + "/");
- Click Enter

This will cause a pop-up window to appear, which will indicate the actual website that is being visited.

Preventing phishing

Phishing can be avoided through a combination of common sense, adherence to good safe practices, becoming aware of the threats, and appropriate self-education. Before responding to an e-mail request for information, think before acting. Why would the organization from which the e-mail purports to be request personal or confidential information when they already have it? If a request is made via an e-mail, call the organization to verify if it requested the information. Never respond to a potential phishing request until verification has been provided.

Other prevention tips include the following:

- Avoid clicking on embedded links
- If responding, type in the company's URL in the browser address bar (such as *www.ebay.com*), which will take you directly to its website where the login can be made safely. Alternatively, login using your own bookmark or URL.
- Never provide the user ID or password when responding to any unsolicited request, as it could be from a phishing site
- Do not be impressed by high-quality graphics or images that look exactly like those from the genuine websites
- Check the text carefully; beware if the text is within a graphic and cannot be selected
- Avoid using non-secure systems. Do not enter important data into any form on a website that is not encrypted (the address of secure websites begins with *https://*, not *http://*, as shown on Figure 7).
- Regularly empty the browser cache using the browser settings or via the menu path: *Internet Explorer > Tools > Internet Option > Temporary Internet files > Delete*
- Convert all incoming e-mail to plain-text, a setting that most e-mail clients now support, which will enable the real URL links to be viewed

Figure 7

As a public service, forward phishing e-mails to anti-phishing organizations, such as *reportphishing@antiphishing.com* and *uce@ftc.gov*.

Anti-phishing software tools

Some utilities can determine the true address of a website that the user plans to visit. *SpoofStick* (*www.spoofstick.com*) is a free software utility that can be installed directly into the Firefox browser, which helps users detect spoofed (fake) websites. EarthLink provides another anti-phishing utility (*www.earthlink.net/home/tools*). A tool from Microsoft, *Microsoft Phishing Filter Add-in for MSN Search Toolbar*, scans the websites being visited to determine if they are fraudulent. It blocks the user from sharing personal information with a known phishing site. Internet Explorer 7 and Firefox 2.0 also provide good defense against phishing.

UNDERSTANDING IM INFECTIONS
What is instant messaging

Instant Messaging, usually referred to as IM, is a communication method. Using IM, a user can send and receive messages to/from an online buddy in real-time. This technique took off as a chatting medium for teenagers. However, it has now become very widespread and is used both by individuals as well as businesses. The well-known and very popular IM programs are AOL AIM, Yahoo Messenger, IRC, ICQ, and MSN Messenger.

IM technology, which was initially used for simple chatting, has now become very sophisticated. It can support the exchange of files, pictures, and videos. Hyperlinks can be embedded within IM messages. With the increase in the versatility and usage of this tool, malware developers have started to exploit it for transmitting viruses and other types of malware. IM attacks have the look and feel of conventional e-mail attacks. The impact to the computer through IM-borne malware is the same as with malware transmitted via e-mail. The type and extent of damage depends on the malware, not the medium used to transmit it.

Modes of infection through IMs

Malware can be transmitted via IM chats with strangers as well as with friends, colleagues, and acquaintances. An IM can transmit viruses and other malware just like an e-mail. Infections can be transmitted by clicking on embedded hyperlinks or by downloading/ opening attachments such as files, games, pictures, etc. The infected and activated file can perform a range of actions including the installation of spyware, Trojans, keyloggers, etc.

Preventing IM infections

Many of the methods and behaviors used to prevent malware infections, described in Chapter I, can also be used to prevent infections via IMs. The following are a few additional tips relevant to IM protection:

- Use respected and safe IM products. Avoid IRC, ICQ, and other more complicated or unregulated programs unless you are very familiar with them.
- Using the latest version of the IM software, as newer versions tend to have improved and built-in protections against spyware and viruses.

Firewalls

UNDERSTANDING FIREWALLS
What is a firewall

A firewall is a piece of hardware or software application that resides between two different security domains, like your computer and the Internet. It supervises all inbound and outbound traffic and prevents unauthorized access to/from the computer. Either type of firewall, hardware or software, can define access control rules for the computer being protected. A firewall is a computer user's first line of defense against hackers and various types of malware.

A firewall prevents a computer from communicating directly with other computers. It typically consists of a device that acts as a barrier through which all communications between the computer being protected and other computers must pass. A firewall monitors the traffic to/from external computers and if the data being transmitted or received does not conform to the specified rules, it blocks its transmission. It also stops hackers who probe the Internet for vulnerable computers. More information about firewalls can be obtained at the firewalls FAQ (*www.faqs.org/faqs/firewalls-faq/*).

Firewall necessity

A firewall provides basic protection that every computer needs. Every user who connects to the Internet should install a firewall to protect against malware such as spyware, viruses, worms, adware, phishing, tracking and monitoring software, etc. While a firewall has long been considered an essential component of business networks, it has now become a requirement for home computers as well due to the proliferation of security threats.

A firewall can reduce risks, not eliminate them. It does not provide protection against all types of malware. For example, Trojans can manage to get through as they can sneak in through legitimate applications and, later on, install themselves surreptitiously when the application is launched. For those items that manage to evade a firewall, other anti-malware tools such as anti-virus and anti-spyware programs can provide protection.

How a firewall protects

A firewall monitors inbound and outbound Internet traffic and flags any suspicious behavior. For example, if a website sends data that was not requested by the user, the firewall will stop it. However, if the user did request it, the firewall will allow the data to pass. Many firewalls do not block outbound traffic.

A firewall enables communications only with those who are given permission, based on specified rules that can be customized. An effective firewall can differentiate between traffic types (good versus bad) and provide alerts when necessary. The alerts provide enough information about abnormal activities so that users can make informed decisions to permit or block them.

Firewalls provide the ability to control the ports that can be accessed. A port is an interface through which data is sent and received. A port number identifies the port's type. For example, port 80 is used for HTTP traffic. A firewall can be configured to keep a specific port(s) open or closed and hence control the data that can come in or go out. Most firewalls are pre-configured with specific security settings that can be customized by the user, if desired, depending on their individual protection requirements (low to high).

Firewall features

Depending on the particular needs and priorities of a user or network, the firewall protection requirements can vary considerably. Since firewalls are characterized by a number of features and functions that can determine the level of protection provided, it is important that users be aware of them so that an informed decision can be made when choosing a firewall. The following sections list desired personal firewall features.

Primary firewall features

- Inbound filtering: Examines incoming data traffic and, based on specified rules or filters, determines if it should be allowed to pass through or be blocked.
- Outbound filtering: Outbound filtering enables outbound traffic to be monitored in order to prevent confidential and personal data being transmitted to an external system on the Internet.
- Intrusion detection: Intrusion detection monitors the legitimacy of incoming data based on known penetration methods, comparison against known attack fingerprints, and behavior evaluation. If intrusion is detected, it notifies the user,

who becomes aware of the hacking method being employed.

- Application integrity: Enables a firewall to monitor file modifications and, also, how applications are launched. When any changes are made, the firewall informs the user and prevents the application from being executed or data being transmitted.
- Stealth mode: Enables the host computer to evade detection by hackers or other computers, when they try to probe the Internet in order to identify unprotected computers, and prevents the establishment of unauthorized communication channels. In this mode, the computer does not respond to probes and, hence, the prober does not become aware of its existence.

Additional firewall features

- Selective filtering: Selective filtering permits filters to be specified so that only certain computers can communicate with the host computer and/or allow it to transmit data to external computers on the Internet. For example, if a remote user is to be permitted to connect to the host computer, a port such as 3389 can be opened for enabling access.
- Security: Includes anti-spyware defenses that can block at every stage (including installation, activation, transmission and re-installation), place attachments in quarantine, prevent transmission of confidential data, and configuration (defining how a particular application communicates over the Internet). It can also include packet filtering (which allows a user to specify the protocols, ports, and remote addresses that can be accessed) and prevent the installation of a third-party scripting code executing stealthily inside a browser.
- Control: Control allows monitoring of all connections between the host machine and other computers on the Internet or the network. If required, an unwanted connection can be terminated. The firewall should also be able to maintain an events log, which can provide a history of the computer's online activities.
- Privacy protection: Ensure protection of user privacy and prevent confidential and personal data being transmitted. Also covers surfing privacy protection, which maintains confidentiality during web surfing. The firewall can hide the IP address and browser during Internet surfing.

Other firewall features and characteristics

The other desirable firewall features include Internet filtering to restrict undesirable content, tracking of all potential and actual threats, data encryption, pop-up ad blocking, e-mail virus protection, reporting and logging, context-sensitive help, pre-defined rules for popular applications, and easy program updates via an automatic update feature.

A firewall should have the capability to notify the user whenever the computer experiences an abnormal activity such as an intrusion or other security issue. Limited and clear alerts should be provided so that the user is not irritated or confused. A firewall should be easy to install and use, an important feature for many inexperienced users. It should be able to perform automatic installation and, for the more experienced users, permit customization and specify various options. The customization should be easy and configuration options should be clearly explained. The firewall should also perform consistently and reliably, be compatible with the installed applications, and not create conflicts or execution problems.

TYPES OF FIREWALLS
Software firewall

A software firewall, also known as a host-based firewall, is a program that protects a computer by monitoring and restricting communications, primarily incoming traffic, though it can also be used to monitor outgoing traffic. It can protect systems from malware that is spread through e-mail, P2P programs, shared drives, etc. A software firewall is essential for laptops that are used in public areas such as hotels and wireless networks. Software firewalls can be used with most operating systems including Windows 2000, Windows 98, Windows ME, and Windows 2000. Windows XP and Vista contain built-in firewalls.

A software firewall, which does not require any additional hardware or computer wiring, is a good option for individual computers. Its advantage over a hardware-based firewall is outbound application checking. A software firewall is more expensive, especially if it needs to be installed on multiple computers, though many free products are also available. It may also need to be installed and configured before it can be used. Typically, a software firewall cannot be used with multiple computers on a network. However, this is possible if the broadband router is attached to a single computer, which is shared.

Hardware firewall

A hardware firewall is a device that is installed between two security domains, like your local network and the Internet. In the case of a network, a hardware firewall is placed between the Internet and the network computers, typically using a hub so that the Internet connection can be shared. The technology used for this purpose is called Network Address Translation (NAT), which prevents external computers from directly communicating with any computer on the network. Hardware firewalls can also be used for home computers.

Hardware routers, which handle Internet traffic, can also provide firewall protection against external attacks. Their benefit is lower cost, as a single router can provide firewall protection for multiple computers. However, even though a router can defend against external attacks and outgoing attacks (if it has the capability to block unauthorized outbound traffic), it will not be effective against internal malware. Host-based firewalls can be easily disabled by malware, which is not true of a hardware-based firewall.

Windows firewall

The latest version of Windows XP, *Window XP Service Pack 2 (SP2)*, has a built-in firewall. The default setting is "on" but can be turned off if desired. To download SP2, visit *www.microsoft.com*. Even without SP2, firewall protection can be enabled by turning on the built-in *Internet Connection Firewall (ICF)*. The latest release of the Windows operating system, Vista, has a built-in firewall along with many enhanced security features.

Firewall with a wireless router

A wireless router enables computers and peripherals to be connected without any physical wiring. Many wireless routers have built-in firewalls. However, to ensure greater protection, a wireless router should be complemented by a standalone firewall.

Firewall types to use

The type of firewall to use depends on the configuration—individual computer or multiple computers on a home network. For an individual computer, a personal software firewall should be adequate. While either a hardware or software firewall may be sufficient for most users, it is advisable that protection be enhanced by using both. The downside of using both types of protective devices is higher cost. Also, in general, hardware-based firewalls are more difficult to configure. For protecting multiple computers, a hardware firewall may be more cost-effective. Another factor is the operating system (Windows with its many flavors, Apple Mac, Linux, etc.), which may or may not provide its own firewall protection. Two software firewalls should not be used simultaneously as they can interfere with each other.

USING AND MONITORING FIREWALLS
Checking firewall protection

To verify if the installed firewall is protecting the computer, an independent tool can be used to perform a check. A useful tool is the ShieldsUp test, available at Gibson

Research (*www.grc.com*), which can scan a computer for browser vulnerabilities, open network ports, and similar security flaws. It can also perform the Leak test, which can identify a computer's vulnerability to Trojans. Symantec also provides a scanning tool that can perform a free online security test (*www.symantec.com/techsupp/home_homeoffice/index_virus.html*).

A tool from Microsoft, Baseline Security Analyzer, can be used to check if the latest Windows security patches and service packs have been installed. It also checks for incorrectly configured security settings. The tool can be downloaded from *www.microsoft.com/downloads*.

Monitoring firewall logs

A firewall log should be monitored periodically to enhance security. When an unusual event occurs, it will be easier to identify abnormalities, such as activity patterns and probes, if they are recorded in the log. Monitoring the log will make it easy to identify the ports and services being targeted by intruders. If any weakness is detected, appropriate protective measures can be taken before any damage is inflicted.

Another benefit is that if the computer is compromised, the firewall log can help determine when and how the penetration was successful. It may even provide the IP address of the hacking computer. Based on the information gathered, the security hole can be plugged to prevent subsequent attacks. One of the best ways to respond to persistent attacks, especially if they originate from the same IP address, is to report them to your ISP.

Re-evaluating custom rules

In general, when configuring custom rules, set a deny-by-default policy whenever possible. These can be relaxed on a case-by-case basis. After custom rules or filters have been configured for the firewall, it should not be assumed that they will remain good for ever. Periodically, these rules should be revisited and re-evaluated to ensure that they are still appropriate, based on any changes since they were initially implemented, as the environment can change fairly rapidly. For example, the security level may need to be elevated due to the unleashing of a new and dangerous malware. Also, it is fairly common for a user to disable some rules for a specific requirement, such as the installation of a new application, and then forget to revert back to the previous more stringent configuration.

Choosing a firewall

Many firewalls are available in the market whose features, functions, prices, strengths, and weaknesses vary quite a bit. Firewall selection should be based on the individual needs for security level desired, number of computers to be protected, and cost. Some available firewalls include:

- Zone Alarm Pro
- Norton Personal Firewall
- McAfee Personal Firewall
- Agnitum Outpost Firewall
- Windows Firewall
- BlackIce PC Protection

A comprehensive list of software firewalls, along with their descriptions, is provided in Chapter 14, which also contains a list of free firewalls. Hardware routers/firewalls are provided by a number of vendors including Linksys, Belkin, Netgear and D-Link.

FIREWALL ISSUES
Some programs do not work as expected
The installation of a firewall or its customized settings can lead to some, or all, features of an application not working as designed. This issue can be resolved by modifying the firewall settings so that traffic to/from the computer is allowed for that particular application. This can involve opening specific ports, which the application requires, on the computer.

Windows NetBIOS file and printer sharing does not work
The installation of a firewall can cause problems in Windows NetBIOS file and print sharing. To enable Windows file and print sharing, some ports need to be opened on each computer that contains the files to be shared. These are the UDP ports (137, 138, and 445) and TCP ports (139 and 445).

IM programs are unable to transfer files
Some IM programs are unable to transfer files due to their port requirements, which can differ from the firewall's default settings. This issue can be solved through IM program configuration so that it always uses the configured ports. Both the firewall as well as the device connecting the computer to the Internet (router, etc.) will need to be configured for those ports. Be aware that sharing files via IM increases the risk of malicious attack.

Firewall issues with Windows XP Professional

If an attempt is made to remotely connect to your Remote Desktop from another computer, a firewall will prevent that connection because, by default, it blocks all incoming
traffic. The solution for this issue is to modify the firewall setting so that TCP port
3389 is opened in order to receive incoming traffic.

PC and Home Network Protection

HOME COMPUTER SECURITY
Risks for home computer users

Personal computers are exposed to three primary risks. The first risk category pertains to confidentiality. Any data available on the computer should only be accessible and available to authorized users. The second risk category involves integrity. No one except authorized users should be able to change any data on the computer. The third risk category is availability. The data stored on the computer should be available to authorized users whenever it is needed.

A computer can be exposed to these risks when it is either online or offline. Offline risks include theft, compromising of passwords, equipment failure, etc. (the first two offline risks imply that the intruder has access to the computer). However, the risks from the Internet are considerably higher. Many of these risks can be reduced or eliminated, as will be explained in subsequent sections.

Objective of computer security

When a computer is compromised many problems can result, the magnitude of which depends on the purpose and type of intrusion. The problems can include identity theft, stealing of IDs and passwords, loss of privacy, user behavior monitoring, attack on other computers, abnormal application behavior, performance degradation, etc. To avoid these and other problems, every computer should be secured.

The objectives of securing a computer are:
- Preventing unauthorized use of a computer by blocking intruder access
- Detecting successful or unsuccessful unauthorized attempts to access the computer
- Determining what an intruder may have done after breaking into the system

How computers can be compromised

It is relatively easy to break into a computer. Many break-ins can be attributed to friends, relatives or others to whom access may have been provided on a limited basis. A very common and simple way is to obtain the user ID and password for booting the computer or launching an application. However, professional intruders perform the most serious break-ins via the Internet. They use the operating system/application security vulnerabilities, or holes, to gain access to a computer. Many of these vulnerabilities can be taken care of by installing fixes, called patches, which the operating system or application vendor provides. Hence, it is important that computers be kept up-to-date with the latest security patches.

Most common intrusion methods

A wide variety of methods are used to gain unauthorized access to computers. These include Trojan Horses, viruses, Java, JavaScript, ActiveX, e-mail spoofing, backdoor and remote administration programs, etc. Another widely-used method is cross-site scripting, a computer security vulnerability. In this method, a developer attaches a malicious script to a transmission to a website, which can be an element in an interactive form (such as a form that a user fills out on a web page). When such a website responds to an Internet user's request, it transfers the script to the user's browser. Sources for such contamination can be e-mails, URL links and HTML tags, website forms, discussion group sites, etc.

Packet sniffing is another method that captures data from information packets transmitted over the Internet. Using this method, IDs, passwords, and other personal and financial data can be compromised. Many attacks, such as the *LoveLetter* worm, exploited hidden file extensions. An extension may appear to be harmless by appearing as a .txt or other extension, when it actually may be an executable (.exe) file or a malicious script. Chat clients (software that resides on a user's computer for handling instant messaging or chat rooms) are vulnerable to intrusion because many of them allow the exchange of executable code. These chat clients also permit the exchange of URLs and files, which carries risks.

How to protect

While many techniques and steps can be taken to protect a computer, there are some basic protective requirements that every user must implement, which are listed in the following sections.

Primary protection techniques

- Update the operating system with the latest service packs, updates, and patches,

such as Service Pack 2 for Windows XP
- Install anti-virus and anti-spyware software and keep them up-to-date; configure them for automatic update of definitions
- Install a firewall
- Perform regular scans for malware
- Keep applications up-to-date by installing available patches and security fixes

Additional protection techniques

The following are additional recommendations for protecting a home computer:
- Do not open e-mail attachments from unknown sources. Be careful when opening any file attachment, even if appears from a known source, as it may be spoofed. If an unexpected file attachment arrives and there is any suspicion at all, ask the sender via an e-mail to confirm the authenticity of the e-mail and the safety of the attachment.
- Before opening a file attachment, save it to the hard disk and then scan it with anti-virus and anti-spyware software.
- Do not execute a program of unknown origin unless it can be trusted.
- Disable the hidden filename extensions setting in the Windows operating system (the default setting is enabled for "Hide file extensions for known file types"). This will cause Windows to display file extensions.
- Disable Java, JavaScript and ActiveX, if possible, as they are common sources of malicious mobile code. Disable all scripting languages to reduce vulnerability to malicious scripts. The downside is that the functionality of some websites will be degraded. Chapter 10 demonstrates how to configure scripting. To view detailed instructions for disabling browser scripting languages, visit the CERT website (*www.cert.org/tech_tips/malicious_code_FAQ.html*).
- Disable scripting features in e-mail programs, which can be impacted just like web browsers running Java, JavaScript, and ActiveX.
- Backup data on a regular basis.
- Create a boot disk for use in an emergency situation. Also, have handy the original installation disk (for Recovery Console).
- Disconnect the computer from the Internet when it is not being used for online activities.

HOME NETWORK SECURITY
Need for home network protection

A home network is a system in which two or more computers are interconnected to form a local area network (LAN). The network permits its components to communicate with each other. The connected computers can share an Internet connection, files and documents, programs, printers and other peripheral devices.

Home networks, like individual computers, are also susceptible to various types of malware and security threats and consequently must be protected. The risk level of a home network depends on its weakest component. For example, if a network has four computers, it will only be as strong as the weakest PC, which will be the easiest one for an intruder to break into. In addition to the protective measures for individual computers, home networks also need to be protected.

How to protect

The basic requirement is to use a router, a hardware firewall, between your network and the Internet. This can be complemented by software firewall protection for each individual computer on the network. If all the computers are connected directly to the broadband modem, which has built-in protection, then the network is protected. To verify that this protection is available and adequate, the ISP should be contacted for verification.

Typically, when a broadband router or a wireless device is used to connect the broadband modem to the network, the router/device configuration should be based on NAT. This should be verified from the available equipment documentation.

Suppose a network has five computers out of which three PCs have been installed with Windows XP, one with Vista, and the fifth one with Windows 98. In this case, the weakest computer is the PC installed with Windows 98 and the best-protected one is the one installed with Vista. However, the network will only be as strong as the PC with Windows 98, as an intruder can initially gain access via the weakest PC and, subsequently, compromise the other four computers. Hence, every individual computer must be protected at the desired minimum level of security.

A network can be additionally secured by implementing these steps:
- If the computer runs Windows with Internet Connection Sharing, install a firewall
- If Windows XP, which has a built-in firewall, is being used, ensure that the firewall is turned on
- Use a broadband router, if:
  - A network hub is being used
  - All the computers are connected to the broadband modem without a built-in firewall
- Use WPA2 or 802.22i on the wireless network. Do not use WEP unless it is the only technology that your wireless hub supports.

For additional information on this topic, visit the CERT website (*www.cert.org/tech_tips/ home_networks.html*).

Broadband and corporate networks

Broadband networks for home users are always connected to the Internet in contrast to dial-up or DSL users. While the ISP provides some level of protection, the responsibility for a protecting a home computer lies with the individual user. Corporate networks have many levels of protection, which can include firewalls, encryption, as well as professional support and service. They also have high availability requirements as they cannot afford to have any downtime. A typical home network user does not have such requirements or resources. However, many of the security protective measures are common for both types of networks. Whenever possible, if cost is not prohibitive, protections implemented for corporate networks should also be implemented for home networks.

Wireless Malware and Network Protection

UNDERSTANDING MOBILE MALWARE
Wireless malware

A wireless worm or virus is a type of malware that infects wireless devices, such as personal digital assistants (PDAs), handheld PCs, cell phones, handheld devices, laptops, etc. Such malware can erase data, cause devices to malfunction, compromise personal and confidential data, initiate cell phone calls, as well as cause other problems associated with conventional viruses and worms. Though wireless worms and viruses are not as widespread as their conventional counterparts, their infection rate is expected to increase.

How wireless viruses and worms are spread

Mobile viruses and worms can be spread just like conventional viruses and worms. Infections can occur through the downloading of infected files, programs, ring tones, video clips, games, photos, etc. Many such malware infections are received via text messages. When a text message is opened, the virus or worm starts its malicious actions, which can include crashing the device, copying and transmitting the message to all phone numbers in the address book, etc. At this time, malware that transfers from a laptop or desktop to wireless devices is not a problem, though it has the potential to develop.

Bluetooth risk

Bluetooth is a wireless technology that enables the transfer of data between different devices over short distances, including mobile devices. While this is a useful technology, it also has associated risks. For example, the worm Cabir replicated through a Bluetooth connection. The Skulls virus disabled applications and replaced screen icons with skulls, causing all functions except incoming and outgoing calls to be disabled. If a Bluetooth-enabled mobile device is in "discoverable" mode, and it is located within a short distance (30 ft) of an infected Bluetooth-enabled device, it can be infected by a mobile virus if both the devices are using the same operating system. By default, the discoverable mode is switched off for Windows mobile devices.

Protecting against mobile viruses

The methods previously listed for protecting against conventional malware should be applied against wireless malware, whenever possible. Those techniques and behaviors can be supplemented by the following tips:

- Secure the phone's operating system
- Keep wireless drivers updated and patched
- Use passwords to protect mobile devices, whenever possible
- Download files, photos, ring tones, etc., only from trusted sources
- Turn off Bluetooth when it is not being used

WIRELESS NETWORKING
What is wireless networking

A home network is used to connect multiple home computers so that they can access the Internet simultaneously. To enable this, the typical method has been to use gateway devices, called routers, to which the individual computers are physically connected by an Ethernet cable. This architecture often requires extensive cabling through walls and crawl spaces, which can be a real issue when the computers are located in different rooms and/or floors in the home.

To provide flexibility and work around physical constraints, routers with wireless capabilities have been developed. The wireless network architecture allows a wireless router to be connected to individual computers equipped with a wireless card. The routers and wireless cards are often preinstalled and available as a standard component in many computers and laptops. Also, they are an inexpensive add-on option. Consequently, they have become very popular in the past few years. The Windows XP operating system, which offers built-in support for wireless network configuration, has also contributed to the popularity of wireless networking.

Connecting to a wireless network

In addition to connecting to your own wireless home network, you can connect to an external wireless network if your computer and/or laptop is wireless-enabled (contains a wireless network card). The prerequisite is that the wireless network's signals reach your computer. For example, you can connect to your neighbor's wireless network, provided it is not secured by a password, if its signals reach your machine. Similarly, you can connect to other networks such as those available at airports, Starbucks, etc.

To access a wireless network, three simple steps are required:

- Locate the wireless network(s) within range (can be one or many networks)
- Select a network
- Access the selected network

In populated areas, if one drives around with a laptop, tens of networks can be identified and any one of them can be accessed provided they are not protected.

Wireless network protection

Wireless networks must also be protected like physically-connected networks. Wireless protection requirements are even more stringent as wireless networks are inherently less secure than wired networks, due to the elimination of physical barriers. A wireless network can be easily accessed by an outsider if it is not properly protected. For example, neighbors can easily pick up a user's wireless network signals. Therefore, if a user's wireless network is unprotected, neighbors can log onto his network, which can have serious consequences. This principle of easy access for anyone is demonstrated at public hotspot locations such as Starbucks. Their wireless networks are unprotected and any user with a laptop can access them. Most users are unaware of this and consequently most wireless networks either have minimal or no security at all.

An intruder accessing a network via a wireless device bypasses the firewall, which is located between the broadband modem and the network. Consequently, the network loses the protection provided by the firewall due to the backdoor entry. This makes it imperative that wireless networks' default settings are changed to ensure a high level of protection.

Enterprises are better at protecting their networks than individuals. However, the level of security across enterprises can vary, ranging from weak to very stringent. For example, some use 40-bit encryption key size while others use 128-bit key, which translates into different protection levels. Some do not use encryption at all. In general, enterprises also have to deal with higher security standards. For example, they have legal, privacy, intellectual property protection, and other requirements that force them to have the highest possible security that they can afford to implement. They also have to deal with corporate crackers who have very high technical skills. Hence, corporate security requirements are far greater than home users.

Consequences of an unsecured wireless network

While an average home user has a greater risk of being hacked from the Internet via a physical connection, the installation of a wireless device adds another means of unauthorized access from the air which does not require an intruder to get past the router firewall. The consequences of an unsecured wireless network are the same as explained in Chapter I. If a computer connects to an unsecured wireless network that does not require a password, a cracker can potentially connect to it without the user being aware of it. Once connected, the intruder can use the computer just like the genuine user and potentially access or steal confidential and personal data. Other consequences include:

- Free access to the Internet
- Impact on bandwidth
- Illegal activities for which the network owner may be held liable
- Backdoor entry to corporate data through a VPN (virtual private network—a secured access path through which company users can access their organization's systems and data)
- Injection of malware
- Network data sniffing
- Capturing of passwords
- Denial-of-service attacks

WIRELESS PROTECTION TECHNOLOGIES
What is WEP

Wired Equivalent Privacy (WEP) encryption is an older technology used to protect wireless networks, which should only be used if it is the only one that is supported by the user's system. WEP is based on encrypting data transmitted between two wireless devices, which can be a combination of devices such as two computers, a laptop and an access point, or two access points. While encrypted data can be intercepted, its jumbled format makes it practically useless to a hacker, especially a casual hacker, who will need to spend an inordinate amount of time trying to decipher it.

Enabling WEP

The steps involved in enabling WEP are:

1. Configuring the wireless access point which is the device connected to the broadband, cable or DSL modem. The specific configuration depends on the manufacturer. Use the longest key that is supported by the available devices (wireless access

point and wireless network adapters).

2. Configuring the wireless network adapter (which may either be pre-installed in the computer or plugged in). Determine the key length it can support (40-bit or 128-bit), configure the WEP using the device's installation documentation, and setup a password.

The configuration section of the documentation for the hardware (router, access point, or the network interface card) provides the necessary information required to enable WEP. It provides information about the type of key, alphanumeric or hex (a numeral system with a base of 16), as well as the key itself. Identical settings for the key length and the key should be used on all devices or they will be unable to communicate with each other.

WEP levels

WEP can be implemented at different levels. The length of the key used for encrypting the data determines the level of protection afforded by the device. The longer the key length used for encryption, the more difficult it becomes to decipher (crack) the transmission. The early versions of 802.11b were implemented using a 40-bit key, which provided the bare minimum protection. Other versions include the 64-bit key (which is effectively the same as 40-bit, as it also uses a 40-bit key) and the 128-bit key. Some of the latest products support 256-bit WEP.

The highest level of protection should be provided for a wireless network. This means that the highest level of WEP supported by the hardware should be used. When different hardware devices that support different WEP levels are used, use the highest level that is common to all components.

WEP weaknesses

There are two major weaknesses of WEP. The first is encryption weakness—WEP encryption is not strong. Unless manually changed, the encryption key of all lengths remains static and, hence, the network's data traffic can be monitored. Over time, if a hacker has powerful computing capabilities, the key can be deciphered, which can potentially expose the user's data. If required, changing the key on all network devices can be a maintenance burden, especially if there are many connected components. The second problem is authentication weakness. WEP does not authenticate network users. The solution for this has been to use MAC address filtering; however, MAC address filtering has its own limitations, as a consequence of it being associated with a network device and not a user.

Avoid using WEP-only segments for home networks as they can be easily hacked and provide a backdoor entry to other computers attached to the network. You can determine if your access point is secure or unsecure from the *Wireless Network Connection (Choose a wireless network)* window (Figure 8). In Figure 8, three of the four listed networks are secured.

Figure 8

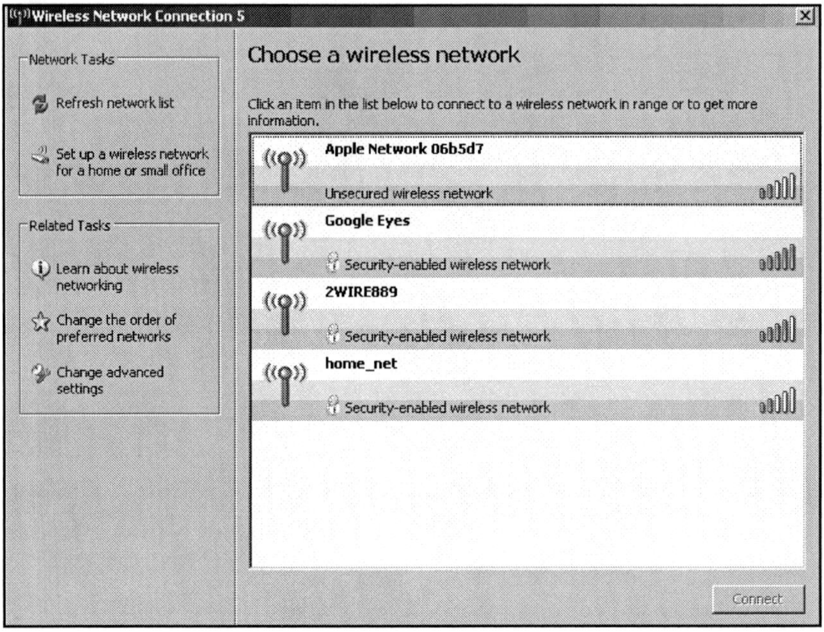

On many networks, the encryption method is displayed below the network name (SSID). A WPA-encrypted network, which is based on an improved standard, is specifically listed as a WPA.

What is WPA

Wi-Fi Protected Access (WPA) is an improved standard for wireless protection, which eliminates some of the weaknesses associated with WEP. Some of its enhanced features include the following:

- User has to provide a master key, a password used for verification and network access
- Master key does not remain a static encryption key
- Master key is the starting point, which is used to derive the key for encryption
- Key is changed regularly (and automatically)

WPA has two types:
- WPA-Enterprise (for large networks)
- WPA-Personal (for small business and home wireless networks)

Most WEP devices can be upgraded to WPA. However, any upgrade should include all network devices including access points and components such as adapters. A partial upgrade will have limited effectiveness as the weaker components will remain the vulnerable intrusion points. WPA is the preferred technology for users and businesses desiring higher security levels, provided their available hardware can support it. For new installations, it is advisable to implement WPA or WPA-2.

What is WPA-2
Wi-Fi Protected Access 2 (WPA2) is an upgraded and stronger version of WPA. It has two versions:
- WPA2-Enterprise
- WPA2-Personal

WPA-2 uses an advanced encryption standard (AES) instead of the temporal key integrity protocol (TKIP) used by WPA. If your wireless network supports it, use WPA2 instead of WEP or WPA.

LOCKING DOWN A WIRELESS NETWORK
Configuring wireless products can be a challenge for most home network users. However, it is worth the effort to implement wireless security features if you want to avoid the repercussions of an unsecured system. The following sections explain the fundamental requirements for securing home wireless networks. Note that while the tips covered in this chapter are applicable to 802.11b networks, which are most widely used, they can be applied to most types of networks.

Establishing the SSID
Select a wireless transmitter that has built-in security features. The first step requires the setup of the Service Set Identifier (SSID)—the wireless network name. It may need to be either established or changed. Do not use the default name as manufacturers tend to use the same SSID name for all their products. For example, Linksys uses the SSID *Linksys* for all its devices. Change the SSID to something that is not easy to guess, like a combination of numbers and characters. The

subsequent steps include:

- Establishing a WPA passphrase on the router or access point.
- Configuring all network wireless computers/devices so that they are associated with the SSID of the router or access point. Use the same passphrase.

Preventing the SSID from being broadcast

The access point or the router typically broadcasts the network name (SSID) over the air, at regular intervals. This is an unnecessary feature that a home network can do without, as it can be an invitation to neighbors and/or hackers. If your network name is broadcast and it gets listed in someone's list of networks, that person can easily select your network and log into it.

The SSID broadcast should be disabled. This will prevent others from knowing that your network exists. Some devices require a firmware upgrade while others do not support this feature at all. If the SSID is disabled and thus is not broadcast, the user will need to remember it as it will be required for connecting new devices to the network. The actual steps required to stop broadcasting vary from router to router and even from model to model. The appropriate device's documentation should be referred to for configuring this step.

Keep in mind that disabling SSID broadcasts provides minimal security as current wireless hacking tools can easily enumerate the SSID. A more effective way to protect is to implement WPA-2 or 802.11i technologies.

Enabling password protection for connecting to the network

A password should be established for connecting to the network. Strong passwords with characters and numbers should be used and they should be changed periodically. User log-ins should be established for each computer and the guest account should be disabled.

Changing the wireless hub's default password

The default passwords provided by the manufacturer for administrator access to the wireless router or access point should never be used, as hackers are usually familiar with them. If possible, the setting should be changed to ensure a unique administrator name and password. If this change is not implemented, it is possible that a wireless network sniffer program can identify the manufacturer from the broadcast, which can enable the hacker to determine the default password from publicly-available sources (like the manufacturer's website). You should also ensure that the wireless hub has updated, patched code.

Enabling MAC address filtering

Every network component has a unique identifier or serial number, a hardware address called the *MAC address*. The router and access points monitor the MAC addresses of all the devices that are connected to them. A network can be restricted by only permitting devices with specified MAC addresses to connect to it. If such a restriction is put into place, all other devices will be restricted from accessing the network. The network administrator can specify the approved MAC addresses in the list of devices that can connect to the network. The list can be updated if a new device needs to be added to the network.

To obtain the MAC address on Windows XP, navigate as follows:

- *Windows > Start > Run*
- Type *command* in the *Open* field
- Click *OK*
- Type *ipconfig /all*
- Hit *Enter*

This will display the MAC address, displayed as a *Physical Address*, which is a 12 digit number identifying the network card installed in your computer. It is usually in the format XX-XX-XX-XX-XX, as shown on Figure 9.

Figure 9

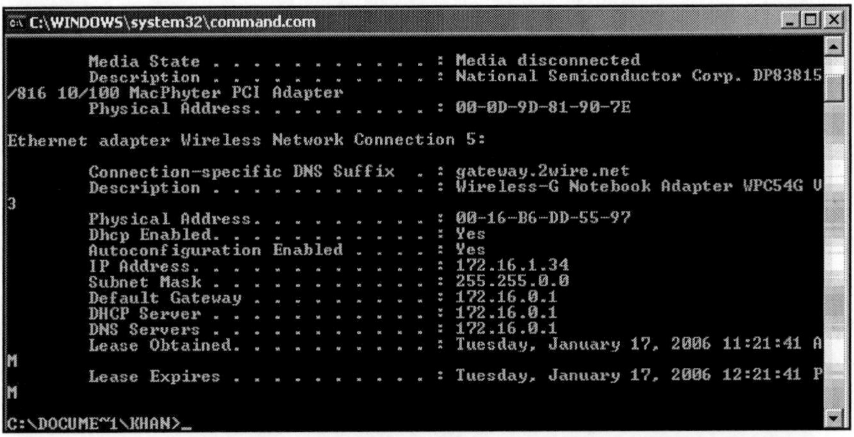

MAC address filtering does not provide a perfect defense as MAC addresses can be spoofed. However, it does provide another element of security. It should be noted that all routers and access points do not provide MAC-filtering capabilities. Some devices can filter based on IP addresses. However, that technique is characterized by a weakness as IP addresses are not always unique and can also be changed, making the filter ineffective. The steps required for enabling MAC address filtering varies from manufacturer to manufacturer and from model to model.

Enabling encryption

Encryption involves the scrambling of data being transferred between two devices so that it cannot be intelligible to anyone monitoring it. Most wireless devices support encryption, though the level of security provided by various encryption technologies varies considerably. The strongest encryption technology should be selected. However, cost considerations and the support provided by the available devices may force the selection of a weaker technology.

When a choice exists for implementing 64-bit or 128-bit encryption, select the latter as it is less likely to be hacked. Use WPA/WPA-2 encryption technology. There exist even stronger encryption technologies such as RADIUS, whose hardware requirements are higher (such as dedicated server). However, for most home users, it is not a practical option at this time.

Disabling DCHP

Dynamic Host Configuration Protocol, DCHP, is a protocol for assigning dynamic IP addresses to devices on a network. With dynamic addressing, a device can have a different IP address every time it connects to the network. When DCHP is enabled, any new network host broadcasting a request for an IP address and TCP/IP configuration information will be provided with such information, which is very convenient for users. However, the downside is that a hacker can easily connect to the wireless network, as he can obtain the TCP/IP configuration information required to connect to the network by setting up his own computer to use DHCP. Therefore, DHCP should be disabled and static IP addresses should be assigned, even though it will cause inconvenience and additional work for the network user. For the hacker, it will create another hurdle for connecting to the network, as it will force manual configuration of the TCP/IP properties.

Turning off setting to connect to non-preferred networks

The setting to connect to non-preferred networks automatically, which used to be enabled by default in older versions of Windows, should be turned off. This will prevent other network users from connecting through your computer's Internet connection. In Windows XP SP2 and Vista, this setting is disabled by default. To ensure that this setting is not enabled:

- Right-click on the wireless connection icon (in the notification area, which is located in the bottom right-hand corner of the monitor)

- Click menu item *Status*
- Click the *Properties* button
- Click the *Advanced* tab
- Remove the checkmark, if it has been placed, for the item *Allow other network users to connect through this computer's Internet connection*

Turning off file-sharing

On Windows XP, it is possible to turn off file sharing for additional network security. To specify the folders that can be shared, navigate as follows

- *Control Panel > Folder Options*
- Click the *View* tab
- Uncheck the item: *Use simple file sharing (Recommended)*

This particular function can be used for any computer to protect against any attack, not just wireless attacks.

MORE WIRELESS PROTECTION TIPS
Turning off remote administrative access

If possible, turn off remote administrative access over the Internet for the router. In such a case, configuration changes can be made after connecting to the router using a wired connection.

WPA passphrase

A WPA passphrase can contain up to 63 characters. The passphrase should contain as many characters as possible, preferably at least 15-20 random characters. It is advisable to use strings and words that are not commonly used and cannot be associated with the user. The usage of strong passwords, such as a combination of upper case and lower case characters mixed with numbers, is recommended. Periodically, the passphrase or password should be changed.

Security when traveling

Additional security precautions should be taken when connecting to public wireless networks and hotspots with a laptop. These networks use very little security and cannot be counted on to encrypt data. If you want to check your work e-mail, use a VPN (which uses an encrypted tunnel) instead of a browser. If a VPN is not available, use the *Remote Desktop* connection.

Positioning the router

To minimize the external area to which the wireless signals from a router or access point can be reached, install the device in the center of the home, rather than at extreme points.

Using when required

Use the network only when it is required. As a security measure, turn off the network when it is not in use, especially during extended periods of non-usage. Disable your wireless network card when it is not being used; this can be as easy as pulling the card out if it is not built-in. Also, configure wireless settings so that automatic connection with nearby networks is disabled.

Using the Windows XP SP2 Wireless Network Setup Wizard tool

Configuration changes to a network can be an overwhelming task for casual users. Novice users can use the Windows XP SP2 Wireless Network Setup Wizard tool, which can create a new wireless network or add another computer or device to the existing wireless network, quickly and easily. More information about this tool is available at *www.microsoft.com/windowsxp/using/networking/getstarted/windowsconnectnow.mspx.*

Browser Protection

SECURING THE BROWSER
Need for browsers to be secured

Web browsers are used to access and surf the Internet. The most popular browsers are Internet Explorer, Netscape, Firefox and Safari, which are installed on most home computers. From a security perspective, the default configuration of most home computer browsers is inadequate. Therefore, it should be modified to make the security settings more stringent. If this step is not taken, the computer will remain vulnerable to external threats and, in the worst-case scenario, can be taken over by an intruder.

Malware developers are aware of browser security vulnerabilities, patches that are released to overcome known browser limitations, and user behavior. Every day, they probe and test potential weaknesses and exploit them when they find them. Hence, even if a browser is secured at some stage, it needs to be updated diligently through the implementation of newly-announced security patches in order to maintain its secure status.

Why browsers are vulnerable

The web browser is a popular gateway for intruders who want to access or control a computer connected to the Internet. The reason is that browsers have vulnerabilities that they can exploit relatively easily. For example, malware developers create websites that install spyware or a Trojan Horse on the visitor's computer. In a more aggressive type of scenario, crackers actively probe computers connected to the Internet, especially those with vulnerable browsers.

Browser vulnerabilities are often caused by features that provide web browser functionality, such as ActiveX, Java, JavaScript, VBScript, etc. The problems can be attributed to a variety of reasons. The most common ones are poor configuration, faulty design, specific weakness of the technology, and inferior software.

The browser vulnerabilities problem has been aggravated by a number of factors, including the following:

- Most users do not possess the skills required to securely reconfigure their browsers.
- Newer threats are developed at a non-stop pace. Hence, even a brand new computer's browser may be vulnerable to a just-unleashed threat.
- Many websites force users to install additional software to enable certain features, which increases the risk.
- Many users are unwilling to disable features that make their browser more vulnerable.
- Many users are unaware or unable to determine if their computer has been compromised.
- In many cases, even when a problem has been identified and a cleanup effort is undertaken, the decontamination is incomplete.

Browser features and vulnerabilities vary considerably

Many types of browsers are available for PC users. Internet Explorer comes installed with the Windows operating system. However, other browsers such as Firefox and/or Netscape can also be installed on the same machine. Vista, which is Microsoft's latest desktop operating system, also includes Internet Explorer 7, which is a browser that is far more secure than Internet Explorer 6. Internet Explorer 7, expected to be released to the general public in early 2007, has a special Protected Mode feature that does a lot to stop drive-by downloads. All these browsers can be configured with different security settings. If two or more browsers are installed on a computer, securing a single browser will not automatically protect the other browsers. Each browser will need to be configured individually.

Since the available browsers differ considerably in their features, users need to be aware of their installed browser's strengths, weaknesses, configuration options, and whether they impact security positively or negatively. Based on that knowledge, a particular feature may be enabled or disabled. For example, many websites require that the ActiveX feature be enabled. However, enabling the browser to permit the ActiveX feature often increases the browser's vulnerability.

Where browser settings are configured

If not correctly configured, the security-related browser settings lead to vulnerabilities most often exploited in browsers and websites. These settings are configured in the Internet Explorer's Security zones, which are used to specify multiple levels of security settings. Subsequent sections of this chapter, as well as Chapter 10 and Chapter 11, demonstrate how to configure these zones. For more information on setting up security zones, visit the Microsoft website at (*www.microsoft.com/windows/ie/using/howto/security/setup.asp*).

Security-related features that can be configured

This section lists security-related features that can be configured for browsers. The description of these features, which will be technically challenging for most readers of this book, has been provided for informational purpose only—for readers who may desire to understand the background and technical aspects of the items that will be configured in subsequent sections and chapters.

- ActiveX: This feature, which allows a web browser to utilize an application or parts of an application, provides enhanced functionality for web browsing. Using ActiveX in a web browser can increase security vulnerabilities considerably. A vulnerability of ActiveX is that an attacker can gain control of the computer. Many vendors use ActiveX for enabling the installation of their software. The default setting causes Windows to prompt a user for permission to install such an application. However, a browser can be setup to automatically run ActiveX controls without obtaining user permission.

- Active Content: These are plug-ins, such as Macromedia's Flash, which are used by browsers. They are used by websites to add functionality to static web pages. However, they can also be used to install malware or hijack a computer. While similar to ActiveX, they cannot be executed outside a web browser.

- Malicious scripting and HTML: Some websites, through underhand means, cause visitors to provide information or perform an action that will enable them to gain privileges, which can be used for subsequent unauthorized or unwanted actions. The mechanism used for this purpose can be Active Content, HTML, or a malicious script.

- Java: This is an object-oriented programming language used for developing Active Content for websites. To execute Java code, a Java Virtual Machine (JVM) is required on the client computer and, hence, may need to be installed before the Java functionality can be used. JVM can contain vulnerabilities that can enable various restrictions, which limit interaction with the rest of the system, to be bypassed.

- JavaScript: This is a dynamic scripting language used for developing Active Content for websites. In contrast to Java, a browser interprets JavaScript directly.

- VBScript: This is a Windows programming language that has limited compatibility with non-IE browsers and hence is not as widely used.

- Cross-site scripting: This website vulnerability enables an intruder to benefit from the trusted relationship that a user has with a website.

- Cookies: These text files are placed on a computer by a website for a variety of reasons including login information, preferences, etc.

- Spoofing: For browsers, this involves the faking of the address or location bar, status bar, or other elements for the purpose of obtaining personal and confidential data. This technique is usually associated with phishing attacks.

- Security models (cross-zone and cross-domain): To prevent a website from accessing a different domain's data, browsers employ security models. An intruder can use a security model vulnerability to access restricted and protected areas and perform actions that normally would not be possible.

GETTING STARTED

This section will demonstrate how to secure a web browser and also disable features that pose a security risk. You should be aware that browsers are updated periodically. Therefore, some of the steps or features shown here may not reflect how a particular feature may work or be configured on your computer. Since Internet Explorer is the most widely used browser, the steps and screenshots shown in subsequent sections are limited to IE, with a few exceptions.

About IE

Internet Explorer is the web browser provided with the Microsoft Windows operating system. IE supports technologies associated with browser vulnerabilities including ActiveX, Java, Scripting, and Active Content. There exist many flavors of the Microsoft Windows operating system including Vista, Windows XP Professional, Windows XP Home Edition, Windows 2000 Professional, Windows ME, Windows 98, etc. The steps that will be demonstrated in subsequent sections for securing and configuring IE will primarily be based on the Windows XP operating system.

To check the IE version that is installed on your computer, navigate as follows (Figure 10):

- *Internet Explorer > Help > About Internet Explorer*

Figure 10

This will lead to the following window, Figure 11, where the desired information is displayed.

Figure 11

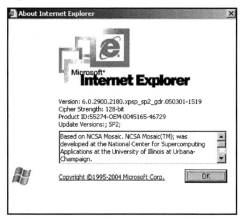

Note the version number (6.0) and update version (SP2 - Service Pack 2).

Where IE settings are made

To change the IE settings, navigate as follows:

- *Internet Explorer > Tools > Internet Options*

Figure 12

Understanding cookies

Cookies are small data tags that are placed on a computer by websites, enabling them to recognize and/or track the user's behavior and navigation, customize displays according to user preferences, pop-up ads, etc. IE can be configured so that only desirable cookies are placed on the user's computer. The configuration steps vary from IE browser version to version. In IE version 5, cookies can be configured within the various security zones (*Security* tab), while in IE version 4, they can be configured on the *Advanced* tab. In IE version 6, cookies are configured on the *Privacy* tab.

Cookies are of two types: permanent and session. Permanent cookies are those that can be permanently stored on a computer's hard drive, where they are available to the website that placed them. Temporary or session cookies are those that are deleted when the browser session is closed.

Cookies are also categorized into:

- First-party cookies: These are placed by the website being visited. For example, you visit Amazon.com and it places a cookie on your hard drive.
- Third-party cookies: These originate from a website other than that being visited. For example, you visit AOL.com and it places a cookie on your hard drive from one of its advertiser's servers.

IE provides the ability to disable stored cookies, and selectively manage and delete cookies.

Deleting all cookies

To delete all cookies, navigate as follows:

- *Tools > Internet Options*

Figure 13

- Click the *Delete Cookies* button, which will delete all cookies

On older versions of IE, cookies can be deleted from the *Temporary Internet Files* directory. Be aware that deleting all cookies can create issues with some websites. For example, they can cause your online banking preferences to be deleted. Consequently, whenever you visit the bank's website, your preferences or data may need to be re-entered unless the cookies are reinstalled.

Cookies can be deleted selectively. They can also be managed through IE browser configuration, so that some cookies are selectively blocked while others are allowed.

Selectively deleting cookies

IE can be configured so that all cookies are rejected. It can also be configured to accept all cookies, which the user can subsequently manage selectively. This can be done by viewing the cookies that are placed on the hard disk, in the *Temporary Internet Files* folder, and then selectively deleting the undesirable ones.

To view the contents of the *Temporary Internet Files* folder, navigate as follows:

- *Tools > Internet Options*

Figure 14

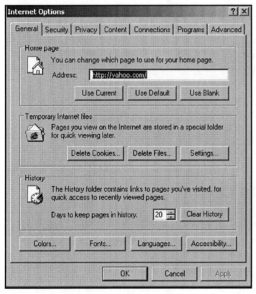

- Click the *Settings* button

This will lead to the following window (Figure 15):

Figure 15

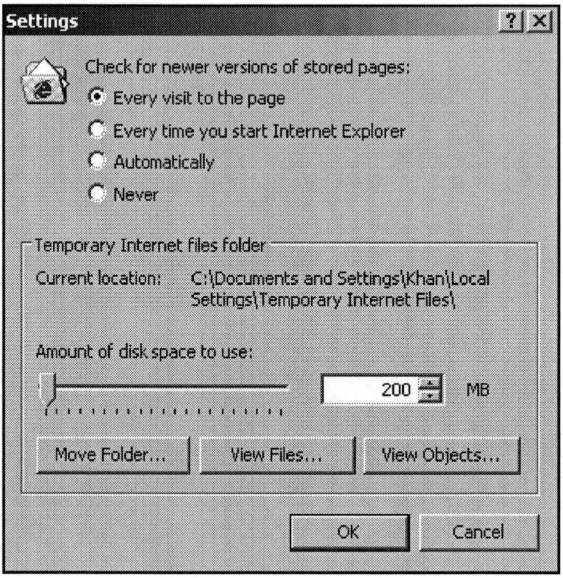

- Click the *View Files* button

This will lead to the following window (Figure 16):

Figure 16

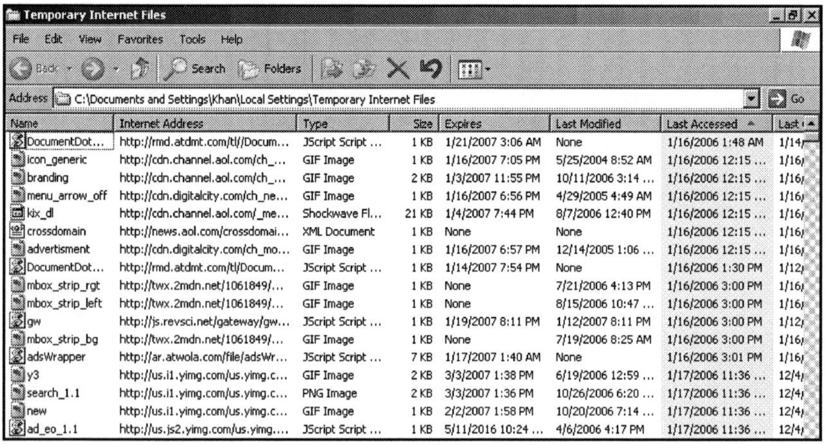

Any cookie displayed in this window, Figure 16, can now be deleted. To delete an item:

- Click on the item to be deleted
- Hit the *Delete* button on the keyboard

Deleting history

To delete a record of the websites that have been visited, i.e., history, navigate as follows:

- *Tools > Internet Options*
- Click the *Clear History* button

C H A P T E R T E N

Internet Zone

SECURING THE INTERNET ZONE

The Internet Explorer 6 configuration options have been split into seven tabs:

- General
- Security
- Privacy
- Content
- Connections
- Programs
- Advanced

Navigating to the security tab

Most of the security settings are configured in the *Security* tab. To access this area, navigate as follows:

- Launch Internet Explorer
- Navigate via the menu path *Tools* > *Internet Options*

Figure 17

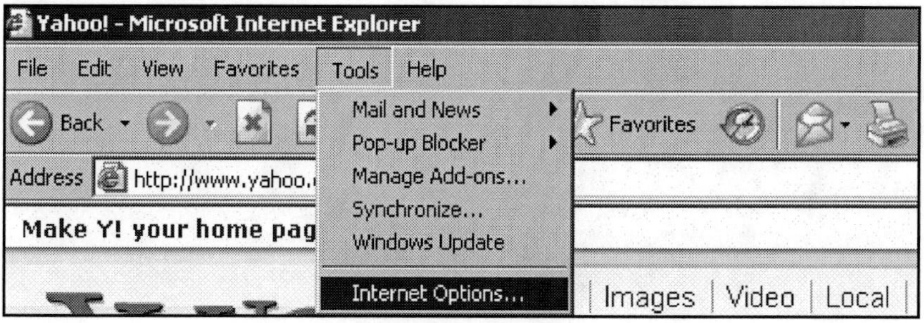

This will lead to the following window (Figure 18):

Figure 18

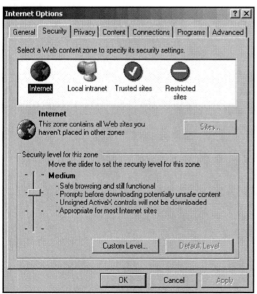

• Click the *Security* tab

This will lead to the following window (Figure 19):

Figure 19

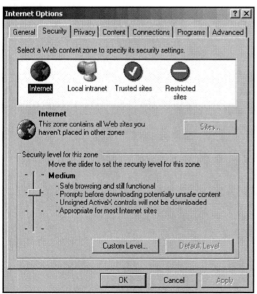

Security tab zones

The security tab contains four different zones that can be used to configure the level of security, depending on the level of confidence that is associated with a website. These zones, which can be accessed via the four icons displayed on Figure 19, are:

- Internet
- Local Intranet
- Trusted sites
- Restricted sites

Most of the security configuration settings will be done in the *Internet* zone, which is highlighted on Figure 19.

Placing websites in various zones

A balance is required between security, privacy, and convenience. Low security increases the risk of unwanted downloads, with obvious consequences. Very restrictive security settings provide maximum security but they can degrade the performance of some websites and render them less useful. By default, all websites fall in the *Internet* zone. Also, by default, all non-local websites are automatically placed in the *Internet* zone unless they are manually placed elsewhere by the user. All local (on the same network) websites are automatically placed in the *Local intranet* zone unless the user manually puts them elsewhere.

A website can be specifically placed under another zone, such as the *Trusted sites* or *Restricted sites*. Only trusted websites should be placed in the *Trusted* zone. When a website is visited for the very first time, it is placed in the *Internet* zone, where it will remain unless it is added to one of the other zones (such as the *Trusted* or *Restricted* zone).

Internet zone settings

Each zone can be configured to the desired level of security. The *Internet* zone can be configured at four levels: High, Medium, Medium-Low, and Low. Medium is the most appropriate level for most websites. The level can be changed by simply moving the slider, shown on Figure 20, up or down to the desired setting. Selecting the *High* setting, the selection that is displayed on Figure 20, will disable ActiveX, Java and Scripting and hence make the browser more secure.

Figure 20

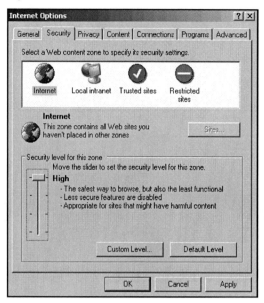

Security (Custom Level) settings

To customize additional settings for ActiveX, Java and Scripting, at the *Custom* Level, navigate as follows:

- *Tools* > *Internet Options*
- Click the *Security* tab, which will display the window shown on Figure 20
- Click the *Internet* icon to select the Internet zone
- Click the *Custom Level* button

This will cause the *Security Settings* window to pop-up (Figure 21).

Figure 21

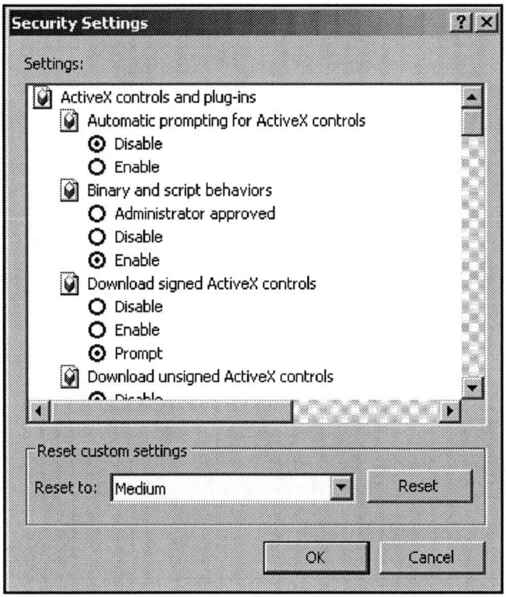

Various customized settings can be configured on this window by simply selecting or deselecting various radio buttons.

CONFIGURING SETTINGS
Settings that are most widely configured

The settings that are most often configured to secure the Internet zone from malicious websites are the following:

- ActiveX controls and plug-ins
- Java permissions
- Scripting

If a website does not work as expected due to the disabling of Active Content, a solution is to add such a site to the Trusted sites zone, where the security is less restrictive.

Configuring ActiveX controls and plug-ins

To configure ActiveX controls, navigate as follows:

- *Tools > Internet Options*
- Click the *Security* tab, which will display the window shown on Figure 20
- Click the *Internet* icon to select the Internet zone
- Click the *Custom Level* button

This will lead to the following window (Figure 22):

Figure 22

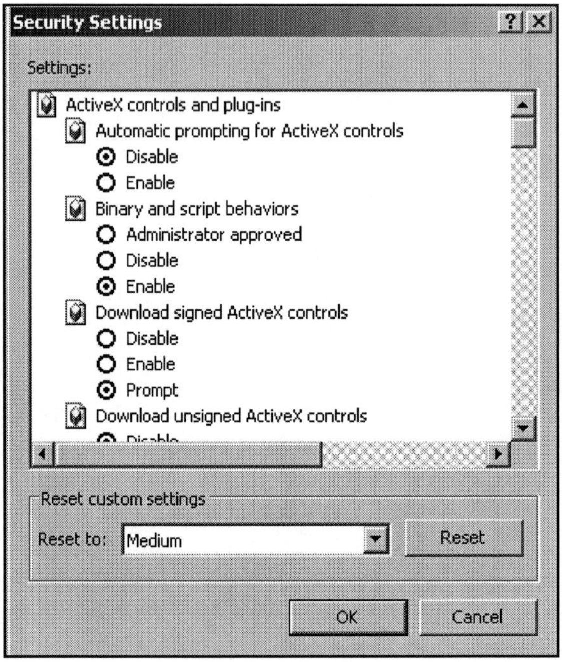

On the *Security Settings* window, Figure 22, configure each option by selecting the appro-
priate radio button. For example, the following three options are currently displayed:
- Automatic prompting for ActiveX controls: *Disable*
- Binary and script behaviors: *Enable*
- Download signed ActiveX controls: *Prompt*

To ensure the highest level of security:
- Change all ActiveX controls and plug-ins settings to *Disable*
- Click the *OK* button (after making the desired selections)

To view additional options, use the scroll bar on the *Security Settings* window. Selecting
the *Prompt* setting will lead to many pop-up confirmations, which many users have
difficulty in coping with. Hence, use this setting only if you can handle the frequent
pop-ups that this setting will generate.

Configuring Java permissions

On the *Security Settings* window (Figure 22), scroll down until the *Microsoft VM* selections are displayed, shown on the following window (Figure 23):

Figure 23

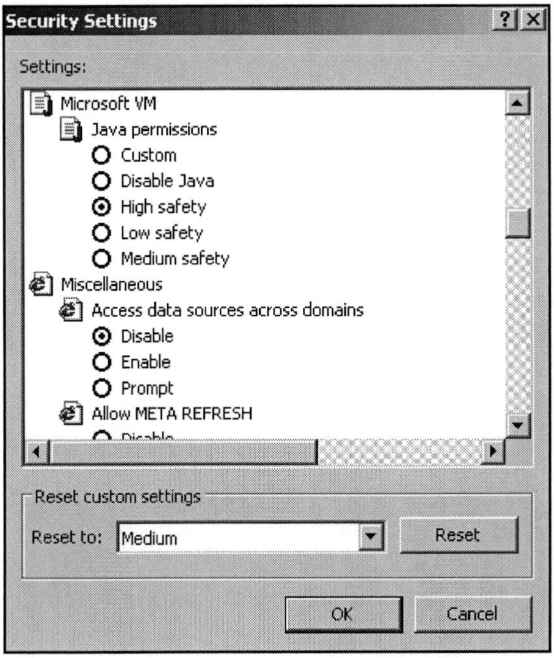

For the highest security level:
- Select the *High Safety* radio button

The Java Permissions can also be configured using another method. On the previous window (Figure 23):
- Click the *Custom* radio button (under *Java permissions*)

This will cause a new button, *Java Custom Settings*, to pop-up on the window as shown on Figure 24:

Figure 24

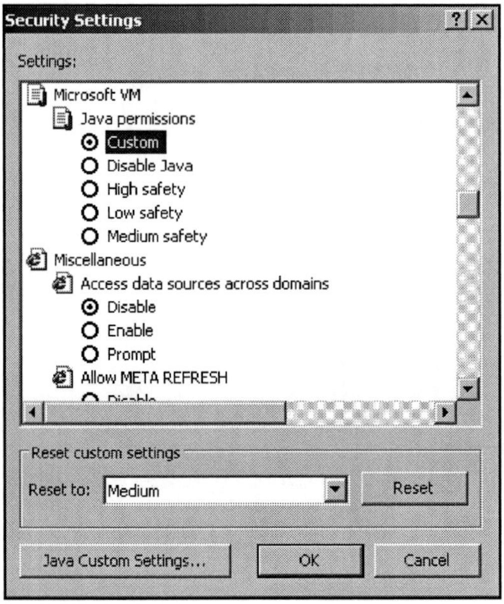

• Click the *Java Custom Settings* button

This will cause the following window to pop-up (Figure 25), provided Microsoft's Java JVM has been installed, where the security settings can be configured under the two tabs (*View Permissions* and *Edit Permissions*):

Figure 25

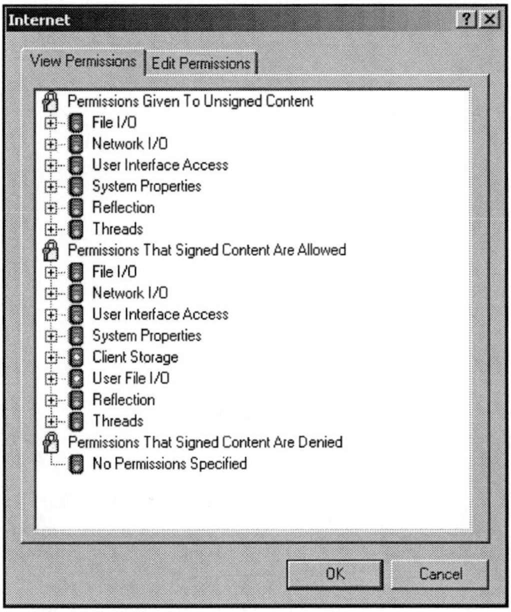

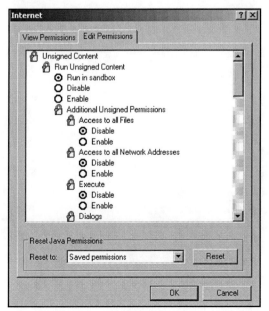

• Click the *Edit Permissions* tab

This will lead to the following window (Figure 26), where the permissions can be set.

Figure 26

- Change the settings, as required
- Click the *OK* button

Configuring Scripting

On the *Security Settings* window, scroll down until the *Scripting* selections are displayed, as shown on Figure 27:

Figure 27

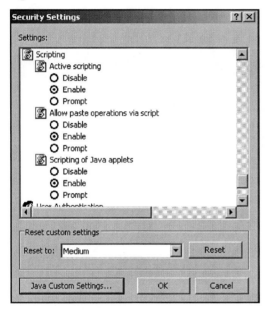

On Figure 27, all the scripting selections are enabled. To ensure the highest level of security:

- Change all *Scripting* settings to *Disable* (by clicking on the appropriate *Disable* radio buttons)
- Click the *OK* button

Configuring Miscellaneous settings

On the *Security Settings* window, scroll down until the *Miscellaneous* selections are displayed, as shown on the next window (Figure 28):

Figure 28

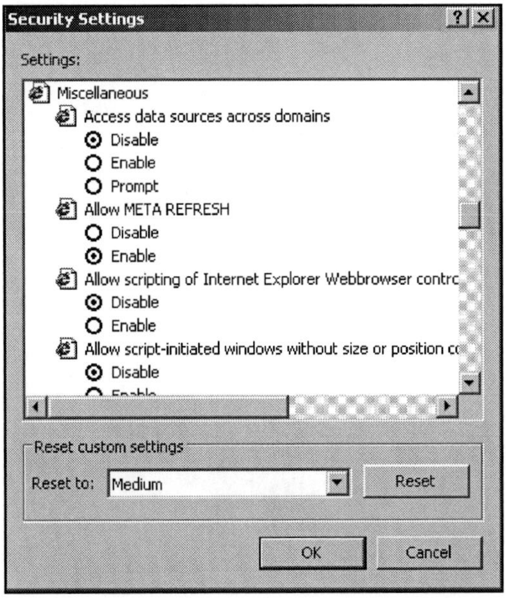

To ensure the highest level of security:

- Change the following *Miscellaneous* settings to *Disable* as they can increase vulnerability:
    - Access data sources across domains
    - Allow META REFRESH
    - Display mixed content
    - Installation of desktop items
    - Launching programs in an IFRAM
    - Navigate sub-frames across different domains
    - Userdata persistence

  Since the *Disable* setting can cause problems with legitimate websites, most of these settings can be set to *Prompt.*

- Click the *OK* button

Example of suggested settings for the Internet zone

Table I Internet Zone		
ActiveX controls and plug-ins	Download signed ActiveX controls	Disable
	Download unsigned ActiveX controls	Disable
	Initialize and script ActiveX controls not marked as safe	Disable
	Run ActiveX controls and plug-ins	Disable
	Script ActiveX controls marked safe for scripting	Disable
Downloads	File download	Enable
	Font download	Prompt
Microsoft VM	Java permissions	Disable Java or High Safety
Miscellaneous	Access data sources across domains	Disable
	Allow META REFRESH	Enable (or disable)
	Display mixed content	Prompt
	Don't prompt for client certificate selection when no certificate	Disable
	Drag and drop or copy and paste files	Enable
	Installation of desktop items	Disable
	Launching programs and files in an IFRAME	Disable
	Navigate sub-frames across different domains	Enable (or disable)
	Software channel permissions	High safety
	Submit nonencrypted form data	Enable
	Userdata persistence	Disable
Scripting	Active scripting	Disable
	Allow paste operations via script	Disable
	Scripting of Java applets	Disable
User authentication	Logon	Automatic logon only in Intranet zone

Trusted and Restricted Sites Zones

TRUSTED SITES ZONE
Objective of the Trusted sites zone

The *Trusted* sites is an IE security zone. Only websites known to be safe, with trustworthy content and not expected to pose a risk to the computer, are added to this zone. By default, websites are placed in the *Internet* or *Local Intranet* zones, which should be configured with a higher level of security, as shown earlier. If a website has not been added to the Trusted sites zone, and the Internet zone has been secured properly, it will be unable to use Active Content like Scripting, Java, and ActiveX. This can reduce the website's functionality. In such a case, three options are available:

- Do not use that website or the missing functionality
- Add the website to the Trusted zone, which will increase the risk
- Lower the security settings of the Internet zone (without adding the site to the Trusted zone), which will increase the risk

Trusted sites zone settings

The Trusted sites zone uses security settings that are different than the Internet zone. These settings have lower security and hence can create vulnerabilities if the wrong websites are placed in the Trusted Sites zone. The default settings in the Trusted zone, which are set to *Low*, enable ActiveX, Java, Scripting, and Cookies. The settings in this zone can also be customized. Some browser hijackers, after taking control, place websites in this zone. This enables them to bypass the Internet zone's higher security settings and execute actions like downloading ActiveX components onto the computer.

Accessing the Trusted sites zone

On the Internet Explorer, navigate as follows:

- *Tools > Internet Options > Security tab*
- Click the *Trusted sites* icon, which will display the following window (Figure 29)

Figure 29

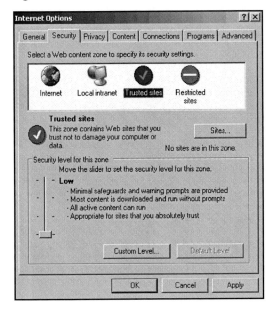

On Figure 29, the current (default) setting is *Low*. To increase the security level (to make it more restrictive):

- Move the slider up

The next figure, Figure 30, shows the window after the slider was moved up (to the *Medium* level):

Figure 30

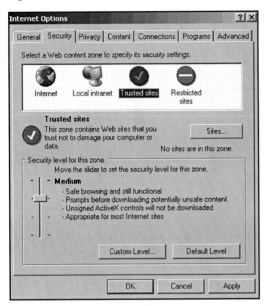

You can start off by selecting the *Medium* level setting for the Trusted zone. If you experience issues with the websites placed in this zone due to the *Medium* setting, such as inability to display web pages, modify the security level by lowering the setting to the *Low* level.

To restore the default setting, i.e., *Low*, after making some change(s):

- Click the *Default Level* button
- Click the *OK* button

Adding a site to the Trusted site zone

To add a website to the *Trusted* zone, navigate as follows:

- *Tools > Internet Options > Security tab*
- Click the *Trusted sites* icon
- Click the *Sites* button (which is shown on Figure 30)

This will lead to the next window, Figure 31, where the *Add* button is grayed out:

Figure 31

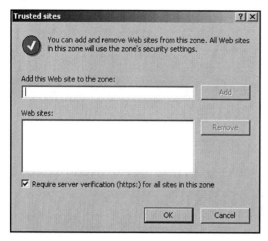

On this window, individual websites can be added to the *Trusted sites* zone by typing the website address in the appropriate field. For example, on the next window, Figure 32, Microsoft's web address has been typed in:

Figure 32

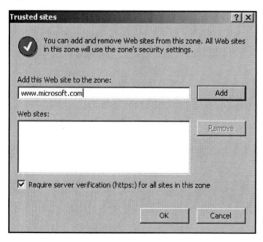

- Uncheck the *Require server verification (https:) for all sites in this zone*

Leave the checkmark in place if you want to ensure that only websites with Secure Sockets Layer (SSL) are added to this zone. SSL provides a secure connection to a website and ensures that the site being visited is the one that it claims to be. The URL address of an SSL-enabled website starts with https:// (not http://), as was shown on Figure 7.

After the website address has been typed in, the *Add* button will no longer be grayed out, as shown on Figure 32.

• Click the *Add* button

This will move the trusted website into the lower section of the window, as shown on Figure 33:

Figure 33

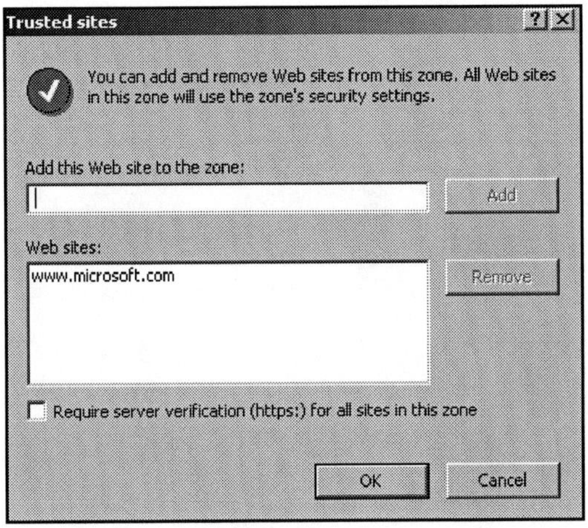

• Click the *OK* button

If required, more websites can be added using the same procedure. To include all websites within a particular domain to the Trusted zone, use a leading asterisk wild card as shown below:

*.microsoft.com

This will ensure that all websites in the Microsoft domain, such as *www.download.microsoft.com* and *www.office.microsoft.com*, will be included—rather than just *www.microsoft.com*.

If you occasionally visit a website that requires scripting and you do not want to add it to the Trusted zone or lower the security settings on the Internet zone, use a second browser such as Firefox whose usage can be limited to infrequently visited sites. However, be aware that scripting can be risky for any browser and, therefore, should only be allowed for trustworthy sites.

The zone (Internet, Trusted or Restricted) to which the current website belongs can be verified by observing the zone icon located at the bottom right-hand corner of the Internet Explorer window.

Figure 34 and Figure 35 are two examples of websites being placed in different zones: Internet zone (washingtonpost.com) and Trusted sites zone (cnn.com).

Figure 34

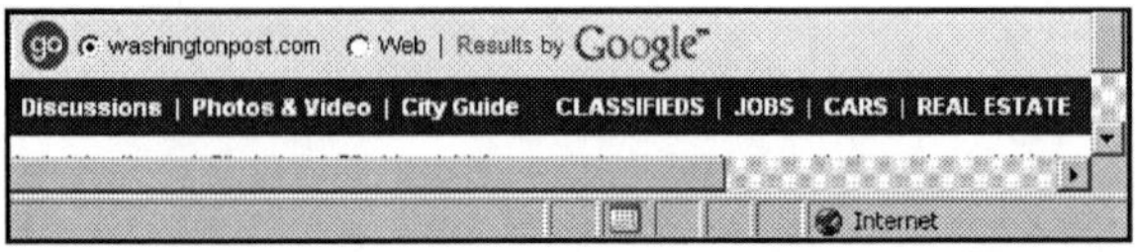

Figure 35

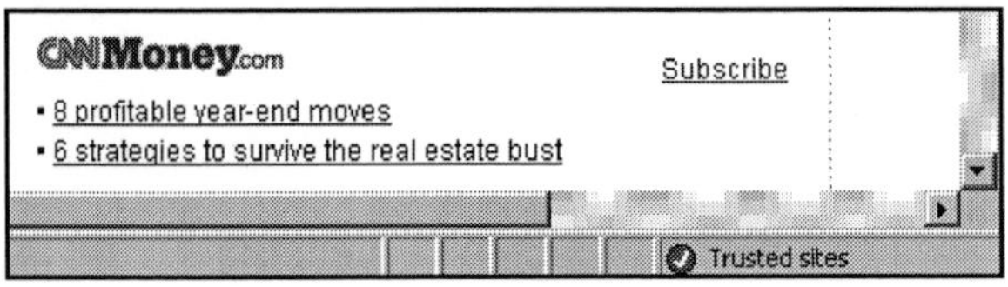

Tips for adding websites to the Trusted sites zone

Adding a website to the Trusted zone has its pros and cons. It lowers security but enables functionality that can be exploited if suspicious websites are added to the zone. The decision to add a particular website should be made after carefully evaluating the potential benefits and risks. Since these are unique and different for each situation, you need to review your own requirements and desired risk level and, subsequently, make a personal decision on whether to add a website to the Trusted zone. For example, when evaluating the placement of your banking website, you will want the enablement of full functionality, including ActiveX. Therefore, you will have few concerns and hence it is expected that you will quickly add the website to the Trusted sites zone. However, if you are visiting a recently-discovered website that you like, you need to be conservative. Be careful and evaluate it for some time before making a decision to add it to the Trusted zone.

In general, add a website to the Trusted zone only if:
- It is extremely important or essential
- It requires features, such as ActiveX or Scripting, which have been disabled in the Internet zone and you do not want to relax that restriction in the Internet zone
- It belongs to a well-known, reputable and trustworthy organization
- Adding the site will not interfere with user experience (such as generating excessive pop-up windows, animation, etc.)

Example of suggested settings for the Trusted zone

Table 2 Trusted Zone		
ActiveX controls and plug-ins	Download signed ActiveX controls	Prompt
	Download unsigned ActiveX controls	Prompt
	Initialize and script ActiveX controls not marked as safe	Prompt
	Run ActiveX controls and plug-ins	Enable
	Script ActiveX controls marked safe for scripting	Enable
Downloads	File download	Enable
	Font download	Enable
Microsoft VM	Java permissions	High safety
Miscellaneous	Access data sources across domains	Disable
	Allow META REFRESH	Enable
	Display mixed content	Prompt
	Don't prompt for client certificate selection when no certificate....	Disable
	Drag and drop or copy and paste files	Prompt
	Installation of desktop items	Prompt
	Launching programs and files in an IFRAME	Prompt
	Navigate sub-frames across different domains	Enable

	Software channel permissions	Medium safety
	Submit nonencrypted form data	Enable
	Userdata persistence	Enable
Scripting	Active scripting	Enable
	Allow paste operations via script	Prompt
	Scripting of Java applets	Prompt
User authentication	Logon	Automatic logon only in Intranet zone

RESTRICTED SITES ZONE
Adding a site to the Restricted site zone

The Internet Explorer's Restricted site zone is used to block undesirable websites that are known to be threats. To add an unwanted website to the Restricted site zone, navigate as follows:

- *Internet Explorer > Tools > Internet Options*
- Click the *Security* tab
- Click the *Restricted* sites icon
- Click the *Sites* button

This will cause the following window to pop-up (Figure 36):

Figure 36

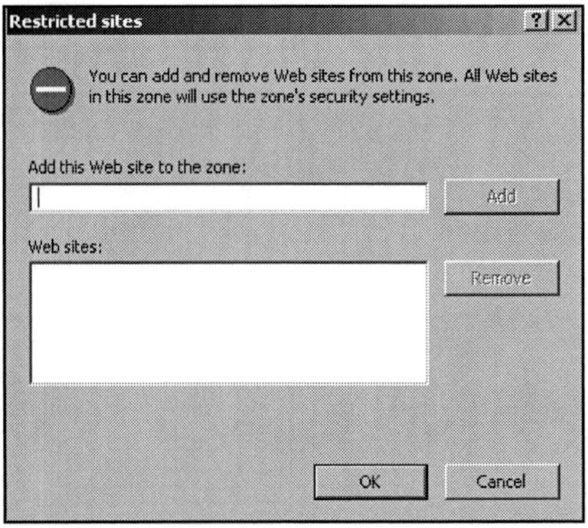

To specify the address of the website that is to be restricted:
- Enter the address (URL) in the appropriate field, as shown in the example on Figure 37

Figure 37

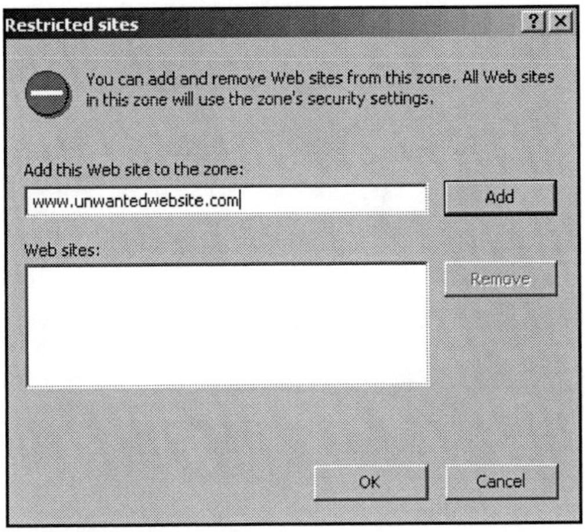

- Click the *Add* button
- Click the *OK* button

This manual procedure of adding known problem websites and domains to the Internet Explorer's Restricted Sites zone can be simplified by using tools like IE-Spyad.

MANAGING WEBSITES IN SECURITY ZONES
Removing a website from a security zone

To remove a website that has been placed in any of the security zones, such as Trusted or Restricted, navigate as follows:
- *Internet Explorer > Tools > Internet Options*
- Click the *Security* tab
- Click the *Trusted sites* icon (alternatively, click the *Restricted* sites zone icon if the site to be removed is located in that zone)
- Click the *Sites* button

This will display the list of websites that have been added to the selected zone in the lower *Websites* section of the window, as shown on Figure 38:

Figure 38

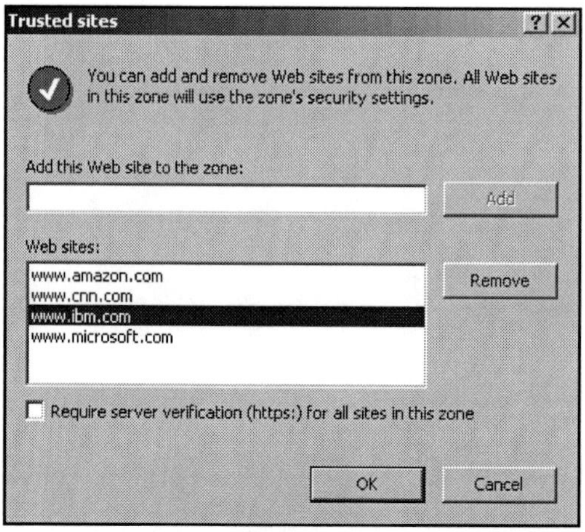

- Click the website that is to be removed (such as *www.ibm.com*)
- Click the *Remove* button
- Click the *OK* button, which will lead to the *Internet Options* window
- Click the *OK* button

Adding the menu option for Trusted and Restricted zones

Microsoft provides a Security zone utility that makes it easy to add websites to the Trusted zone or the Restricted zone. The utility adds two additional menu items, *Add to Trusted Zone* and *Add to Restricted Zone*, to the Tools menu on the Internet Explorer as shown on the next window (Figure 39).

Figure 39

To use this utility to add the website being visited to the desired zone, Trusted or Restricted, navigate as follows:

- *Internet Explorer > Tools*
- Select the appropriate IE menu item (*Add to Trusted Zone* or *Add to Restricted Zone*), which will cause the website to be added to the desired selected zone

This utility, known as *Internet Explorer Power Tweaks Web Accessories*, can be downloaded from Microsoft's website *(www.microsoft.com/windows/ie/previous/webaccess/default.mspx)*.

CHAPTER TWELVE

More Browser Security Settings

CONFIGURING COOKIES ON IE

Managing cookies

Cookies can be managed in the Internet Explorer browser. To access this feature, navigate as follows:

- *Internet Explorer* > *Tools* > *Internet Options*
- Select the *Privacy* tab, which will lead to the following window (Figure 40)

Figure 40

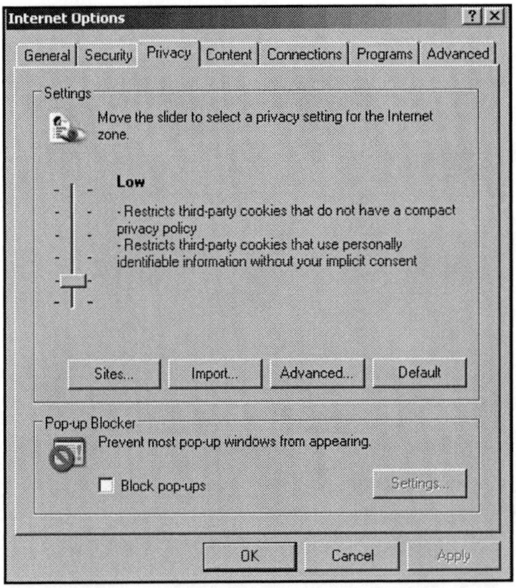

On this window, cookies can be configured via:
- Adjustment of the slider bar
- *Advanced* button
- *Import* button

These three methods are mutually-exclusive, which means that only one method can be used at any one time. Notice that this window can also be used to perform a useful function—users can block pop-ups simply by placing a checkmark located next to the text *Block pop-ups.*

Using the slider bar to configure cookies

The setting displayed on the previous window, Figure 40, can be modified by moving the slider up or down to the desired setting. Using the slider, any of the following options can be selected:
- Accept all cookies
- Low
- Medium
- Medium High
- High
- Block all cookies

Consequences of adjusting the slider bar settings

The slider bar is an easy way to configure cookies. However, it does not allow a user to selectively block cookies from some sources while accepting beneficial cookies from desirable sources. The slider bar's various settings can also create some problems. For example:
- If all cookies are blocked, some websites may not operate as designed. The website may be unable to recognize the user (as any registration/other data will not be saved on the computer), surfing may not be as smooth or uninterrupted as desired, etc.
- Despite the *High* setting, third-party cookies may still be stored.

Overriding automatic cookie handling

The cookies setting can also be customized to override automatic cookie handling. To customize, navigate as follows:
- *Tools > Internet Options*
- Click the *Privacy* tab
- Click the *Advanced* button, which will lead to the next window (Figure 41)

Figure 41

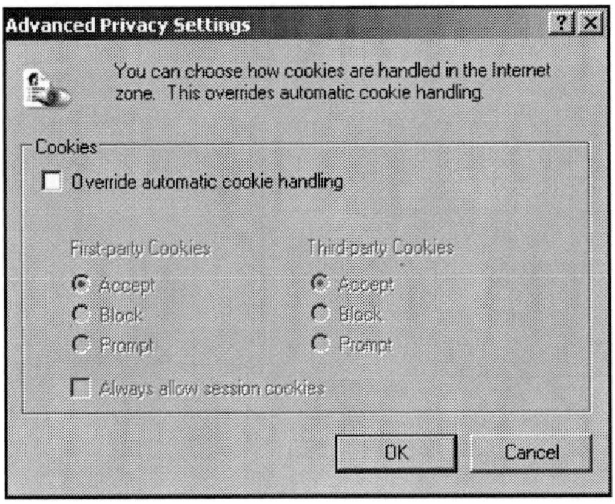

• Place a checkmark next to *Override automatic cookie handling*

This will enable the selection of the various radio buttons that were previously grayed out, as shown on the following window (Figure 42):

Figure 42

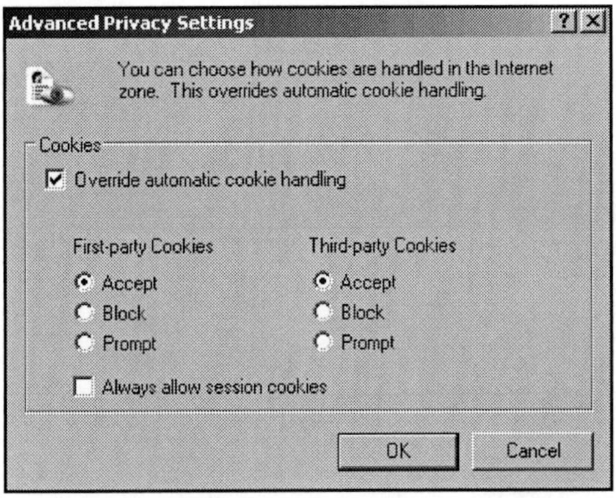

• Select the desired radio button for the *First-party* cookies
• Select the desired radio button for the *Third-party* cookies
• Click the *OK* button

These cookie settings will apply only to the Internet zone. By default, cookies are accepted in the Trusted sites zone. In the Restricted sites zone, all cookies are blocked by default.

To start with, select the *Prompt* option for first-party and third-party cookies, which will provide a better understanding of how and which cookies are being installed on the computer. With experience, users can modify the settings so that there is no need to intervene every time a cookie is about to be installed.

The settings made via the *Advanced* button provide a more effective way to protect the computer. You should note that the configuration settings made on the *Advanced* button override the settings made via the *Settings* slider bar.

Managing cookies for specific sites

In addition to the three methods for configuring cookies, listed previously, IE provides the flexibility to add specific websites on the *Per Site Privacy Actions* window. Cookies from such websites will always be allowed or blocked despite any other setting made by using the slider bar, because the *Per Sites Privacy Actions* configuration overrides those settings. The only exceptions are two slider bar settings: *Accept All Cookies* and *Block All Cookies.*

To access the *Per Site Privacy Actions* window, navigate as follows:
- *Tools > Internet Options > Privacy tab*

This will lead to the *Internet Options* window, displayed on Figure 40.
- Click the *Sites* button, which will cause the following *Per Site Privacy Actions* window to pop-up (Figure 43)

Figure 43

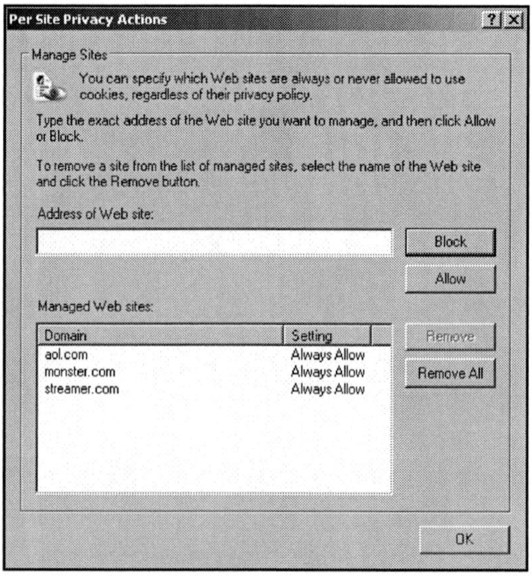

To block (or allow) cookies from a website:
- Add the website's address in the *Address of Website* field
- Click the applicable *Block* (or *Allow*) button
- Click *OK*

To remove a website:
- Click the website (in the lower *Managed Websites* section of the window)
- Click the *Remove* button

Configuring using the XML Privacy Import file

Cookies can also be configured using a special XML Privacy Import file. The XML files to be imported need to be built before this procedure can be implemented. Therefore, due to its high skill level requirement, only advanced users should use this method. The XML Privacy Import file contains pre-configured settings that can be used to configure two zones: Internet zone and Trusted sites zone. The XML Privacy Import settings override the settings made with the slider bar.

To import an XML Privacy Import file, use the following steps:
- *Tools > Internet Options > Privacy tab*

Figure 44

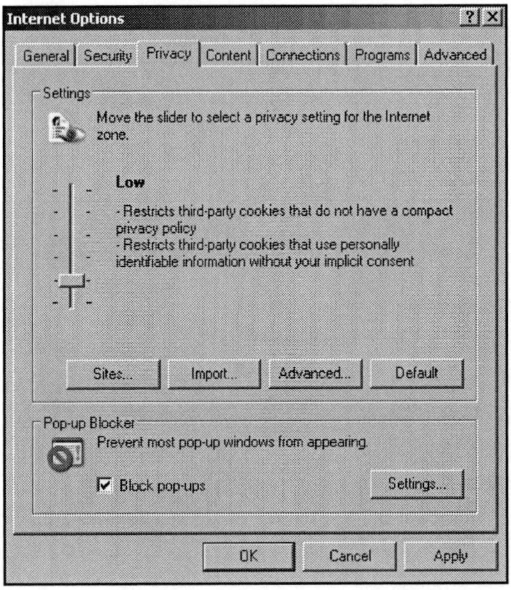

- Click the *Import* button

This will cause the *Privacy Import* window to pop-up.
- Navigate to and select the XML file to be imported
- Click the *Open* button

Consequences of changing Privacy tab settings

Changing the Privacy tab settings can impact the web surfing experience and also increase or decrease the risk to the computer. Some of the negative impacts of changing the Privacy tab settings to increase security include difficulty in logging into websites that require a login and password or some other type of authentication, blocking of promotions from websites, broken websites, frequent interruptions at some websites due to pop-ups requiring confirmations, etc. Since individual requirements and risk tolerance varies considerably, every user must decide how to strike a balance by evaluating the risk of a liberal/restrictive security policy versus the benefits to be gained or lost due to its implementation.

MANAGING COOKIES USING
WINDOWS EXPLORER
Displaying the contents of the cookies folder

The Windows Explorer can also be used to manage cookies. To display the folder where the cookies are stored, navigate as follows (for Windows XP or Windows 2000):
- *Windows > Start > Explore*
- Navigate to the folder via menu path: *Documents and Settings > User name > Cookies*

Note that cookies are stored at a different location (*\Windows\Cookies*), on other Windows operating systems like Windows 98, Windows ME, etc.

Cookies should not be deleted from the cookies folder. Instead, they should be deleted from the *Temporary Internet Files* folder. Deleting cookies from the cookies folder will not remove them from the *Temporary Internet Files* folder. Hence, cookies should be deleted there, which will automatically remove them from the cookies folder.

Deleting cookies from the Temporary Internet Files folder

To display the Temporary Internet Files folder for Windows XP or Windows 2000, navigate as follows:
- *Windows > Start > Explore*

- Navigate to the folder via the menu path: *C:\Documents and Settings\User name\Local Settings\Temporary Internet Files*

Figure 45

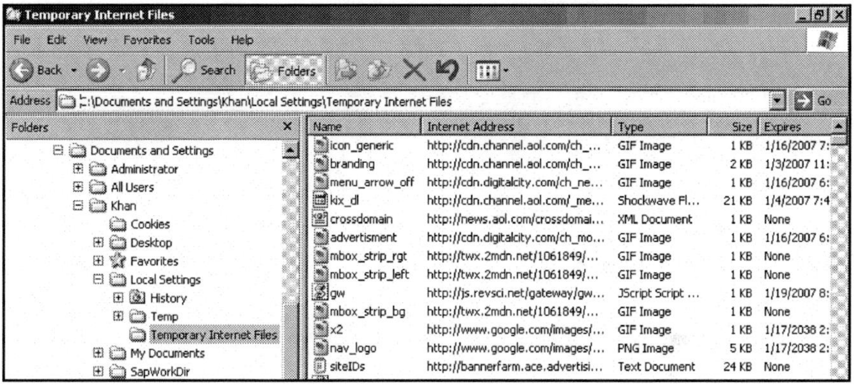

The Temporary Internet Files can also be displayed by navigating as follows:
- *Internet Explorer > Tools > Internet Options*
- Click the *Settings* button
- Click the *View Files* button

After the Temporary Internet files are displayed, they can be selectively deleted. To delete:
- Click on the file that is to be deleted
- Click the *Delete* button

SECURING MOZILLA FIREFOX

Firefox is another widely-used web browser that has better security than IE 6. However, its user base is considerably smaller. Firefox can also be configured to disable various features according to specific user requirements.

Navigating to the settings area

To configure security settings for Firefox, navigate as follows:
- *Mozilla Firefox > Tools > Options*

Figure 46

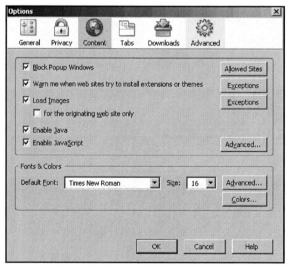

This will lead to the following *Options* window, Figure 47, where the settings can be made:

Figure 47

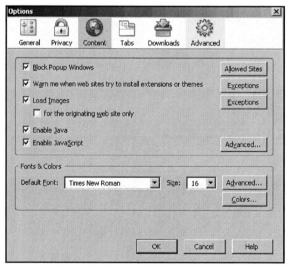

Privacy settings

- Click the *Privacy* icon on Figure 47, which will lead to the following window (Figure 48)

Figure 48

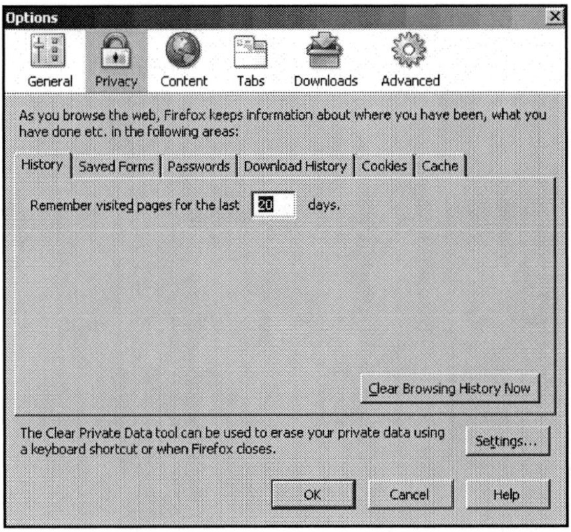

• Click the *Cookies* tab, which will led to the following window (Figure 49)

Figure 49

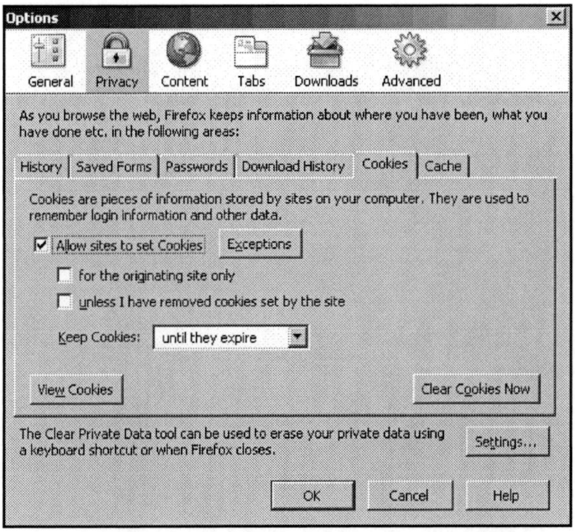

On this window, cookies can be managed by specifying preferences, as shown in the following example:

• Place checkmarks for the appropriate selections, as shown on Figure 50

Figure 50

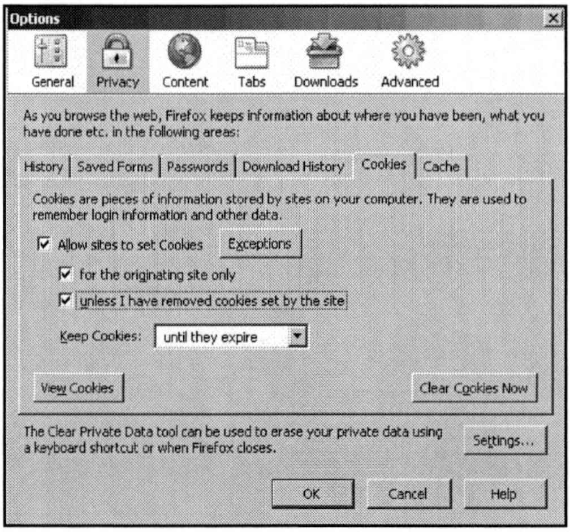

• Click the *OK* button

It is advisable to allow cookies for the originating site only. The option *unless I have removed cookies set by the site* blocks a website from placing cookies after its cookies are removed manually.

Passwords can be managed under the *Passwords* tab. Avoid the *Remember passwords* option. The master password protects all passwords.

Content settings

For additional, advanced, settings:

• Click the *Content* icon, which will lead to the following window (Figure 51)

Figure 51

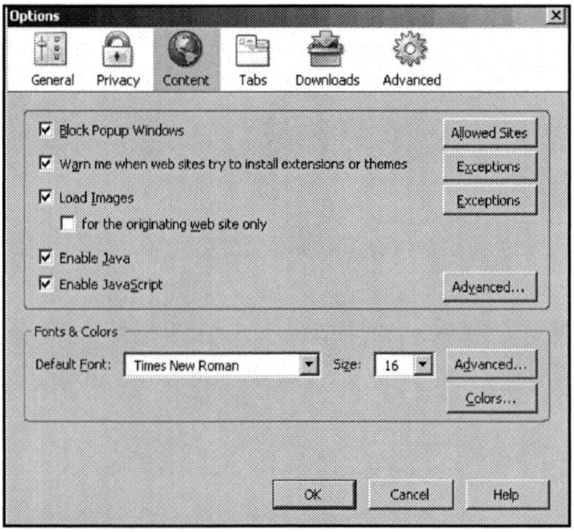

On this window, Java and JavaScript can be enabled or disabled by simply placing or removing a checkmark next to the displayed option. These features should be disabled. If a website requires it, you can enable it and subsequently disable it when the site visit has been completed.

- Click the *Advanced* button, which will lead to the next window (Figure 52)

Figure 52

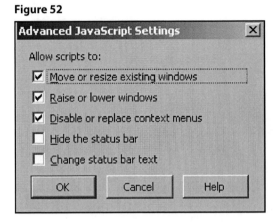

It is recommended that all the options on this window should be disabled.

- Click the *OK* button after making the selections

This will lead back to the *Options* window.

Downloads settings

- Click the *Downloads* icon, which will lead to the next window (Figure 53):

Figure 53

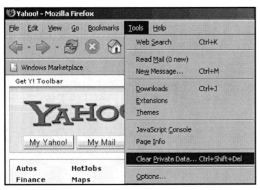

This window can be used to define how downloads are to be handled. For example, the automatic launching of an attachment, which can be risky as it can lead to the installation of malware and/or lead to the exploitation of loopholes, can be disabled on this window.

Private data

Another useful Firefox feature is the ability to *Clear Private Data*, which removes confidential or sensitive data from the web browser. To access this feature, navigate as shown on the following window (Figure 54):

Figure 54

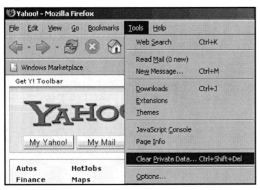

- Click the menu item *Clear Private Data*

This will lead to the following window, Figure 55, where the various options can be selected or deselected, as desired.

Figure 55

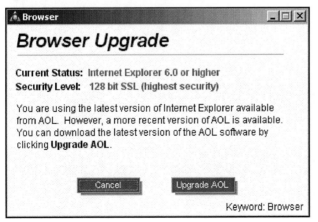

SECURING OTHER BROWSERS
AOL browser

Internet Explorer is actually the browser that AOL uses, even though it has it own unique front end that makes it look very different than IE. To determine the Internet Explorer version that is installed, use the AOL keyword *Browser*, which will cause the following window, Figure 56, to pop-up with the required browser information:

Figure 56

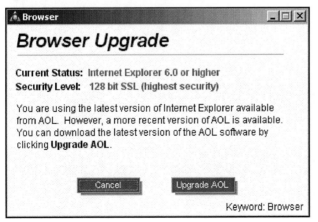

To configure the AOL browser setting, follow these steps:

- On the AOL menu bar, navigate via menu path: *Keyword > Go to Keyword*
- Type in the keyword *Preferences*
- Click on the *Go* button, which will launch the *Settings Main* window
- Click on *Browser Settings* (from the list of keywords that are displayed)

This will launch the *Internet Preferences* window (Figure 57):

Figure 57

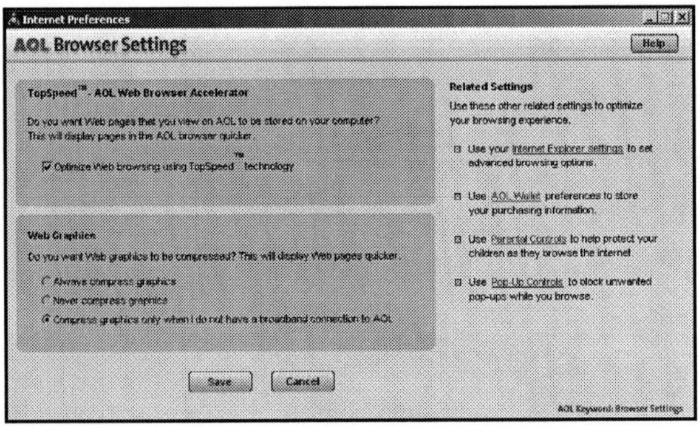

- Click the *Internet Explorer settings* hyperlink, which is displayed on the right-hand side of the pop-up window

This will cause the following familiar *Internet Options* window to pop-up, Figure 58, where the security settings can be configured.

Figure 58

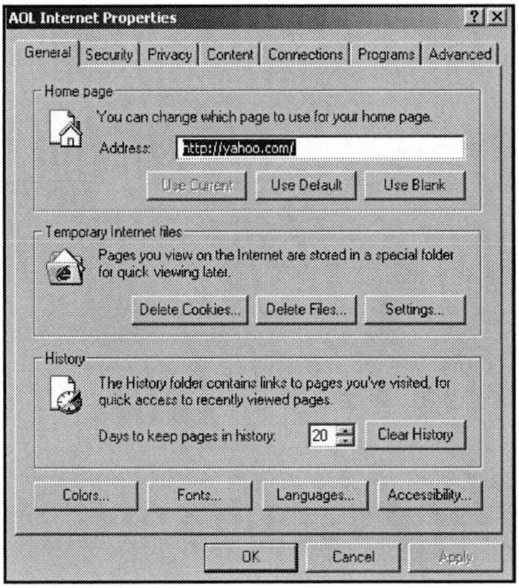

Other browsers

Many of the IE features for disabling various functions that can place a browser at risk, described in the previous sections, can also be implemented for other browsers such as Netscape, Opera, etc. To determine the specific procedures and options that can be configured, refer to the applicable browser's documentation.

Selecting Anti-Malware Tools

SELECTION BASICS
Tool limitations

Anti-spyware, anti-virus and other types of anti-malware software applications can be quite effective in identifying existing threats. Each one is fairly specialized and targets specific types of threats; anti-virus software targets viruses and worms, anti-adware applications target pop-up ads, and anti-spyware software targets spyware. While there do exist dual-purpose software applications, such as an anti-spyware cum firewall product, no existing software application targets all types of malware.

No anti-malware program should be expected to be useful, effective, or appropriate for every user. An anti-malware product cannot provide protection against every threat that exists within its category. For example, you should not expect any anti-spyware product to provide protection against every spyware threat—existing as well as new infections—because they are programmed, transmitted, installed, and hidden in different ways.

The effectiveness of individual products varies considerably. Some have very high detection rates, in the high 90% range, while some are barely able to identify 50% of the existing threats. The percentages for newly-released malware detection are considerably lower. Also, since new malware is being released at a non-stop pace and newer transmission techniques being introduced, the detection rate of a previously-effective product can quickly degrade significantly if the anti-malware program is not upgraded to keep up with new threats and developments.

Selection methodology

Dozens of variables can be used to evaluate and select anti-malware products. The importance attached to a particular variable can vary from user to user. For example, a casual user may be very cost-conscious, while a home office user may be willing to spend a lot in order to protect his computer and/or small business. Hence, the importance and value attached by the two users, who have different requirements, to the cost variable will be quite different.

A technique for evaluating products is based on the following two steps:

- Identifying the most important variables to be used in selecting the anti-malware product. For example, the five most important variables for selecting an anti-spyware product can be effectiveness, cost, real-time protection, ease of use, and customer support.
- Providing a score for each variable, which is determined by its importance to the user. For example, each variable can be scored in a range from 1 (worst) to 5 (best).

In the simplest case, the total score for a product can be calculated by adding the individual scores for each variable. Suppose that only the top five variables are being considered in an evaluation. If the scores for Product A's five variables are 4, 5, 5, 5 and 3, then its total score will be 22. Similarly, as shown in Table 3, the scores for the other products can be tabulated and, subsequently, the product with the highest total score will be selected. In this case, Product E will be selected based on its highest overall score (23).

Table 3					
Variables	Score Product A	Score Product B	Score Product C	Score Product D	Score Product E
Effectiveness	4	4	5	3	4
Cost	5	4	4	5	5
Real-time protection	5	5	5	5	5
Ease of use	5	4	4	3	3
Customer support	3	5	3	3	4
Total	22	22	21	19	23

Selection variables

In general, users evaluating an anti-malware product should consider some, or most, of the variables listed in the following two sections.

Primary variables

- Effectiveness of the tool
- Ability to prevent and remove infections
- User's risk tolerance
- Desired product features
- Cost
- Real-time protection
- Automatic updates
- Type of browser being used
- Ease of use
- Scanning configuration
- Customer support
- Ratings from review sites

Additional variables

- Resources used by the application (memory, hard disk storage, etc.)
- Compatibility with the operating system
- Compatibility with other applications and other anti-malware products that are installed
- User's online activities and behavior
- Versatility (ability to deal with multiple types of malware)
- Type of applications used (P2P, IM, etc.)
- Type of access (cable, DSL, wireless, etc.)
- Ease of installation (manual versus automatic)
- Surfing time
- Vendor reputation

Basic guidelines and tips

The following two sections provide tool selection guidelines and tips.

Basic tips

- Protection effectiveness should be given the highest priority.
- Use best-of-breed applications, which can increase the overall cost of protection, whenever possible.
- Use two anti-spyware products. Be aware that some products can interfere with one another. Do not run both products simultaneously.
- Do not compromise essential and fundamental product features, such as the

ability to protect, in order to gain additional or cosmetic features in a product. For example, it does not make sense to select a product with a lower detection rate, over one that has better detection capabilities, because it has the auto-update feature or its interface is intuitive and has a better look and feel.

- Use different software packages for different malware types.
- Use a proven product. Do not depend on products that are relatively new and untested.
- Use product reviews and test results with care. Only use reviews from well-known organizations.

Additional tips
- Evaluate a wide range of products
- Investigate the tool vendors
- Tool should have minimal or no impact on computer or browser performance
- Avoid freeware and shareware products as they are risky and more likely to be outdated than commercial products

Quick selection guide to products

If you desire to protect your computer without conducting comprehensive product research and want to select a few tools that can provide fairly good protection, you can implement the following two steps:

1. Protect your browser and configure it as per the settings in Table 1 and Table 2
2. Install anti-malware tools using one of the following three options:
   - Option A: Use a comprehensive product that will cover most of the bases. It can be supplemented with secondary tools that will cover its shortcomings.
   - Option B: Use best-of-breed products that are the leading tools within their categories. They can be expected to provide the best protection against every type of malware.
   - Option C: Use an assortment of free products.

Option A: Protection based on comprehensive products
- Symantec Norton Internet Security
- Evidence Eliminator

Option B: Protection based on best-of-breed products
- Anti-spyware: Spy Sweeper
- Anti-virus: BitDefender 9 Standard or McAfee VirusScan
- Firewall: Zone Alarm Pro

- Privacy: Evidence Eliminator
- Anti-spam: Spam Shield

Option C: Protection based on free products
- Anti-spyware: ewido or Spybot Search & Destroy. Supplement with Ad-aware Personal.
- Anti-virus: AntiVir Personal Edition Classic and BitDefender Free Edition (virus scanning)
- Firewall: Zone Alarm
- Prevention: SpywareBlaster and SpywareGuard. Alternative to these two products is Microsoft Windows Defender.
- Anti-spam: Choice Mail or Spambayes

Which option to use
Each of the three options (A, B and C) has its pros and cons. Option A is a simpler option as a single product, the security suite, will provide comprehensive protection that can be supplemented by a secondary tool. Option B will require the installation and maintenance of multiple tools. However, their installation will result in the most effective protection against all types of malware. Option C will appeal to those who cannot afford to buy protection.

PROTECTION REQUIREMENTS
An anti-malware product's *primary* function is to protect a computer from malware. As a minimum, it should identify malware that has already been installed on the computer. Additionally, it should prevent the installation of newer threats. The level of protection that security products provide, and their available features, varies depending on the type of program (anti-spyware, anti-Trojan, anti-virus, etc.). The following are the desired features of anti-spyware tools.

Basic protection features
- High detection rate
- Detecting and removing a wide range of threats including spyware, keyloggers, adware, Trojans, dialers, drive-by downloads, tracking cookies, toolbars, ActiveX configuration, browser hijackers, etc.
- Product effectiveness and selectiveness. It should identify and manage (quarantine or delete) real threats and have limited false positives. It should remove only the

threats, not non-harmful items. The contamination removal should be effective and complete. No traces of the threat should remain after removal.

- Real-time blocking and protection
- Real-time protection of the operating system
- Boot-time scan, which enables checking before the spyware is activated
- Scan memory, Windows registry, and all drives
- Ability to protect the web browser by setting ActiveX kill bits, which is a flag that prevents websites from being able to load and run a particular ActiveX control, for known threats. For more information about this technique, visit the Microsoft website *(http://support.microsoft.com/default.aspx?scid=kb;en-us;240797&sd=tech)*.
- File system protection to prevent any spyware from being launched on the computer
- e-mail protection
- Scan scheduling
- Auto-updates
- Monitoring the registry (for browser hijacking and modifications to system startup settings) and the HOSTS file (for any modifications or additions). A HOSTS file is a database that contains a list of remote hosts' IP addresses which, in simplified terms, is like an address book.

Additional protection features

- Prevent installations from blacklisted websites
- Add known untrustworthy websites to the browser's restricted sites
- Enable different settings, such as the ability to specify which files should be scanned during copying or which file extensions should be scanned
- Quarantine management that allows control over what is to be retained, quarantined, or deleted
- Rollback/restore capabilities (permits the reversal of removals through the quarantine/recovery feature)
- Create a scan log/report
- Indicate the level of spyware severity
- Ease of installation, use, and customization

Some of these features are not available in all anti-spyware tools, as the range of available features can vary considerably. Most of the protection features, such as real-time blocking and scan scheduling, are also desirable in other protection categories such as anti-virus and anti-Trojan tools.

DESIRED FEATURES OF ANTI-MALWARE PROGRAMS

Anti-malware software applications are characterized by a number of common features described in the following sub-sections. Some features, like the ability to provide protection, are mandatory. Note that all the features described in this section are not required for all anti-malware product categories. For example, a particular requirement for anti-spyware tools, such as update of definitions, may not be required or necessary for anti-spam products or tools in other categories.

Regularly updated definitions

An anti-malware product should be updated regularly to retain the ability to recognize and fight newer threats. The updates can be to the program itself or to the database (which stores the malware definitions). Preferably, the updates to the database should be incremental, which means that only newer definitions should be downloaded in order to bring the database up-to-date.

Updates can be performed via the live update feature, whenever the computer connects to the Internet or as scheduled within the program. An alternative method is to initiate a manual update. It is essential that the anti-malware product support either manual or auto-updates. Many shareware and freeware programs do not have the ability to update and, hence, may not be able to recognize and block new malware. Therefore, such a program's user can be misled into a false sense of security.

Scan configuration

A user should be able to configure the scans. Frequently configured items include timing of scans (system start scan at every PC bootup), components to be scanned (memory, registry, drive, etc.), whitelists (items to be excluded), frequency of scans, and updates. Customized scans can limit the scanning to specific components. For example, a user can specify that the scan be limited to the memory or only to a particular drive.

Dedicated research team to enhance the product

The anti-malware vendor should have a dedicated team of researchers at its disposal. The existence of such a team ensures that the product will continue to improve to meet the new and constantly-evolving anti-malware software requirements. A product that is free or is being developed on a casual basis can have updates that are non-existent, shoddy, and/or delayed (which can make the product practically useless). Such a product will leave gaps in protection that a user cannot afford.

Availability of customer support

The software should be backed by good customer and technical support that is provided in a number of ways including phone, e-mail, and instant messaging (live chat). Some companies use an Internet-based workstation remote control program to monitor and/or troubleshoot the user's computer. Since the average computer user has limited technical skills, the availability of technical support is very important. Many product reviews penalize companies that have limited or poor customer service, which is reflected in their overall ratings.

User-friendly

The product should be easy to install and use. It should have a user-friendly interface so that even casual users can operate it without any problem. The product should support customization and enable configuration settings, such as scan and update options, to be changed easily and intuitively.

Vendor reputation

The product should be backed by a stable and well-established vendor. The vendor should have a reputation for providing quality products. Such a software provider is expected to quickly take care of any shortcomings in the product, provide regular updates, and provide support when needed.

Pricing

Most home computer users are very price-conscious and thus many of their purchase decisions are driven by this factor. The purchase price of the product, as well as renewals and upgrades, should be reasonable. The comparison of product prices becomes complicated due to variations in pricing from different sources (online, retail, or reseller), cost of updates during and after expiry of the typical 12-month subscription period, type of product (trial versus full-feature), etc.

System Integration

The product should integrate and operate smoothly with the operating system. Its launching should be possible via different means such as a mouse click on a folder, Windows system tray, Start Menu, etc. It should also be compatible with other installed anti-malware products. For example, the anti-spyware product should not cause conflicts with the installed firewall or the anti-virus program being used.

Diagnostic tools

The software program should contain tools that enable users to investigate their computer system more thoroughly. This can include the browser settings that can be configured, entries in the Windows HOSTS file, installed Browser Help Objects (BHOs), installed ActiveX controls, installed programs, etc. While this feature will primarily appeal to advanced users, some novices can also use and benefit from the more user-friendly diagnostic tools.

Supports Windows

The anti-malware program should ideally support the various versions of Windows, ranging from the old (Windows 95) to the newer ones (Windows XP and Vista). If the product supports 64-bit Windows, it will enable the application to execute faster and with greater efficiency.

Versatility

An anti-malware product can specifically target a particular type of malware or be more versatile. For example, the primary and essential objective of an anti-spyware product is to protect against spyware. However, it can be more versatile and have additional features such as the ability to detect other malware (viruses, worms, adware, Trojans, hijackers, etc.), protect IM and P2P programs, act as a basic firewall or detect intrusion, scan traffic (network or incoming Internet HTTP), block or warn when visiting websites known for phishing and pharming attacks, etc.

Primary Protection Tools

ANTI-SPYWARE TOOLS
Leading anti-spyware applications

A number of well-known organizations and computer publications, listed in Appendix A, periodically review anti-spyware applications. The following is a list of the best anti-spyware applications, which has been compiled after reviewing the ratings and comments posted by those entities:

1. Spy Sweeper
2. Spyware Doctor
3. Ad-Aware SE Personal
4. ewido anti-spyware (AVG Anti-Spyware)
5. Pest Patrol
6. SUPERAntiSpyware
7. Windows Defender
8. StopZilla

Many of the commercial anti-spyware products that are available, including the leading products, provide a free version, though with limited functionality. For those who cannot afford the full-blown versions, the free versions are a good alternative. Some of the applications also provide free scanning service.

Features of leading anti-spyware applications
Spy Sweeper

Webroot's Spy Sweeper (*www.webroot.com/consumer/products/spysweeper/*), with a list price of $29.95, is one of the best anti-spyware product. It blocks new spyware installations and outperforms most of its competitors in detection and removal of spyware and other malware including Trojans, adware, keyloggers, system monitors, dialers, toolbars, drive-by downloads, and BHOs. It has a user-friendly intuitive interface and is easy to download and install.

The product is suitable as the primary anti-spyware tool, which can be complemented with a secondary tool like Ad-Aware Personal. The features of this product include a very high success rate (90+%), advance detection and removal capabilities, removal of most threats at first pass, real-time blocking and protection, automatic updates, rollback/restore, spyware severity indicator, scan scheduling, scanning of removal media, and blocking of tracking cookies. Spy Sweeper provides an overview of each threat, enabling accurate risk assessment, and also maintains log files.

SpySweeper product support is free via a toll-free number. Support is also provided through built-in application help, knowledge base/FAQs, and e-mail.

Spyware Doctor

Spyware Doctor from PCTools *(www.pctools.com/spyware-doctor/)*, with a list price of $29.95, is another leading anti-spyware product with a high success rate in removing spyware. It is also effective against other types of malware. Spy Sweeper, with superior ease of use, has overshadowed Spyware Doctor, which is cumbersome to update, even though some reviews place them on the same level. Spyware Doctor blocks the installation of malware rather than just identify and remove it.

Spyware Doctor, which provides real-time blocking and prevention, is able to detect and block various types of spyware, adware, keyloggers, hijackers, Trojans, dialers, toolbars, tracking cookies, and system monitors. It provides protection against ActiveX, BHO threats, phishing and drive-by downloads. Spyware Doctor, which includes a pop-up blocker, also provides advanced system scanning and immunization against browser infections.

Spyware Doctor is easy to install and use and has an excellent user interface. Its other features include regular live auto-updates, log file, spyware severity indicator, and scheduling. Any suspicious files discovered by a user can be forwarded to the company's research center for investigation. Support is provided via a toll-free number, built-in application help, knowledge base/FAQs, and e-mail.

Ad-Aware SE Personal

The Ad-Aware product, from Lavasoft *(www.lavasoft.de/)*, is provided in four versions. The free Ad-Aware SE Personal version provides protection from a variety of threats including spyware, adware, Trojans, browser hijackers, keyloggers and tracking software. It can scan removable and fixed drives, memory, and the Windows registry. The product supports quarantine functionality and allows customizable scans. However, it does not provide real-time protection or scheduled system scans.

Ad-Aware is not as effective or robust as some other competing products. It does not provide free customer support or detailed scan reports. However, since this is a free product, it can find good use as a supplement to the primary anti-spyware tool. For users who desire advanced features, Ad-Aware SE Professional, Lavasoft's alternative product listed for $39.95, is a good option.

ewido anti-spyware (AVG Anti-Spyware)

ewido is a new product from Grisoft (*www.ewido.net/en/*)—the developer of AVG (the anti-virus software program). It is sophisticated and yet easy to use. ewido is available in free as well as paid versions. It includes a real-time scanner that identifies as well as removes infections, which many scanners do not. The program does not conflict with anti-virus programs and has a file shredder, which ensures that deleted spyware is completely removed from the system. ewido provides very comprehensive results that may be too detailed for basic users. It can also create individual exceptions.

ewido anti-spyware is being replaced by AVG Anti-Spyware 7.5, which has a paid as well as free version. The paid version, which costs $39.95 for two years, provides real-time protection and active memory scanning. It also supports automatic online updates and scan scheduling.

Pest Patrol

The Pest Patrol anti-spyware application from CA (*www.ca.com/products/pestpatrol/*), which lists for $29.99, detects and removes a variety of malware including spyware, Trojans, adware, RATs, keyloggers, probing and monitoring tools, toolbars, drive-by downloads, tracking cookies, and BHOs. The features of the product, which is easy to install, include real-time blocking and protection, automatic updates, an easy to use interface, rollback/restore, and scan scheduling. Pest Patrol supports customization, such as scan settings and real-time tracking settings, though with limited options. The product complements anti-virus and firewall applications. Pest Patrol provides detailed scan results but lacks a spyware severity indicator. Product support is provided through built-in application help, knowledge base/FAQs, and via e-mail.

SUPERAntiSpyware

SUPERAntiSpyware from SuperAntiSpyware.com (*www.superantispyware.com*), is a free anti-spyware program that protects against spyware, Trojans, adware, keyloggers, hijackers, and other types of malware. The product is capable of detecting, protecting, and removing threats. SUPERAntiSpyware's features include browser hijack protection (protects web browser settings), ability to quarantine, customizable scan options, ability to restore settings changed by malware, and real-time protection. The free version for home users does not support real-time protection, hijack protection, or other advanced options.

SUPERAntiSpyware can scan removable media as well as system components, which can be manually selected. The scan reports provide useful information. The product's definition updates are available regularly. SUPERAntiSpyware is easy to install and has a user-friendly interface, though it could be improved. The professional version of the product, which lists for $29.95, supports quick, complete, or custom daily or weekly scans. It also provides daily definition updates.

Windows Defender

Windows Defender, previously called Microsoft Anti-Spyware, is a free anti-spyware program from Microsoft (*www.microsoft.com/athome/security/spyware/software/default.mspx*). It will be incorporated into the Windows Vista operating system. Windows Defender features include real-time protection, monitoring system, configuration options including automatic scans, and pop-up blocking. Its installation is fast and easy. Defender is easy to use and has a very good interface. The product is not difficult to manage and its updates can be implemented quickly. The product's weakness is that it does not look for or remove browser cookies.

StopZilla

StopZilla (*www.stopzilla.com*) is a very effective anti-spyware program with real-time protection that also works against adware, browser hijackers, BHOs, Trojans, dialers, keyloggers, and other types of malicious software. It has advanced pop-up protection, includes some firewall features, and also provides phishing protection. StopZilla also permits the selective retention or deletion of adware, provides automatic updates, and can erase cookies and history. It is easy to download and install, has a good interface, and is easy to operate. StopZilla's customer support and service are excellent. The product lists for $29.95.

Features of other anti-spyware applications

In addition to the best eight products described in the previous section, a number of good but less-effective tools are also available, which are described in this section.

Counter Spy

Counter Spy, from Sunbelt Software, is a spyware-removal program that can also detect adware, keyloggers, Trojans, dialers, toolbars, drive-by downloads, tracking cookies, and

BHOs. Its capabilities include a spyware severity indicator, scan scheduling, auto-updates, tracking cookie blocking, as well as real-time blocking and protection.

Counter Spy has an easy to use interface. It requires low computer resources, even though the program runs in the background. The program retains its effectiveness through regular updates. Its negatives are that its malware removal rate has decreased and requires improvement. Also, its pop-up blocking capabilities are not fully effective. Support is provided through a toll-free number, built-in application help, knowledge base/FAQs, and via e-mail.

Privacy Defender

Privacy Defender is an effective anti-spyware program that also works against adware. The features of this program include easy blocking, prevention of home page hijacking, compatibility with all browsers, and scanning of memory, hard drive, and registry. Privacy Defender has a user-friendly interface and it allows users to control which programs are run. It also enables easy reporting of new spyware.

Spyware Eliminator

Spyware Eliminator is a very effective anti-spyware program with excellent detection capabilities that also provides protection against adware, browser hijackers and other malware types. Its features include evidence elimination, elimination of registry changes made by unauthorized programs, and easy updates. It also provides free scanning. Spyware Eliminator has a heavy memory overhead during routine operations. It may appear somewhat complex to novice users and its installation process could be improved.

McAfee Anti-Spyware

McAfee Anti-Spyware, from the leading security vendor, works against spyware, browser hijackers, keyloggers, BHOs and adware. The product has improved since its last release and its detection and removal rates have increased. However, it is still not nearly as good as its competitors. Anti-Spyware, while offering basic features, provides real-time protection and auto-updates. It is easy to install and use, has few customizable features, allows rollbacks of changes, and supports scan scheduling. Installation is easy but time consuming. The product's effectiveness is limited and it does not match the level of the superior anti-virus product that McAfee also provides. Customer support, which needs improvement, is provided through a toll-free number, built-in application help, knowledge base/FAQs, e-mail, and online chat.

Spy Zooka

Spy Zooka is an effective and feature-rich anti-spyware software. The program is easy to download and install, has an intuitive interface, and is easy to use. A useful feature provided by Spy Zooka is the data shredder. The company develops definitions within 24 hours for new threats discovered by users.

Spybot Search & Destroy

Spybot Search & Destroy is a basic, free anti-spyware software program that can remove spyware, adware, Trojans, and keyloggers. Its features include real-time protection, complex registry backup, fixing of registry inconsistencies, clearing of usage tracks, blocking of ActiveX downloads and cookies, and backup of removed problems. Spyware Search & Destroy has advanced and easy (default) modes that can permit advanced users more flexibility and control. It also provides selection options for ignoring specific items as well as for automating scans, removals, and updates. Though users can adjust the interface, the update process is more complex than that of competing products.

CWShredder

The CWShredder product's main objective is to target the CoolWebSearch spyware toolbar, which has the ability to hijack the web browser and subsequently steer the user to the websites of various advertisers. For this specialized purpose, CWShredder is the best tool.

Spy Striker

The Spy Striker tool combats spyware, adware, Trojans, keyloggers, tracking software, and other types of malware. It also includes a firewall and an anti-phishing utility. Spy Striker is also capable of removing bundled software components.

Free anti-spyware tools

The following is a listing of freeware anti-spyware products:

- Ad-Aware *(www.lavasoftusa.com/software/adaware)*
- Keylogger Hunter *(www.styopkin.com/)*
- KL Detector *(http://dewasoft.com/privacy/kldetector.htm)*
- Spybot Search & Destroy *(http://spybot.safer-networking.de/en/)*
- X-Cleaner *(www.xblock.com)*

FIREWALLS
Leading firewall applications

The nature of the problems that a firewall has to protect against, which include internal as well as external threats, has changed as the techniques for malware transmission, installation, propagation, and hiding have changed and become more sophisticated. As firewalls have become practically mandatory, standalone firewall products are becoming less common because their features are being incorporated in security products that provide comprehensive protection against spyware, adware, Trojans, hijackers, viruses, worms, and other types of malware. Therefore, users have the option to select either a:

- Standalone product
- Comprehensive security suite product that includes a firewall as one of its components

A number of well-known organizations and computer publications, listed in Appendix A, periodically review firewall applications. The following is a list of the best firewall applications, which has been compiled after reviewing the ratings and comments posted by those entities:

- Zone Alarm Pro
- Norton Personal Firewall
- McAfee Personal Firewall
- Agnitum Outpost Firewall
- Windows Firewall
- BlackIce PC Protection

Features of leading firewall applications
Zone Alarm Pro

Zone Alarm, from ZoneLabs, is a powerful and reliable software firewall program that protects the computer from hackers, viruses and Trojans, ads and cookies, mobile code (such as ActiveX and scripts), and other types of malicious attacks. The feature-rich and very effective product, which vies for the best personal firewall product status, provides excellent tools for prevention and detection that are better than the McAfee or Norton products, besides being easier to work with. It provides automatic protection against advanced hacking techniques, including distributed denial-of-service attacks as well as intrusion detection and prevention, which are not available in the Norton and McAfee products.

Zone Alarm features include hiding the computer from external attacks by putting the system ports in stealth mode, solid inbound filtering, limited outbound filtering, solid application integrity monitoring, e-mail protection (inbound and outbound), blocking of suspicious e-mails (too many in a short period, too many recipients, etc.), encryption, and preventing protected personal information from being transmitted via e-mail or web forms. Personal information that needs protection can be stored in MyVault, where attempts to access it are thwarted. The program works well with anti-virus programs from other vendors, which widens the choice of anti-virus programs that can be used. Also, an installed anti-virus software program can be incorporated into the firewall.

The product, listed for $49.95, has an intuitive interface and is easy to install and use. Zone Alarm can be customized, with easy configuration and rule modification. Reporting and logging is good, with detailed warnings and full packet logging. The company website provides comprehensive well-organized documentation. Phone support is not free. The freeware edition can be used to provide basic protection. The Pro version of the program, which includes anti-virus software, provides a warning whenever the anti-virus software is outdated. However, the free version does not include the anti-virus software.

Norton Personal Firewall

Norton Personal Firewall (NPF) is a software firewall program from Symantec, a leading security vendor. The product has good features, though not as comprehensive as some competing products, and integrates well with other Symantec products. NPF provides solid inbound filtering, outbound filtering and application integrity monitoring.

Norton Personal Firewall can block ActiveX controls and Java applets, hide the computer from intruders and hackers, and prevent the transmission of confidential data. Some personal information can be marked so that it cannot be transmitted over unsecured connections. NPF enables easy and quick configuration of security settings and permits different security levels to be selected. It permits the selection of programs that can connect to the Internet.

NPF provides robust configuration and rule modification. Customization can be based on connection type. The program enables flexible configuring of options, such as turning off ads and pop-ups, etc., for visiting unknown websites. It provides clear and concise reporting and logging.

The program, listed for $49.99, is easy to install and use. The support documentation available is very informative. However, customer support is not free.

McAfee Personal Firewall Plus

McAfee Personal Firewall (MPF) is a software firewall program, whose functionality is limited compared to the top firewall products such as ZoneAlarm and Norton. For example, it does not provide privacy or anti-virus protection that competing products have built into their firewalls. Also, while the program has good reliability against known threats and blocks significant port attacks, it does not protect well against brand new threats.

McAfee Personal Firewall provides solid inbound filtering, limited outbound filtering, and solid application integrity monitoring. It is also able to trace and map intrusions. MPF provides limited options for advanced users for customizing security levels. Configuration and rule modification is robust. MPF provides separate alerts for inbound and outbound program requests. It also provides different levels of alerts. Reporting and logging needs improvement, as warnings can be confusing.

The product, priced at $49.99 with a cheaper download version, is easy to install. While it is easy to use for beginners, the advanced features of its interface are difficult to navigate. Customer support is expensive, at $39.95 per incident, and is also available via e-mail and online chat. Comprehensive documentation and help is available at the company website.

Agnitum Outpost Firewall

Agnitum Outpost Firewall (AOF) is a software firewall program that provides reliable protection. It is available in two versions: free and Pro. The free version provides basic protection, while the Pro version has far more comprehensive functionality. Agnitum provides protection against spyware, hackers, hijackers, Trojans, worms, pop-ups, and malicious programs. The program includes an on-demand scanner and free regular updates are provided. AOF does not monitor application integrity or provide encryption. It is better at detecting spyware than either removing or preventing it.

Agnitum features include stealth mode, solid inbound and outbound filtering, ID blocking for preventing transmission of personal data, quarantine protection, protection of web privacy and personal information, monitoring of network activity, easy configuration and rule modification, as well as ability to block images or content. The program provides the ability to customize security, such as selective port settings.

The program, listed for $39.95, is easy to install, configure, and use. It has a highly-customizable user interface. It maintains a log and its reporting and logging is clear and concise. The help documentation is excellent and customer support is available via phone and e-mail.

Windows Firewall

Windows Firewall, provided by Microsoft, is designed to integrate with Windows. It is available when the Windows XP SP2 update is installed. The free product, which is easy to install and simple to use, provides minimal protection. The Windows Firewall reporting is poor and it provides no alerts. The product does not protect against spyware, viruses, worms, adware, keyloggers, monitoring software, spam, or suspect attachments.

Windows Firewall, which is turned on by default, provides basic inbound filtering and no outbound filtering. It provides no application integrity monitoring. The product can block incoming attacks and some types of connection requests. Windows Firewall permits very limited customization, though it provides easy configuration and rule modification.

BlackIce PC Protection

BlackIce, *www.blackice.iss.net*, was the one of the first personal firewall products to be released. The program, which has limited features, provides good protection and works against Trojans, hackers, worms, etc. The program monitors both inbound and outbound traffic. It is characterized by solid inbound and outbound filtering as well as solid application integrity monitoring. BlackIce features include stealth mode, limited privacy protection, good customization options, ability to specify different protection levels, easy configuration and rule modification, and periodic free updates.

BlackIce, listed for $39.95, does not provide encryption or virus protection. However, it works well with anti-virus applications. BlackIce is easy to install, though the installation is somewhat time-consuming. It is easy to use and has a simple interface, though other leading products have better ones. It provides clear and concise reporting, logging, and traceability. BlackIce will appeal to novices, though advanced users will also like it due to its customization feature. Customer support is very good as is the documentation.

Free firewalls

The following is a listing of freeware firewalls:
- Agnitum Outpost Firewall *(www.agnitum.com/products/outpost/)*
- AnalogX *(www.analogx.com/contents/articles/ipsec.htm)*
- AShampoo Firewall *(www.ashampoo.com)*
- BlackIce PC Protection *(www.blackice.com)*
- CHX-I Packet Filter *(http://products.enterpriseitplanet.com/security/firewalls/index.html)*
- Comodo Personal Firewall *(www.comodogroup.com/products/free_products.html)*
- Eagle X *(www.engagesecurity.com/products/eaglex/)*
- FirePanel XP *(www.router19.org/software.aspx)*
- Firestarter *(www.fs-security.com/)*

- GhostWall *(www.ghostsecurity.com/ghostwall/)*
- Kerio Personal Firewall *(www.kerio.com)*
- Look'n'Stop Lite *(www.looknstop.com/En/index2.htm)*
- NetVeda Safety.Net *(www.netveda.com/consumer/safetynet.htm)*
- Omniquad Personal Firewall *(www.omniquad.com/downloads.htm)*
- PeerGuardian *(http://phoenixlabs.org/)*
- Premidius Firewall Lite *(www.primedius.com/PersonalFirewall.htm)*
- R-Firewall *(www.r-firewall.com)*
- Securepoint Personal Firewall *(http://usa-01.securepoint.de/)*
- SensiveGuard *(www.sensiveguard.com)*
- Simple TDI Based Open Source Personal Firewall *(http://tdifw.sourceforge.net/)*
- Snort *(http://www.snort.org/)*
- SoftPerfect Personal Firewall *(www.softperfect.com/products/firewall/)*
- SOHOConnection *(www.servlet.com/soho2/)*
- Tiny Personal Firewall *(www.ca.com/tinysoftware)*
- Windows Firewall *(www.microsoft.com)*
- Winsock Firewall *(http://winsockfirewall.sourceforge.net/)*
- WyvernWorks Firewall *(www.download.com)*
- ZoneAlarm *(www.zonelabs.com/)*

ANTI-VIRUS APPLICATIONS
Leading anti-virus applications
A number of well-known organizations and computer publications, listed in Appendix A, periodically review anti-virus applications. The following is a list of the best anti-virus applications, which has been compiled after reviewing the ratings and comments posted by those entities:

- Norton AntiVirus 2006
- McAfee VirusScan 2006
- BitDefender 9 Standard
- Panda Titanium 2006 Antivirus and Antispyware
- F-Secure Anti-Virus 2006
- Kaspersky Anti-Virus Personal
- AntiVir PersonalEdition Classic 6.32
- Avast Home Edition 4.6
- Grisoft AVG Free Edition 7.1

Features of leading anti-virus applications
Norton AntiVirus 2006

Norton AntiVirus (NAV) is an excellent top-selling anti-virus tool from Symantec. The product is highly effective and provides superior performance with excellent threat detection and blocking. NAV is able to detect and remove viruses, worms, and Trojans. It is also able to detect and remove spyware, keyloggers, and other monitoring software. NAV's other product features include checking inbound and outbound e-mail and IM attachments for viruses, preventing home page hijacking, checking compressed file archives for viruses, and automatic updates.

NAV detects worms and other threats before updates are installed. It automatically scans for viruses upon downloading updates. Prior to installation, it disinfects the system. While the product is easy to install and use, its many features many overwhelm some novice users. NAV, which is priced at $39.99, is widely available through many channels. Technical support is limited. Additional information about this product can be obtained at *www.symantec.com/home_homeoffice/products/index.jsp.*

McAfee VirusScan 2006

McAfee VirusScan is an excellent anti-virus tool from McAfee. It is the leading dedicated anti-virus software application. The product, which has an extensive list of features, is highly effective and provides superior performance with solid protection. McAfee VirusScan, which is effective against viruses and spyware, can be bundled with a personal firewall. The application is characterized by low hard disk utilization, though system memory is higher.

McAfee VirusScan, which is priced at $39.99, is easy to install and use. It is available through many channels. Limited customer service is provided primarily through the company website, though it is also available via e-mail and live chat. Additional information about this product can be obtained at *http://download.mcafee.com/eval/evaluate2.asp* or *http://us.mcafee.com/root/catalog.asp.*

BitDefender 9 Standard

BitDefender, an excellent anti-virus tool, is highly effective and characterized by superior performance. It has many features including fast scanning, automatic or manual updates, ability to quarantine infected files, and low system usage. It can recover infected files rather than just delete them. BitDefender's configuration settings, which provide flexibility, can be used to turn off/on many of its features. The product is inexpensive, with a list price of $29.95, and is easy to install and use. The product also has a free version. Technical support is free and provided through online chat and e-mail. Additional information about this product can be obtained at *www.bitdefender.com.*

Panda Titanium 2006 Antivirus and Antispyware

Titanium Antivirus, from Panda Software, is a product with average performance that provides protection against viruses and spyware. It also protects against hackers, phishers and Trojans. The protection of Titanium's anti-spyware component is not as good as that of its anti-virus component. It also has fewer options than many anti-virus programs, with more options being available in the Platinum version that also includes a firewall. The product features include very fast scanning, automatic updates, and relatively high disk and system memory utilization. The program lacks scheduled scan capability, which is available in the Panda Platinum 2006 Internet Security Suite.

Titanium is easy to install and use. It is expensive compared to competing products, being recently priced at $44.99, and is available through limited procurement channels. Online and e-mail customer service is limited and no phone support is provided. Additional information about the product can be obtained at *www.pandasoftware.com.*

F-Secure Anti-Virus 2006

F-Secure Anti-Virus is an anti-virus tool that provides very good detection and cleanup of various threats. Its features include real-time protection, anti-spyware scanner, protection against hackers, registry protection, automatic updates, e-mail and IM scanning, registry startup scanning, and real-time scanning of incoming and outgoing e-mails. F-Secure's resource consumption can be high due to multiple processes running simultaneously. It also has the fastest response to new threats and its scan time is average.

Scans cannot be scheduled with F-Secure, which also includes a firewall utility in its home edition. The product has a simple interface, with basic and advanced views, that is easy to navigate. Advanced users can customize it extensively as per their personal preferences. F-Secure is easy to install and use, though not as much as competing products. It is also preset, ready for use, and automates key tasks. The all-in-one security suite, F-Secure Internet Security 2006, also includes a personal firewall.

F-Secure Anti-Virus is expensive, as it was recently priced at $64, though a trial version of the software is available. Technical support is provided via phone, e-mail, and the company website where tutorials, FAQs and documentation are available. Additional information about this product can be obtained at *www.f-secure.com.*

Kaspersky Anti-Virus Personal

Kaspersky Anti-Virus Personal is an excellent anti-virus tool that is very effective and has a high detection rate. It scans for viruses, spyware, web-based port 80 traffic, and e-mail. It also protects against other malware including Trojans, adware, dialers, rootkits and remote access utilities.

Kaspersky Anti-Virus Personal's performance is superior, it scores well in performance tests (scan speed), and has good heuristic capabilities. Other features include on-demand and scheduled scanning, option to scan only new and modified files, ability to rollback updates in case of software conflict, locking of system registry keys, fastest response to new threats, low hard disk space and very limited system resource requirements, and automatic hourly updates.

The program has free and paid versions. It has an intuitive interface design that supports personal preferences, depending on needs. Kaspersky is easy to install and use, especially for beginners. Advanced users will like its customization features. Free technical support is provided online, via e-mail, and through a toll-free number. The website contains excellent and extensive documentation. The list price is high at $49.95, but it is available at a considerable discount. Additional information can be obtained at www.kaspersky.com or www.kasperskylabs.com.

AntiVir PersonalEdition Classic 6.32

AntiVir PersonalEdition is a free anti-virus product that provides basic protection. The tool, which also protects against spyware and Trojans, is characterized by average performance, though it ranks high among the free products. AntiVir has a scanner, which launches when an attachment is saved or launched, that takes care of threats before attachments are opened. Its scan speed is average. AntiVir does not quarantine; it only repairs or deletes infections. It also does not scan incoming or outgoing e-mail attachments.

AntiVir, which has a fair number of features, is easy to use and has a simple interface. It provides a comprehensive scan report. Support is provided through online forms, not via phone. Additional information can be obtained at www.free-av.com.

Avast Home Edition 4.6

Avast Home Edition is an anti-virus product from Alwil Software that is free for non-commercial home users. It offers good features but below-average performance. It protects against worms and Trojans, as well as P2P and IM programs. The product includes real-time scanning and protection. It can scan before Window boots. Avast also has an on-demand scanner with two interfaces (for novices and experienced users).

It protects e-mails (inbound and outbound messages) and blocks suspicious e-mail activity such as numerous messages within a short time span or spam-like behavior (too many recipients per message).

The Network Shield analyzes network traffic and acts as a lightweight firewall. The Web Shield monitors and filters all HTTP traffic coming from Internet websites. A hard disk area for storing files, called the Virus Chest, ensures that the files cannot be infected by providing complete isolation from the rest of the operating system. Avast supports automatic and incremental updates, through with only new or missing data downloads, that can be manual or scheduled. Both the program and virus database are updated automatically. The scan speed is slow, regular scans cannot be scheduled, and there are limited configuration options. Files can be removed or quarantined and infected files can be repaired using the Virus Recovery Database.

The product has a stylish interface whose appearance users can change. The product is easy to use. The Pro version of the software covers some of the shortcomings, such as scan scheduling and script blocking. Additional information about this product can be obtained at *www.avast.com*.

Grisoft AVG Free Edition 7.1

Grisoft AVG is another free anti-virus program with below-average performance and limited effectiveness. It has limited features and lacks key features. Its spyware detection is good and the product does not include a firewall. Grisoft AVG features include automatic updates, boot scanning (manual or scheduled), scanning of incoming and outgoing e-mails, ability to delete all or specified attachments, ability to quarantine, and low system resource utilization. Scans cannot be customized and scheduling is limited to daily full scan.

The product is easy to install. The interface, which is clunky and awkward, needs improvement. Support is provided though e-mail as well as online via the knowledge base and FAQs. Some of the missing features are available in the paid version of the product. Additional information about this product can be obtained at *www.grisoft.com* or *http://free.grisoft.com*.

Free anti-virus applications

The first five products in the following list, which have paid as well as free versions, were described in the previous section. They have been included in this list only with the objective of providing a standalone list of free anti-virus applications.

- BitDefender 9 Standard
- Kaspersky Anti-Virus Personal

- AntiVir PersonalEdition Classic 6.32
- Avast Home Edition 4.6
- Grisoft AVG Free Edition 7.1
- Antidote SuperLite *(www.vintage-solutions.com/indexeng.html)*
- ClamWin Free AntiVirus *(www.clamwin.com/)*
- MicroWorld Free AntiVirus Toolkit Utility *(www.mwti.net/products/mwav/mwav.asp)*

More Protection Tools

SECONDARY TOOLS
Scanners

The anti-virus and anti-spyware applications installed on the computer should be used to scan for problems. However, if such programs have not been installed, a dedicated scanner can be used as an alternative. A simple scanner will only detect installed malware and then display the list of infections. However, such a scanner will not remove the identified malware, for which a removal component is also required.

Some vendors bait users with a free scan offer. After the malware is identified, the user is steered towards buying the removal component in order to remove the infections. In some cases, many of the items listed by the scan are harmless cookies. However, the novice user is often unaware of that fact and is panicked into buying the product.

Most currently-available scanners are capable of both scanning and removing malware, though they have limited functionality compared to dedicated tools such as anti-spyware and anti-virus programs. Therefore, standalone scanners, while serving the basic purpose of identifying malware infections, should be complemented by other essential protection tools: anti-virus software, anti-spyware software, and a firewall.

Spyware scanners

The following are the leading standalone spyware scanners that can be used to identify spyware that has found its way onto the computer:

- Spyware Doctor: A very effective and probably the best spyware scanner that is currently available. This product, from PC Tools, is one of the fastest scanners that along with its accuracy makes it a superior product.
- McAfee VirusScan: An excellent product, that provides spyware protection as well as virus scanning.

- Spy Sweeper: An effective product, from Webroot, that works especially well against unwanted BHOs and toolbars.
- Sunbelt CounterSpy: An easy to use product, that provides inexpensive, above-average, protection.
- Spybot Search & Destroy: A free product that is very effective in preventing adware and spyware, though it falls short on removal rates.
- Hijack This: A free product, that provides a full system report of the installed malware active on the computer. The user can then disable the malware manually or by using the tool.
- Windows Defender: An above-average free product, from Microsoft, that is currently in beta mode and not recommended as a primary scanner.

Two other spyware scanners, which are free, that can be used to scan as well as remove adware and spyware are:
- Ad-aware Personal Edition *(www.lavasoftusa.com/software/adaware/)*
- SpyCatcher Express *(www.tenebril.com/consumer/spyware/spycatcher-express.php)*

Anti-virus scanners

An anti-virus scanner searches for virus-infected files and stops threats that come through file downloads, e-mail, etc. Anti-virus scanners primarily depend on finding an exact match with a known virus. They also utilize heuristics, which use telltale characteristics to identify malware. However, this hit-and-miss technique provides limited success. Therefore, scanners should be complemented by other protection tools.

A dedicated anti-virus program should be installed on the computer for scanning, detecting and removing viruses. However, if such a tool has not been installed, a stand-alone scanner can be used for detecting viruses and, in some cases, for cleaning the PC as well. Some of these scanners, many of which are online, are available for free.

Never assume that a scan will be 100% effective as a typical scanner will only detect known viruses or virus patterns. Also, while a scanner may be able to detect a virus, it may or may not be able to clean it. For serious contaminations such as an infected boot sector, a utility like Norton Utilities can be used.

Leading anti-virus scanners
The following is a list of well-known scanners which can be used for detecting viruses:
- Command on Demand *(www.commandondemand.com/)*
- eTrust AntiVirus Web Scanner *(www3.ca.com/securityadvisor/virusinfo/scan.aspx)*

- McAfee FreeScan *(http://us.mcafee.com/root/mfs/default.asp)*
- Microsoft Malicious Software Removal Tool *(www.microsoft.com/security/malwarer-emove/default.mspx)*
- Panda ActiveScan *(www.pandasoftware.com)*
- Spybot Search & Destroy *(http://spybot.safer-networking.de/en/)*
- SpyCatcher Express *(www.tenebril.com)*
- Trend Micro HouseCall *(http://housecall65.trendmicro.com/)*

Free anti-virus scanners

The following is a list of free anti-virus scanners:
- Antidote Super Lite version *(www.vintage-solutions.com/English/Antivirus/Super/index.html)*
- Avast *(www.avast.com)*
- Avira AntiVir Personal Edition *(www.free-av.com/)*
- AVG Free Edition *(http://free.grisoft.com/doc/1)*
- BitDefender ScanOnline *(www.bitdefender.com/scan8/ie.html)*
- ClamWin *(www.clamwin.com)*
- Comodo Anti-Virus *(http://antivirus.comodo.com/)*
- HandyBits *(www.handybits.com/vsi.htm)*
- Vcatch *(www.vcatch.com)*

Online scanners

An online scanner is a tool that typically does not need to be downloaded and installed before it can be executed. Such a tool, which is characterized by easy execution, can be run directly from a web browser. The usual procedure for using such a tool is to visit the scanner's website, where a button or link is provided for executing the scan. All that the user has to do in order to launch the scan is to click on the Scan button or link. In some cases, an intermediate step like providing permission might be required.

Online scanners, while being simple and useful, are not as effective as non-online products in detecting and removing existing malware.

Spyware scanners

The following is a list of scanners that can be used for spyware detection. Some provide both detection and removal capabilities, while others can only be used for detection.
- Aluria - Free Spyware Scanner *(www.aluriasoftware.com/index.php?menu=litescan)*
- Anti-Spyware for the Web (free) *(www.trendmicro.com/spyware-scan/)*
- EarthLink Spy Audit *(www.earthlink.net/software/nmfree/spyaudit/)*
- eTrust PestScan *(www.pestpatrol.com/pestscan/)*

- ewido online scan *(www.ewido.net/en/onlinescan/)*
- Fortinet Online Virus Scanner *(www.fortinet.com/FortiGuardCenter/virus_scanner.html)*
- Panda SpyXposer *(www.pandasoftware.com/products/spyxposer/)*
- Parasite Check (www.doxdesk.com/parasite/)
- SpywareGuide.com Free Scanner *(www.spywareguide.com/onlinescan.php)*
- SpywareInfo (free) *(www.spywareinfo.com/xscan.php)*
- Tenebril Spyware Scan (free) *(www.tenebril.com/scanner/main_start.php)*
- Webroot Spy Audit *(www.webroot.com/services/spyaudit_03.htm)*
- X-Cleaner Free *(www.xblock.com/freeware)*

Virus scanners

The following are well-known online scanners that can be used in conjunction with a conventional anti-virus tool:

- Kaspersky Online Scanner: An excellent and very reliable scanner for drives, folders, and individual files. Can be configured for custom scanning. Is the best scanner for detecting new, unknown viruses.
- Kaspersky File Scanner: A good detection tool that can check files up to 1 MB. You can upload a suspect file from your computer to the Kaspersky server, where it will be scanned using the Kaspersky Anti-Virus program.
- Trend Micro HouseCall: Provides a complete computer scan. Also cleans and deletes infected files.
- Virustotal: Provides detection capabilities. Individual files can be checked online or sent via e-mail. Scanning is performed by a number of scan engines.
- Jotti Online Malware Scan: Provides detection capabilities. It operates like Virustotal, though with different scanners.

The following is a list of other available online anti-virus scanners:

- BitDefender ScanOnline *(www.bitdefender.com/scan8/ie.html)*
- Command on Demand *(www.commandondemand.com/)*
- E-Trust AntiVirus Web Scanner *(www3.ca.com/securityadvisor/virusinfo/scan.aspx)*
- ewido online scan *(www.ewido.net/en/onlinescan/)*
- F-Secure Online Virus Scanner *(http://support.f-secure.com/enu/home/ols.shtml)*
- McAfee FreeScan *(http://us.mcafee.com/root/mfs/default.asp)*
- Microsoft Malicious Software Removal Tool *(www.microsoft.com/security/malwareremove/default.mspx)*
- Panda ActiveScan *(www.pandasoftware.com/products/activescan.htm)*
- Trend Micro Spyware for the Web *(www.trendmicro.com/spyware-scan/)*

Spyware and virus removers

Spyware removers

A number of spyware removers are available for getting rid of spyware infections. The leading products are capable of detecting and removing a variety of malware, spyware, adware, keyloggers, ActiveX controls, tracking cookies, spyware in registry, BHOs, etc. Common tool features include spyware detection, scan scheduler, automatic updates, blocking cookies, real-time monitoring, backup/restore capabilities, home page protection, etc. Many of the available tools can be downloaded for free.

The following is a list of the leading products in this category:

- Spyware Detector: Feature rich, easy to use, and very effective. Provides superior customer support.
- Spy Sweeper: Feature rich, easy to use, and very effective. Provides good customer support.
- Spyware Doctor: Good features, easy to use, and effective. Provides good customer support.
- XoftSpy: Less effective than the first three products, though it does eliminate key spyware and adware. Provides frequent updates, is very easy to use, and has good customer support. The company website maintains a spyware dictionary (*http:// paretologic.com/xoftspy/lp/17*).
- Noadware: Has fewer features, removes both spyware and adware, and is highly effective. The tool provides real-time monitoring, installation detection, and is very easy to use. It may interfere with some programs. Provides frequent updates and has fair customer support (*www.noadware.net/?hop=freeadware*).
- AdWareALERT: An effective and easy to use spyware and adware remover, especially for novice users (*www.adwarealert.com/index.php?hop=battlecat*).
- PCorion: A very good spyware remover, which is somewhat more advanced and provides customization options. Is not as easy to use and is more suitable for advanced users (*www.pcorion.com*).
- AlertSpy: A good spyware remover that is backed by good customer service (*www. alertspy.com*).
- Windows Defender: A good free product (*www.microsoft.com*).

Virus removers

A number of virus removers are available for getting rid of virus infections. The following are some free standalone virus removal tools:

- avast! Virus Cleaner (*www.avast.com/eng/avast-virus-cleaner.html*)
- AVG vcleaner (*www.grisoft.com/doc/112/lng/us/tpl/tpl01*)

- BitDefender *(www.bitdefender.com/site/Download/browseFreeRemovalTool/)*
- McAfee AVERT Stinger *(http://us.mcafee.com/virusInfo/default.asp?id=stinger)*
- Microsoft Malicious Software Removal Tool *(www.microsoft.com/security/malwarer-emove/default.mspx)*
- Panda PQRemove *(www.pandasoftware.com/download/utilities/)*
- Sophos SAV32CLI *(www.sophos.com/support/disinfection/pedis.html)*

Detection and removal

Detection and removal tools perform a dual function:
- Scan and identify the malware
- Remove the malware from the system

Due to the functionality that is required for meeting these two objectives, and the wide-ranging functionality of some anti-malware programs, tools from more than one previously-identified category can be used for this purpose.

The detection and removal tools in this section have been grouped in the following categories:
- Free scanners for detection and removal
- Leading detection and removal tools
- Free virus removers
- Free uninstall products

Desired features and operation

The features of the detection and removal tools can vary quite a bit. Typically, these tools can perform the following tasks:
- Scan and/or remove
- Detect monitoring spyware, keyloggers, chat monitors, Trojans, browser hijackers, etc.
- Disable unwanted software programs
- Keep e-mails private and provide an alert if they are being monitored
- Protect online chats and IMs
- Hard disk shredding
- Protect privacy and cover footsteps
- Protect from unknown BHOs
- Scan registers
- Basic firewall functions
- Remove toolbars and toolbar icons
- Disable or eliminate browser add-ons

A detection and removal program should be run at least weekly. However, if risky sites are being visited, then this frequency should be increased considerably as the risks are higher due to such behavior. As a rule, the updated versions of at least two programs should be used. It makes no sense to use a program that has not been updated for two or three months because it will be ineffective.

Free scanners for detection and removal
The following are some of the free leading and widely-available scanners that can be used to detect and remove spyware and/or adware:
- Ad-aware Personal *(www.lavasoft.de/support/download/)*
- ewido anti-spyware *(www.ewido.net/en/)*
- Spybot Search & Destroy *(http://spybot.safer-networking.de/en/mirrors/index.html)*
- SUPERAntiSpyware *(www.superantispyware.com/)*
- Windows Defender *(www.microsoft.com/athome/security/spyware/software/default.mspx)*

Leading detection and removal tools
X-Cleaner
X-Cleaner *(www.xblock.com)* is a web-based multi-purpose tool that is easy to install and use. It can perform a quick and comprehensive scan for detecting and removing spyware and adware. X-Cleaner can also provide protection against future installations. It clears caches, temporary files, chat logs, cookies, history of URLs visited, recycle bin, and activity logs. The tool also has a file shredder and can be configured for various scan options. The company website contains a useful spyware database.

RegBlock
RegBlock *(www.regblock.com)* is a tool that can perform quick and deep scans for detecting and removing unwanted programs which have been installed on the computer, such as spyware, keyloggers and adware. The program also prevents the installation of malware. It is integrated with the spywareguide.com encyclopedia, where threat information is quickly available. The program has a safety check feature, which ensures that the PC is not seriously impacted and crippled if a program is removed.

Pest Patrol
This product was described previously in Chapter 14.

Ad-Aware
This product was described previously in Chapter 14.

Norton Anti-virus
This product was described previously in Chapter 14.

Free virus removers
The following is a list of some free standalone virus removers:
- avast! Virus Cleaner *(www.avast.com/eng/avast-virus-cleaner.html)*
- AVG vcleaner *(www.grisoft.com/doc/1)*
- Dr. Web CureIT *(http://download.drweb.com/drweb+cureit/)*
- McAfee AVERT Stinger *(http://vil.nai.com/vil/stinger/)*
- Microsoft Malicious Software Removal Tool *(www.microsoft.com/security/malwarer-emove/default.mspx)*
- Panda PQRemove *(www.pandasoftware.com/download/utilities/)*
- Sophos SAV32CLI *(www.sophos.com/support/disinfection/pedis.html)*

Free uninstall products
- About-Blank *(www.aboutblank.com.au/)*
- B3D/BDE Killer *(www.wilderssecurity.com/B3DKiller.html)*
- Backdoor Autoupder Removal Tool *(www.symantec.com/enterprise/security_response/removaltools.jsp)*
- Backdoor.Agent.B *(www.symantec.com/security_response/writeup.jsp?docid=2004-081016-3824-99)*
- BDEcid *(www.spywarewarrior.com/uiuc/soft6.htm)*
- BugHunter *(http://bughunter.it-mate.co.uk/)*
- CoolWebSearch Shredder *(www.trendmicro.com/cwshredder/)*
- Cydoor Dummy Files *(http://cexx.org/dummies.htm)*
- DLDER.EXE Remover *(http://cexx.org/dlder.htm)*
- Doug Knox - Internet Explorer Fixes *(www.dougknox.com/xp/file_assoc.htm)*
- EliteToolbar Remover *(www.wilderssecurity.com/archive/index.php/t-100872.html)*
- GetRight Ad Remover *(www.getright.com/remove_ads.html)*
- HandyBits/Teknum Updater Disabler *(www.spywarewarrior.com/uiuc/soft6.htm)*
- Kill2Me *(www.majorgeeks.com/download4166.html)*
- Look2Me/VX2Finder *(www.spywarewarrior.com/uiuc/soft6.htm)*
- LOPcide *(www.spywarewarrior.com/uiuc/soft6.htm)*
- Mattel Brodcast DSSAGENT Removal Utility *(http://cexx.org/dssagent.htm)*
- Netsetter/MarketScore *(www.windowsstartup.com/doc.php?id=8)*
- Netster *(www.spywarewarrior.com/uiuc/soft6.htm)*
- NewDotNet *(www.newdotnet.com/removal.html)*

- Peper *(www.scanspyware.net/info/Peper.htm)*
- RapidBlaster Killer *(www.wilderssecurity.com/showthread.php?t=10059)*
- Scumware.com *(www.scumware.com)*
- ShopNav *(www.spywarehub.com)*
- Showbehind *(http://paretologic.com/resources/definitions.aspx?remove=ShowBehind)*
- ThiefWare.com *(www.thiefware.com)*

Prevention

You must be proactive and implement steps to prevent malware from being installed on your computer. Even if malware was installed and subsequently removed successfully, you must never become complacent. Always be vigilant and take steps to prevent malware re-installation. Two very good tools, from JavaCool, that can be used for basic free protection are:

- SpywareBlaster:

  SpywareBlaster *(www.javacoolsoftware.com/spywareblaster.html)* prevents web pages from installing ActiveX-based spyware, adware, hijackers, monitoring software, cookies, dialers, etc. It can restrict the actions that some websites execute. SpywareBlaster has a feature that takes a snapshot of the system. If infection occurs, this feature enables the changes made by the spyware or other malware to be reversed—so that the system reverts back to its original status (when the snapshot was captured).

- SpywareGuard:

  SpywareGuard *(www.javacoolsoftware.com/spywareguard.html)* complements Spyware-Blaster protection by providing real-time protection. It protects against download risks and browser hijacking. SpywareGuard scans a file for spyware before it is opened and executed. This is in contrast to an anti-virus program which performs the same action but directs it against viruses. SpywareGuard can be run simultaneously with an anti-virus program.

These two tools, which can be installed very easily, provide protection in different ways. SpywareBlaster protects the browser from the installation of unwanted programs, while SpywareGuard monitors the computer and prevents spyware installation. Therefore, both tools should be used simultaneously.

Leading malware prevention tools

The following is a list of leading prevention tools:

- NoAdware *(www.noadware.net)*

- Pest Patrol (*www.pestpatrol.com*)
- Spyware Doctor (*www.pctools.com/spyware-doctor/*)
- SpyHunter (*http://spyware.software.programsbase.com/*)
- Spyware Eliminator (*www.aluriasoftware.com*)
- SpySubtract (*www.intermute.com/products/spysubtract.html*)
- SpySweeper (*www.webroot.com/consumer/products/spysweeper/*)
- SpyRemover (*www.itcompany.com/*)

Free prevention tools
- AdAware Checker (*www.wilderssecurity.com/aawchecker.html*)
- Browser Hijack Blaster (*www.wilderssecurity.com/bhblaster.html*)
- Browser Hijack Retaliator (*www.zamaansoft.com/products/bhr/*)
- BrowserSentinel (*www.browsersentinel.com/*)
- DSOstop2 (*www.nsclean.com/dsostop.html*)
- Enough is Enough! (*www.wilderssecurity.com/archive/index.php/t-862.html*)
- Home Page Monitor (*www.exits.ro/*)
- HTAstop (*www.nsclean.com/htastop.html*)
- ID-Blaster (*www.wilderssecurity.net/idblaster.html*)
- IE Restrictions (*http://camtech2000.net/Pages/Restrictions.htm*)
- Prevx (*https://www.prevx.com/*)
- Process Patrol (*www.processpatrol.com/*)
- Smog's Ad Kill (*http://smog.cjb.net/html/adkill.htm*)
- Spychecker (*www.spychecker.com/home.html*)
- SpywareGuide Blocklist (*www.spywareguide.com/blockfile.php*)
- StartUp Monitor (*www.windowsstartup.com/startupmonitor.php*)
- StartupList (*www.spywareinfo.com/~merijn/*)
- StartupListUI (*www.spywarewarrior.com/uiuc/soft21a.htm*)
- XP-AntiSpy (*www.xp-antispy.org*)

Privacy and covering your tracks
This section provides a list of well-known tools that protect privacy and help cover your tracks. It may be interesting to know that hackers and crackers use some of the tools described in this section to hide what they are doing to your system.

Tool features
The tools in this category vary in their effectiveness, functionality, and features. Typically, they perform some or most of the following tasks:

- Internet browser cleaning: Can include the address bar, cookies, favorites list, downloaded files, plug-ins, URL error logs, temporary files (cache), URL drop-down list, and auto-complete
- Windows cleaning: Can include application log, recycle bin, clipboard content, history of find/search, recently used documents list, MS-Office history, registry backups and other files, temporary files/directories, media files, index files, etc. Can also include wiping the hard disk's free space.
- Cleaning options for startup/shutdown and browser close, as well as automatic task scheduler
- Multiple levels of erasing
- Spyware detection
- Password protection
- Scrambling files and folder properties
- File shredding
- Home page protection
- Retention of required cookies
- Stealth mode
- Creation of various types of log files
- Support for various browser plug-ins

Leading privacy tools

- Evidence Eliminator:
  Evidence Eliminator is probably the most comprehensive privacy product, which is very expensive ($99.95) and has most of the required features. This very effective product has many options that technically-savvy users can use. It is easy to install though not as easy to configure as some competing products.
- Window Washer:
  Window Washer is an excellent and effective product that is a better choice than Evidence Eliminator for those who are not as technically-oriented. It is very easy to install, configure and use. It has fewer features and options than Evidence Eliminator such as stealth mode, hide/unhide browsers, URL error logs, registry backups, etc.
- CyberScrub:
  Another easy to use leading product with many of the desired protection features. It is good enough for novices and also has advanced options that the more technically-savvy users can utilize.

- Max PC Privacy:

An easy to use privacy software application with many commonly desired features. It is easy to install, though novice users will not find it as easy to use.

Other good privacy tools

- Windows Internet Cleaner:

Windows Internet Cleaner is very good privacy product that is easy to install and use. It has fewer features and options than the leading products in this category but still covers the privacy needs of most users.

- Privacy Guardian:

Privacy Guardian is a good privacy product, which is easy to install and use. It has limited advanced features and options compared to the leading products in its category.

- Privacy Eraser:

A very good product that is very easy to install and use, though it is not as effective as some of its leading competitors. However, it does provide most of the desired privacy functionality required by most users.

- Privacy Protector:

A good product that is easy to install, configure and use. It has limited options and features compared to other products in its category, which limits its effectiveness.

- Tracks Eraser Pro:

A good product that is easy to install and use. The product has limited options and its customization options are not as easy to use. Its lack of some privacy features limits its effectiveness.

- Internet Washer:

A very good product, widely used, that is easy to install and use. Its features are limited compared to competing products, which limits its effectiveness, though it covers the essentials of privacy protection. Customization options are not easy to use. Internet Washer contains a preview mode that shows the effect of a cleanup without actually deleting anything.

- GhostSurfPro:

GhostSurfPro is a comprehensive privacy tool that routes information through anonymous proxy servers, enabling anonymous surfing. It can clear browser cookies, history files and temporary Internet files. It also prevents spyware infections and pop-ups.

Anti-Trojan
Tool features

Many of the tools covered in the previous categories also provide anti-Trojan defenses in addition to their primary purpose. The available anti-Trojan tools vary in their effectiveness, functionality, and features. Typically, they perform some or most of these tasks:

- Search for Trojans
- Remove Trojans
- Protect against downloads from the Internet
- Scan memory
- Scan registry
- Scan ini files (configuration files)
- Scan ports
- Scan resident memory
- Perform live updates

The next two sections provide a list of well-known dedicated anti-Trojan tools.

Leading anti-Trojan tools

The following is a list of leading products available in this category:

- Trojan Hunter:

  The Trojan Hunter, *www.trojanhunter.com*, is a sophisticated tool with excellent detection capabilities. It is easy to install, has an easy to use interface, and its system utilization is low. It supports the addition of custom Trojan definitions and detection rules. Trojan Hunter has a wide feature set that includes a high-speed scan engine, registry scanning, memory scanning, port scanning, configuration files scanning, live updates, etc.

- ewido:

  The ewido tool (*www.ewido.net*), which was described previously, detects Trojans almost as effectively as Trojan Hunter. It is quite easy to use and has the advantage of also being able to work against spyware.

- A Squared (a2):

  A Squared (*www.emsisoft.com/en/*) can scan and remove Trojans, keyloggers, rootkits, worms, adware and spyware. It is easy to use and has a live update feature. However, this product has fewer features than the leading products in its category.

- BOClean:

  BOClean (*www.nsclean.com/*) is an effective tool that works against Trojans, worms, and other types of malware. This real-time tool is designed for individual users as well as networks. It detects, removes, and repairs automatically. BOClean can be configured to run in stealth mode.

- Tauscan:
Tauscan (*www.agnitum.com/products/tauscan/*) is a good anti-Trojan tool that can detect and remove many types of malware. This tool is easy to use, has an intuitive interface, and its consumption of system resources is low. Though it has an effective scanner, Tauscan does not match the performance of the top tools in its category.
- Pest Patrol:
The Pest Patrol tool (*www.pestpatrol.com*), described previously in Chapter 14, also works against Trojans.

Free online virus and Trojan scanners
The following is a list of free online virus and Trojan scanners:
- GFI online Trojan scanner (*www.windowsecurity.com/trojanscan/*)
- McAfee VirusScan online (*www.mcafee.com*)
- Panda Active Scan (*www.pandasoftware.com/products/activescan.htm*)
- PC Pitstop (*www.pcpitstop.com/antivirus/default.asp*)
- RavAntiVirus (*www.ravantivirus.com*)
- Symantec Security Check (*www.security.symantec.com*)
- TrendMicro HouseCall (*http://housecall.trendmicro.com/*)

Anti-spam and pop-up filters
Anti-spam features
A number of tools have been developed to fight the serious and pervasive spam problem. Spam management and prevention tools typically attempt to incorporate the following desired features:
- Spam detection capabilities
- Removal of malicious code
- Selection of security levels
- Filter configuration
- Whitelist and blacklist
- Message preview
- Ability to block by domain, IP address, address, etc.
- Support for different e-mail clients
- Removal of tracking and privacy bugs

- Quarantine
- Multiple filtering techniques
- Spoof fraud protection
- Challenge/response (e-mail is blocked until a sender responds to a challenge that is sent whenever an e-mail arrives from a new sender)

Leading anti-spam tools

The following is a list of the leading tools available in this category:

- Benign:

  Benign is a user-friendly application that provides protection against malicious and undesirable e-mail as well as e-mail attachments. It removes the programming code that malware, like viruses and scripts, require for their execution. Benign can strip out malicious code hidden in an HTML message. It has many configuration options that permit various security levels to be selected as desired. The program supports a number of e-mail programs including Outlook and Netscape.

- MailWasher Pro:

  MailWasher Pro is a fairly-effective anti-spam program that provides protection against spam and unwanted e-mails. It protects users from these threats and ensures safe and secure e-mail management. The product is simple to use and has a number of features such as message preview, deleting e-mails before the whole message is downloaded, bouncing e-mail back to the spammer, blacklisting of e-mails and/or domains, filtering, friends list, etc. MailWasher Pro supports Hotmail, MSN and AOL. It uses both powerful rules-based and Bayesian (statistical) filters to detect spam. It is also configurable, which enables users to configure their own filters.

- Mail Box Guard:

  Mail Box Guard is an anti-spam tool, with a user-friendly interface, that is easy to install and use. It provides good e-mail protection against spam, viruses and obscenity. Its features include the ability to see e-mails before downloading, preview mail at the server, rank the risks into categories (including x-rated, spam, virus and foul language), protect against viruses, user-definable lists, blacklist (senders to be rejected), etc. The tool, which has customizable options, is more effective against obscenity and viruses, though its ability to block spam is limited.

- Spam Shield:

  Spam Shield is an effective anti-spam tool that is easy to install, configure and use. It has many features such as rules definition, management of approved sender lists, removal of tracking and privacy bugs, safe message preview, etc.

- Qurb:

  Qurb is a very easy to install and use anti-spam tool, which has a good interface for reviewing blocked mail. The product can be used immediately without any configuration as it creates a whitelist (approved senders), from the user's contact list, which is updated over time. This feature also creates the potential for e-mails from other senders to be filtered initially, as the inbox will only accept e-mails from the approved sender's list. The challenge/response option is optional. Suspect messages are quarantined, not deleted. The product also provides spoof fraud protection. Qurb integrates quite well with the e-mail client—the application used to send/receive/view e-mails.

- Choice Mail:

  Choice Mail is an effective anti-spam product. It uses a permission-based method that contains the option to block e-mails by domain, IP address, as well as well-known spammers. While the setup for novices is not easy, the program is fairly simple to use. Messages are filtered using a whitelist and a blacklist. The product does not integrate as well as Qurb with the e-mail client. Choice Mail supports the setting up of customized rules.

- Spam Bully:

  Spam Bully is another efficient anti-spam product that uses multiple filtering techniques, which is easy to install and use. It uses the address book for import into the approved sender list. Its features include requesting confirmations from new senders, good integration with Outlook and Outlook Express, detailed logging, keyword filtering, and the ability to configure for challenge/response operation.

- SpamBayes:

  SpamBayes, the product of an open-source project, is an intelligent anti-spam tool for Outlook, which uses an advanced Bayesian filtering method. It does not require manual setup and is pretty good at classifying incoming messages. Over time, the product tends to get smarter.

Leading anti-pop-up products

- SuperAdBlocker:

  SuperAdBlocker is an excellent tool for blocking all types of pop-up advertising. It also includes, free of charge, the SuperAntispyware application for removing adware and spyware. The product has many features including real-time protection, the ability to protect home page hijacking, automatic updates, blocking of sponsored and search ads, as well as the cleaning of cache, cookies and browser history. The tool is easy to install and use.

- GL AdPopup Terminator:

  The GL AdPopup Terminator application takes care of undesirable pop-up windows generated by web pages. The product is easy to use and can be customized. A custom list of websites can be built so that pop-ups from specified sites are not blocked.

- PanicWare Popup Stopper Pro:

  The PanicWare Popup Stopper Pro tool blocks browser pop-up and pop-under ads. It can also block IM and desktop ads. The tool also cleans the cache, histories, etc. for privacy protection. Installation is easy and the product is easy to use. The application also comes in a free version, which is also quite effective.

- Adshield:

  Adshield is an Internet Explorer ad and pop-up blocker that blocks flash and animated ads, though with limited effectiveness. The product features include the optional suppression of ad images, pop-up displays and downloads, detection and disabling of web bugs, block and exclude lists, etc. The blocking features are easy to implement.

- Internet Explorer 6 SP2:

  Both Internet Explorer 6 and Internet Explorer 7 provide good protection against pop-ups.

SECURITY SUITES
Understanding security suites
What is a security suite

A security suite is a single comprehensive software application that includes a number of tightly-integrated components such as anti-virus, anti-spyware, anti-spam, firewall, etc. The objective of such an application is to provide users with a single application that can replace a number of individual programs and, thus, provide comprehensive protection against various types of malware and intruders.

Features of security suites

The following is a list of the features and capabilities that are desired in comprehensive all-in-one security suites.

- Firewall
- Anti-malware including anti-spyware, anti-virus, anti-worm, anti-Trojan, anti-adware, anti-backdoor programs, anti-keylogger, anti-spam, etc.

- Ability to detect all *WildList* threats (malware items that are spreading as a result of day-to-day operations)
- Browser protection, including home page and search page hijack protection
- Anti-phishing and fraud protection
- e-mail and IM protection
- Wireless protection
- Content filtering
- Parental controls
- Privacy protection
- Identity theft protection, such as an ID vault for storing confidential data, credit card information, and passwords
- Shredding utility
- Automatic updates
- Scanning: Real-time and on-demand scanning, scan configuration, and fast scan speed
- Low system resource utilization
- Integration with installed applications

The leading security suites incorporate most of these features, while the second-tier applications only include a relatively limited set of features. The selection of the security suite should be based on the requirements that the user considers most important such as anti-virus or firewall protection, parental controls, cost, ease of use, customer support, etc. Typically, advanced users prefer applications that provide more options for configuration and customization.. However, novice users prefer an application that is easy to install, configure, and use.

Limitations of security suites

Many of the previously-listed features are available in all the security suite applications, though their effectiveness varies. For example, a firewall is a common component in all the comprehensive applications. Also, most security suites provide parental controls (for restricting access to undesirable websites) as well as privacy controls (for protecting sensitive and confidential data). However, the quality and effectiveness of the individual firewalls, parental controls, and privacy controls varies considerably from suite to suite.

While many of the comprehensive security suites excel in a particular area, no application exhibits superior performance in every area. Although security suites provide much broader protection, their anti-spyware modules are often inferior to standalone anti-spyware applications. Therefore, even if a comprehensive security suite is being used, it is recommended that a dedicated anti-spyware application be installed for protection against spyware.

Since there is no security suite that has the best component in every area, the alternative strategy is to use the best-of-breed applications: best firewall, best anti-virus program, etc. However, that approach can require more installation and configuration skills compared to the all-in-one suites. Also, that strategy will result in a higher cost, as more tools are needed to provide comprehensive protection equivalent to that provided by a security suite. However, the benefit of the best-of-breed approach is that it will provide a more robust defense against different types of malware.

Leading security suites

All the comprehensive all-in-one security suites exhibit varying degrees of protection effectiveness in various areas. Most of them are very successful in detecting well-known viruses, worms, and script malware. However, according to the PC World reviews, the top two suites that consistently perform well in various areas are Symantec's Norton Internet Security and the McAfee Internet Security Suite. The detailed comparison of the various features of the leading security suites and their rankings are available at *www.pcworld.com*.

Comprehensive applications

The following are the leading and well-known popular products in the security suites category:

1. Symantec Norton Internet Security 2007
2. McAfee Internet Security Suite 2007
3. Panda Internet Security 2007
4. F-Secure Internet Security 2007
5. Trend Micro PC-cillin Internet Security 2007
6. Zone Labs ZoneAlarm Security Suite
7. CA Internet Security Suite 2007
8. BitDefender Internet Security v10
9. Kaspersky Internet Security 6.0
10. BullGuard Internet Security 7.0
11. Windows Live OneCare

It should be noted that the firewalls of all suites reviewed in this section permit some sort of general security level, whitelisting and blacklisting of individual applications, and enabling of specific ports and network protocols.

Symantec Norton Internet Security 2007

Overall, the Norton Internet Security (NIS) suite is probably the best application currently available, with a full range of security features, whose overall performance is excellent. It includes Norton AntiVirus, Norton Personal Firewall, Norton Privacy Control, Norton AntiSpam, and Norton Parental Control. The application detects and blocks spyware, worms, viruses, adware, Trojans, backdoor programs, and other types of malware. It has excellent detection and cleanup capabilities. It automatically filters spam, though not very effectively, and phishing e-mails. The suite is characterized by superior features which makes it a very effective tool against various malware types. The NIS firewall, which monitors and controls all connections to the Internet, is extremely effective in blocking both inside and outside attacks.

Norton Internet Security's scanning is not very fast and its real-time protection can impact performance. The product provides IM protection, parental controls and data privacy. Users have the flexibility to selectively choose to block or allow ActiveX controls and Java applets. They can also select from three default security levels or create a custom control level.

The NIS product, which has a simple interface, is easy to install and configure. The negatives include an interface that needs to be improved and a poor anti-spam feature. The number of pop-up alerts could be reduced as an improvement. Technical assistance, which includes 24-hour phone support, is very expensive and can cost $30 per incident.

Norton Internet Security 2007, which lists for $69.99 and is not available for a single-user license, can be used for protecting three PCs. It does not include a file shredder or a backup utility, which the McAfee product has. The product has a larger footprint than its leading competitors (ZoneAlarm and McAfee), taking up about 350 MB on the hard drive. It provides automatic system protection without prompting the user excessively. Its Auto-Protect feature does come at a price—degradation of system performance.

McAfee Internet Security Suite 2007

The McAfee Internet Security Suite, which incorporates a full range of security features, is one of the best suites. It includes McAfee VirusScan, McAfee AntiSpyware, McAfee Firewall, McAfee SpamKiller and McAfee Privacy Service. The application detects and blocks spyware, worms, viruses, adware, Trojans, backdoor programs, spam, and other types of malware. McAfee Internet Security Suite's performance is superior and it excels in malware detection, where it ranks the highest, and cleanup. It is one of the best suites for detecting viruses and spyware and is also very effective at detecting adware. It also provides IM protection as well as anti-phishing defense. The firewall can be configured to handle inbound and outbound connections independently. It is very effective, though not to the level provided by competing suites (Symantec and ZoneAlarm), and has good intrusion tracing capabilities.

The McAfee suite also provides protection from identity theft. It provides the ability to store private data, such as passwords and credit card numbers, in an encrypted database from where external transmission via e-mail, IM or web forms is prevented. To delete sensitive files, McAfee provides a shredding utility. It also provides content filtering and parental controls. The product also provides automatic backup, one-click restore, and extensive wireless networking utilities. It installs daily updates automatically.

McAfee's installation is quite cumbersome and its anti-spam protection is poor. The anti-spam filter tends to slow e-mail downloads. However, the product is easy to navigate and use. It also provides comprehensive configuration options. Technical support is expensive and costs $3/minute. The latest release of the product, McAfee Internet Security Suite 2007, which lists for $69.95, has been available at a considerable discount ($39.95).

Panda Internet Security 2007

Panda Internet Security 2007 is one of the leading security suites. It provides very good performance and superior features, though it has not improved much over its previous release. The suite includes Panda Antivirus, Panda AntiSpyware, Panda Firewall, Panda Identity Protect, Panda AntiSpam, and Panda Parental Control. The tool provides varying levels of protection against spyware, viruses, and other malware types. Panda's features include anti-spam, e-mail and IM protection, web content filtering, identity theft protection, online fraud protection, parental controls, automatic daily updates, and Wi-Fi intrusion reporting.

An effective firewall and a very fast scanner are also provided in the Panda suite, which lists for $69.95. Panda's heuristic scanning for detecting new malware threats is quite superior. However, its spam filter is mediocre. The suite also provides privacy protection for confidential data such as passwords and credit card information. However, it does not prevent such data from being transmitted via an IM or a web form. If such data is transmitted via e-mail, it provides a warning. The product is easy to install and use.

F-Secure Internet Security 2007

The F-Secure Internet Security 2007 suite is one of the leading security suites. It is characterized by good performance, has very good features, and ranks among the best suites in its ability to detect viruses (using the Kaspersky anti-virus engine) and spyware. The product's heuristic scanning is excellent. Other features include Trojan and anti-spam protection, protection against backdoor programs, anti-phishing defense, parental controls, and rootkit detection. However, its cleaning capability does not match its detection capabilities. F-Secure's firewall is solid and it is very effective in responding to external as well as internal attacks. It has eliminated annoying confirmation pop-ups that characterized the previous release of the product.

The virus scan is slow compared to its competitors. This is attributed to its multiple scan engines used against different types of threats. F-Secure Internet Security has limited effectiveness against adware and it also has an ineffective anti-spam feature. The product is easy to install, has a simple interface, and is easy to use. It provides many configuration options that are not very intuitive, though it can be used with minimal configuration.

The F-Secure Internet Security 2007 release, listed for $79.90 but available at a good discount, provides improved integration between its anti-spyware and anti-virus engines.

Trend Micro PC-cillin Internet Security 2007

PC-cillin Internet Security 2007, characterized by fair performance and features, provides protection against viruses, spyware, hacker intrusions, phishing, spam, and online threats. Though the product provides good security, it is not among the leading products in its category because the effectiveness of its modules varies significantly. The level and quality of its powerful and excellent anti-virus protection is not matched by its other modules.

PC-cillin provides substandard spyware protection. Its privacy protection (which prevents personal information from being transmitted) and Website Filter (which blocks specific sites or website categories) features are superior. Web-content filtering protection enables the blocking of undesirable, inappropriate, and dangerous sites. The program provides real-time scanning as well as on-demand or scheduled checks for any Wi-Fi intruders. Scanning can be scheduled for various periods, along with different settings.

PC-cillin does not protect against home page hijacking or similar attacks. It scans incoming and outgoing e-mail and attachments. Fraud protection is good but the firewall and anti-spam modules are inferior. The firewall fails to stealth important file-sharing ports and it is difficult to manage. It has vulnerabilities in blocking outside attacks, controlling program access to the Internet, and protecting itself from malware.

The program provides too many pop-up security messages. It reduces system resource requirements by turning off some security options, such as Website Filter, by default. Even after turning on all options, it is faster than some of the leading products. The program is easy to install and has a well-organized interface. It provides many configuration options but is easy to use and control, which makes it suitable for advanced users as well as novices.

Since the quality of the modules varies considerably in terms of protection and ease of use, a good option might be to use the tool only for anti-virus protection.

With a list price of $49.95, the product is cheaper compared to the competing all-in-one security suites. Phone technical support is free via a toll-free number. The available documentation is excellent and the company's knowledge base is a very useful source for information.

Zone Labs ZoneAlarm Internet Security Suite

The ZoneAlarm Internet Security Suite is a comprehensive application that performs very well and has a wide range of good features. It provides good security protection, though the performance of its various components varies. ZoneAlarm protects against spyware, viruses, spam, identity theft, and phishing. The product also has a mode for gamers, which removes interruptions. The suite provides IM and e-mail protection, privacy settings, parental controls, identity protection, and Wi-Fi security protection. The program uses an encrypted vault and protects private data such as passwords and credit card numbers, whose transmission it blocks via e-mail, IM or web forms.

The firewall is the best one available and provides protection from external as well as internal attacks. The anti-virus component, which is based on the eTrust EZ anti-virus engine, is relatively inferior and ineffective. Spyware removal and adware detection are also not as effective. ZoneAlarm's spyware and virus scans are not integrated. The tool also scores low in heuristics.

The suite is easy to install and has an intuitive interface. The footprint is small and its impact on performance is slight. Technical support is available at $2.95 per minute, which is similar to other competitors' charges. The latest release of the product, with a list price of $69.95, is available at a considerable discount.

CA Internet Security Suite 2007

CA's Internet Security Suite is a comprehensive application with a list price of $69.99. It offers good features and is characterized by average performance. The product provides inferior protection against malware, where it ranks quite low compared to the leading all-in-one security suites. Its protection against viruses and spyware is average. The anti-spyware component is ineffective in blocking spyware installation. The product has weak real-time protection, its spyware scan is fast, and it provides solid protection against adware and spam (using the Qurb anti-spam product). The suite's firewall, licensed from Zone Labs, provides solid protection against internal and external attacks.

The product's other features include inbound and outbound e-mail protection, browser cache cleaning, privacy settings, parental controls, web content filtering, and fraud protection. It encrypts stored confidential data and also prevents personal information from being transmitted via e-mail or web forms.

The anti-virus scheduling options are limited and the product is light on system resource utilization. The suite is less integrated compared to the other leading comprehensive suites. Technical support is expensive at $30 per incident.

BitDefender Internet Security v10

BitDefender Internet Security is a comprehensive security suite from Softwin, a Romanian company. It includes anti-virus, anti-spyware, and firewall protection. The suite, with a $59.95 list price, has good features and is marked by average performance. However, the performance of its various modules varies significantly. Anti-virus protection is solid, while spam protection is mediocre. Its heuristic capabilites are better than the average among the security suites. Other features include rootkit detection and removal, P2P and IM application protection, filtering of web traffic in real-time, anti-hacking and phishing protection, limited parental controls (different restrictions cannot be applied to different users), and home page hijack prevention.

The ability to disinfect a spyware-infested system is poor. The adware scanner is mediocre and its scanning speed is slow. The firewall provides protection against internal and external attacks. It is also able to operate in stealth mode, which hides the computer from intruders. However, it generates too many pop-ups.

The application is easy to install and use, with a well-organized interface. Novice users will not find it easy to select configuration options. Overall, the product ranks at the lower end of the all-in-one comprehensive security suites.

Kaspersky Internet Security 6.0

Kaspersky Internet Security 6.0 from Kaspersky Labs, with a list price of $69.95, is a comprehensive application that provides solid protection against spyware, viruses and other threats. It includes a solid firewall and provides effective malware and adware detection, though its anti-spam protection is mediocre. Its heuristic capabilities are good. The product's other features include web protection tools, scanning of files and e-mail, on-demand and scheduled scanning, phishing protection, rootkit detection, and detection of other threats originating from the web.

The Kaspersky application does not include privacy protection or parental controls, which are provided by most of the comprehensive suites. It cannot scan IM messages and it is not very good at disinfection either. Other negatives include a high price and an interface that is not intuitive and needs improvement. Scanning is somewhat slow and the application also impacts system performance. The product uses unconventional naming conventions which can cause confusion, especially for novices.

BullGuard Internet Security 7.0

The BullGuard Internet Security 7.0 suite, with a list price of $59.99, provides anti-virus and anti-spyware protection, a firewall (based on the Outpost firewall engine), as well as a spam filter. However, the missing features include parental controls and privacy protection. The anti-virus module is quick and very effective, the firewall component is average, while the spam filter is mediocre. The suite provides, for a payment, a unique feature—an online encrypted backup of the most important files. BullGuard 7.0 can be configured to perform scheduled backups to external hard drives, network drives, USB drives and other removable media. Technical support is excellent and live chat is available round-the-clock.

Windows Live OneCare

The beta Windows Live OneCare is a subscription-based security package from Microsoft that costs $49.95 for one year for up to three PCs. It is cheaper, has limited features, and is not as configurable as the other comprehensive security suites. Windows Live OneCare features include anti-virus, anti-spyware, firewall, performance tune-up, backups, and automatic windows patch management.

The performance of Live OneCare is good. However, the product does not provide protection that is comparable to the broad and comprehensive protection provided by its competitors. The anti-virus component is superior to its anti-spyware component. Its heuristic ranking is the lowest among the security suites. However, it does cleanup effectively. Though it is an effective firewall that provides both inbound and outbound protection, it does not protect against spam or provide privacy or parental controls. The product also provides backup and tune-up tools.

The application is easy to use and configure, which is due to the limited configuration options that are available. However, the integration of its application components needs to be improved.

Tips and Good Practices

Online threats cannot be eliminated. However, they can be minimized to a large extent by following the good behavior and habits described previously throughout the book. In this chapter, in order to enable easy and quick reference, important good practices and tips have been organized into different categories and presented in a summarized format.

PROTECTING THE COMPUTER
Keep Windows security patches up-to-date

Install the latest security patches for the computer's operating system. Microsoft regularly issues critical updates to rectify flaws that are detected in its Windows operating system versions. The Windows XP Service Pack 2 (SP2), which provides significant privacy and security features, should be installed along with the latest security patches. As a habit, run the Windows update program once a week at least. It should also be run whenever Microsoft or one of the security companies, such as Symantec and McAfee, issues a warning regarding the operating system.

Periodically visit the *Microsoft Windows Update* site, *www.windowsupdate.microsoft.com*, which lists recommended updates along with the latest patches and fixes. The update process is fairly simple and takes only a few minutes. When the update process is started, as per the update website instructions, the computer is analyzed and a menu of applicable downloads is listed. All that the user has to do is select the updates that need to be installed and then click the appropriate download button, which will start the download and installation process. After the installation is complete, the computer will need to be rebooted.

The Windows operating system can be configured so that the updates are installed automatically. Before turning on automatic updates, be aware of the risk that was explained in Chapter 1. To automate the installation of updates, Windows XP can be configured by navigating as follows:

- *Control Panel > System > Automatic Updates*
- Select the *Automatic* radio button
- Click *OK*

Use a firewall

Individual computers as well as networks must be provided with hardware or software firewall protection. Both types of firewalls can be used simultaneously for extra protection. Firewalls can be configured to block the transmission of data from your computer to other computers or the Internet. Windows XP with SP2 has a built-in firewall. However, a commercial firewall should be used for even better protection.

Use anti-spyware and anti-virus software

Use effective and reliable anti-spyware and anti-virus products from reputable vendors. Use products that can be updated easily, as such software can quickly become outdated and ineffective. Anti-spyware and anti-virus software product updates should be installed at regularly-scheduled intervals.

Avoid using freeware and shareware, as many of these act as vehicles through which malware is delivered. However, if cost makes it impractical to buy a commercial anti-spyware and/or anti-virus product, it makes sense to use a free product that provides basic protection. Before running or downloading a product that is not provided by a well-known and trusted source, check it out. Conduct a search on the Internet and check for any warnings that may have been posted by the products' previous or existing users, review sites, anti-malware forums, etc.

Scan at startup and installation

The anti-spyware and anti-virus software should be configured so that that they are launched every time the computer is booted. The scan at startup will protect the computer every time it starts and tries to launch an executable file, which can be a potential source of malware. Executable files are a major source of malware and you should never take any chances by installing a program without subjecting it to a contamination check. Additionally, *without exception*, every new program that is installed should be scanned for viruses and spyware.

Be aware of programs limitations

Different types of anti-malware programs, such as anti-spyware and anti-virus software, specialize in identifying specific infection types. They do not take care of all types of malware. For example, an anti-virus program will be unable to detect a Trojan horse program. Similarly, an anti-spyware program will not be as effective as a dedicated anti-virus program in detecting viruses and worms.

Limit administrative rights

When you are logged in as an *Administrator* on your PC, your authorization will be the maximum permissible for that machine. However, a user logging in as a guest is provided minimal authorization and, consequently, cannot make changes to many important Windows settings. Therefore, if you login as a guest, it significantly reduces the potential for malware infection. Hence, you should maintain two accounts: *Administrator* and *General User*. Use the *General User* account for routine tasks. You should login as an *Administrator* only when essential tasks need to be performed, such as configuration and installing software applications, which the *General User* cannot perform. After patching, this is one of the most effective ways to protect computers.

If a single computer on a network is contaminated, it has the potential to spread the infection to every computer on the network. Therefore, administration rights for users of enterprise computers and laptops should also be restricted. This will prevent the installation of spyware and other malware on network computers.

Disable vulnerable features

The ability to automatically execute JavaScript, macros, and other executable code that might be embedded in an e-mail or attached to it should be disabled due to reasons explained in Chapter 9.

Disable Scripting

Disable Scripting due to reasons explained in Chapters 1 and 9. If the Internet Explorer is being used, turn off its ability to execute scripts without permission, which can be done by navigating as follows:

- *Tools > Internet Options*
- Click the *Security* tab
- Select the *Internet* icon by clicking on it
- Click the *Custom Level* button, which will cause the *Security Settings* window to pop-up
- On the *Security Settings* window:
  - Select the *Disable* radio button for the following items:
    - *Download unsigned ActiveX controls*
    - *Initialize and script ActiveX controls not marked as safe*
    - *Active scripting*

- *Scripting of Java applets*
- Set the *Java permissions* to *High safety*

This change can cause some websites to become unusable. To rectify such an issue, add the blocked website (if it can be trusted) to the list of Trusted sites using the following steps:
- *Tools > Internet Options*
- Click the *Security* tab
- Select the *Trusted sites* icon by clicking on it
- Click the *Sites* button
- Add the URL of the desired safe site that requires scripting
- Uncheck *Require server verification (https:) for all sites in this zone*
- Click *OK*

Update application software

Applications can also be vulnerable to malware. Therefore, any patches provided by the software vendor must be implemented for identified vulnerabilities. These updates and information about releases are provided through a variety of means including the company's website, e-mails, distribution lists, manuals, other notification methods, etc. Two of the most effective methods for ensuring that you are informed about updates and patches released for your applications is to register the product when you buy it and to periodically visit the vendor's website to check for relevant news about the application.

Learn from online sources

A number of websites and blogs provide valuable information and tips for securing computers. You should visit such sites periodically to educate yourself. A useful site for starters is the CERT website (*www.cert.org*). Two helpful documents available at this site are *Home Network Security* and *Home Computer Security*. Another good site for more knowledgeable users is *www.sans.org.*

Practice safe behavior and communications

Avoid unsafe online behavior and habits pertaining to surfing, opening attachments, file downloading and sharing, randomly clicking on hyperlinks, entering personal information at unfamiliar websites, etc. Create multiple e-mail accounts and share the primary account only with friends and people you know and trust. Use such an account for personal banking, transmitting and/or receiving sensitive data, and other important tasks. The other accounts can be used for miscellaneous purposes such as entering an online form at a website, newsgroups, mailing lists, Internet directories, etc.

PROTECTING THE BROWSER
Use a more secure browser

The Internet Explorer browser is a common source of security problems and must be secured. It is the most commonly-used browser, which is embedded in the Windows operating system, and the favorite target of malware developers due to its popularity and availability on such a large number of computers. IE has many vulnerabilities that have been widely exploited by hackers and spyware developers. However, a fully-patched Internet Explorer 6 SP2 is a strong and secure browser.

A far better option is to use the latest version of the Internet Explorer, IE 7, which is a very secure browser. If you do not want to use the Internet Explorer, alternative products are Firefox (*http://www.mozilla.com/en-US/*) and Opera (*http://www.opera.com/download/*). These browsers are free and provide good protection, especially against adware and spyware. Firefox is secure and does not permit software installation, thus preventing drive-by downloads. However, it is also vulnerable to attacks, as was widely demonstrated during the past year. As more users have started using Firefox, and as its user base has increased considerably and continues to grow, they have gained more unwanted attention from those who see financial benefits in exploiting them.

Lock down the browser

To prevent or reduce security risks, lock down the Internet Explorer browser. The procedure for lockdown has been described previously. If a non-IE browser is being used, it should also be locked down. If you have installed two browsers, such as IE and Firefox, both should be locked down.

Make IE security settings more stringent

To provide greater protection from various security risks such as drive-by downloads and the installation of programs without permission, increase the browser's security settings to a higher level—medium or high. The security settings can be changed by navigating as follows:

- *Internet Explorer > Tools > Internet Options*
- Select the *Security* tab, where the settings can be made

Note that the default security setting for the Internet Explorer, running with Windows XP (SP2), is medium.

Use a tool to lock down the browser

You can use a tool to help lockdown the IE browser. A number of utilities are available for this purpose including *Enough is Enough* and *IE LockDown* (freeware). The *Enough is Enough* software locks down two zones, Internet and Restricted, with restrictive settings that disable features like Scripting, ActiveX, etc. It also restricts the use of cookies and disables several advanced settings. The *Internet Explorer Power Tweaks Web Accessories* is a tool that adds two menu items to the IE toolbar menu, which can be used to quickly add websites to the Trusted and Restricted zones.

IE-SPYAD is another tool that can be used to add a list of domains, marketers and advertisers, and sites associated with adware to the Internet Explorer's Restricted Sites zone. It blocks cookies and disables ActiveX, Java and Scripting. It can also prevent home page hijacking, browser settings from being changed, and drive-by downloads. PivX Solutions also provides an advanced software tool for protecting Windows-based desktops and servers from malware *(www.pivx.com)*.

DOWNLOADING

Malware transmitted via downloads is a common problem which can be minimized, though not eliminated, by performing a few checks and following safe risk-reduction practices before downloading, which are described in the following sections.

Be aware of P2P risks

P2P software has two main issues. First, it often downloads spyware and adware. Second, the files swapped through P2P often contain malware. Learn how to manage adware pop-ups often associated with P2P software. Do not click on an "Agree" or "OK" button to close a window. Instead, click the "x" on the top right-hand corner of the window or use the Alt+F4 keys on the keyboard.

Learn to identify download sources and methods

Educate yourself and be aware of the risks associated with different download sources such as P2P, websites, freeware, application software, files, games, etc. Also be aware of the risks associated with various installations methods such as ActiveX, which were explained in Chapter 9. Carefully review the differences between free and paid versions of the software because the free versions often contain adware. Do not take the "no spyware" or "adware-free" claims by a vendor at face value.

Avoid downloading files from unknown sites

Do not download files from unfamiliar websites, especially if they ask you to download software that you are unfamiliar with. If the product or company is familiar, such as

Acrobat or Flash, the risk is minimal. However, any other software from an unknown source can be a risk that should be avoided, unless absolutely necessary. It is recommended that downloading should be limited to trusted well-known sites only. Before downloading from an unknown source, investigate by performing a Google search to determine if there are any complaints against the product to be downloaded or its vendor. For this purpose, use the products's name as the keyword, along with additional keywords such as spyware, malware, and review.

Avoid free software

Avoid installing free software programs as they are a very common source of malware, especially adware. While many free software applications are legitimate and provide many benefits to those who cannot afford to buy commercial software, it is difficult to distinguish between good and bad software freeware providers. Hence, as a rule, avoid free software applications unless you are able to confirm their safety via research or through acquaintances or reputable online sources. To determine if a freeware product has been flagged as malware, perform a search using one of the well-known search engines like Google and Yahoo.

Check education and online sources

A number of online sources provide very useful information and education about security threats. Periodically visit such sites and educate yourself about the latest trends, threats, download risks, protection methods and tools, etc. Visit anti-malware forums and sites to educate yourself about security risks in general, as well as download risks from specific applications. Some of the sites that can be visited for this purpose include:

- Doxdesk.com *(www.doxdesk.com/)*
- PC Pitstop.com *(www.pcpitstop.com/)*
- Spywareguide.com *(www.spywareguide.com/)*
- Spywarewarrior.com *(http://spywarewarrior.com/)*
- Spywareinfo.com *(www.spywareinfo.com/)*
- Stopbadware.org *(www.stopbadware.org)*

A more comprehensive list of sources is provided in the appendices.

ANONYMOUS SURFING
Why surf in anonymity

When you visit a website, it can monitor and gather a vast amount of information about you and your computer including habits and actions, websites visited, operating system, Internet browser, applications installed on the PC, other computer specifics and vulnerabilities, cache content, IP address, etc. This monitoring is not limited to the time that is spent at a particular website. You can continue to be monitored in the future as well, through tracking software that gets installed on your computer when you visit that website.

A number of websites including *www.anonymizer.com*, *www.proxyway.com*, and *www.2privacy.com* provide free privacy tests. The tests display some of the information that a website collects about its visitors, which can include the IP address, current geographic location, Windows Clipboard contents, browser language, operating system, pages visited, etc.

How to surf in anonymity

To surf anonymously and in privacy, a proxy server can be used. Such a server sits between the user and the websites that are to be visited. When such a server is used, the user's browser does not establish direct contact with the website. Instead, the browser passes a message to the proxy server, requesting connection to that website. The proxy server then connects to the desired website, after filtering out the address from the user's request packets and replacing it with its own. Therefore, the user's IP address does not get transmitted to the website being visited. In such a case, the website is able to view the proxy server's IP address—not the IP address of the user's computer, which is hidden. This prevents the website from accessing the user's computer for any purpose. The downside of using a proxy server is that it can slow down web surfing.

In addition to Anonymizer Inc., many companies provide web-based anonymous surfing services. To find an anonymous proxy service, visit the website *www.atomintersoft.com/products/alive-proxy/proxy-list*. This list provides detailed information such as uptime percentage, which can be used to select a more reliable proxy server.

Typically, an anonymous service will install a toolbar on the Internet Explorer browser, which can be used to turn on anonymous surfing whenever anonymity is required. Some anonymous services are available for free, while others charge a fee. To setup a proxy server:

- Select the proxy server that has the highest uptime percentage. Note the following two items for the proxy server to be used:
    - IP address (example: 137.168.114. 15)
    - Port (example: 8080)
- Navigate as follows: *Internet Explorer > Tools > Internet Options*
- Click the *Connections* tab
- Click the *LAN Settings* button

- Enter the appropriate values for the proxy server's IP address and Port, that were noted previously (in the first step), in the *Address* and *Port* fields (as shown on Figure 59)

Figure 59

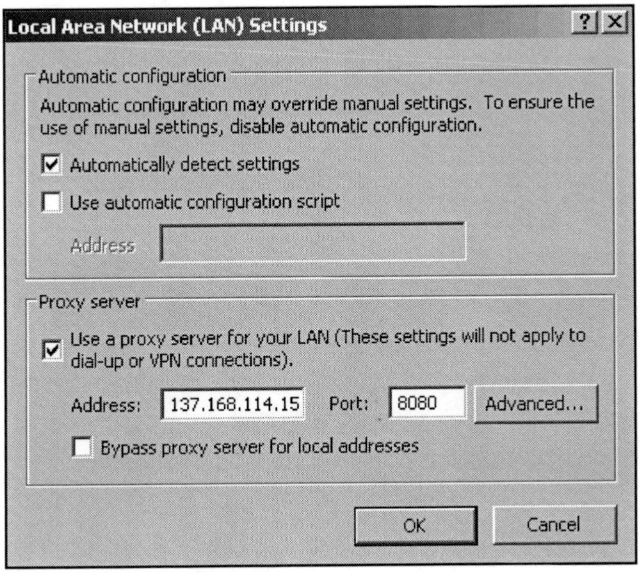

- Click *OK*, which will close the *Local Area Network (LAN) Settings* window
- Click *OK*, which will close the *Internet Options* window

The browser can be automatically configured to use anonymous proxy servers by using tools such as GhostSurf, which is available at *www.tenebril.com/products/ghostsurf.* It lists many anonymous proxy servers and is able to determine and connect to the fastest one. The products that can be used for this purpose are listed in Chapter 15, in the *Privacy* and *covering your tracks* section.

OTHER GOOD HABITS AND PRACTICES
Read the EULA

The End User License Agreement (EULA) is usually very long and covers many pages. It is written in legal and/or ambiguous terms, that most users are unfamiliar with, and provides vendors with many rights such as monitoring the computer/user, installing toolbars and/or additional programs, etc. In many cases, the EULA is not displayed prominently.

Before agreeing to download any software, carefully review the EULA's terms and conditions and the vendor's Privacy Policies. If there is any doubt or suspicion, do not agree and abort the installation. Adware vendors benefit from known user behavior, which is to quickly agree by clicking the Accept button without checking what they are agreeing to. Therefore, do not accept any agreement unless there is a fairly good understanding of what will be downloaded or installed. For this purpose, you must carefully read the EULA and Privacy Policies.

You can use EULA scanners that can evaluate an EULA for risky language. Two such tools are:

- EULA Scanner (*www.halfbakery.com/idea/EULA_20Scanner*)
- EULA Analyzer (*www.javacoolsoftware.com/eulalyzerdl.html*)

Use and protect passwords

Passwords should be used to protect the computer as well as your personal and confidential information. They should not be left on sticky notes or papers on the desk where anyone can view them. Keep passwords safe and do not share them with family members, friends, and others. Also, never transmit a password to others via e-mail. Passwords should be changed periodically and a different password should be used for different accounts.

Never use the same password between unrelated websites. Some applications, such as AOL, allow passwords to be stored so that it can be launched without entering the password. Do not enable this feature. If a password is compromised, act without delay to take corrective action.

Use strong passwords that are not easily guessed or cracked. Tips for creating a strong password include using both upper and lower case characters, numbers and characters, and using a minimum of 8 characters. An example of a strong password is My86Vote. When in doubt, go for a longer password and forget about complexity. A non-complex 10-character password is more secure than a complex 8-character password.

Use trusted sites for malware research

When using search engines for identifying anti-malware software and review sites, be wary of sponsored links and ads that vendors have paid for. Do not assume that an ad or hyperlink appearing during a Google search will lead to a legitimate site. Whenever possible, use the websites of well-known and organizations such as Symantec, CNET, PC World, PC Magazine, Information Week, SpyWarrior, PC Pitstop, and Stopbadware.org, which can be trusted to provide good security information and/or product reviews.

Beware of misleading ads and techniques

Many ads for anti-spyware software offer to scan the computer for spyware, viruses and other malware. Their objective is to identify and display existing malware so that the user is steered into buying the product. The problem is that the results provided by some of these tools are questionable. Be aware of such misleading tactics as well as other shady ones, such as phishing.

Prevent e-mail virus infections

Practice behaviors that prevent e-mails from becoming a source of infections that can compromise personal and confidential data. Some of the steps that can be taken to ensure this include the following:

- Convert all incoming e-mail to plain text; this disables Active Content and also reveals malicious phishing. This can be easily implemented in most e-mail clients.
- Do not open an attachment unless it is from a known sender
- Even if the sender is known, check the attachment to determine its potential risk (type of attachment-such as executable, need for the attachment, etc.)
- Avoid clicking on links; type the URL instead of clicking on the embedded link
- Scan all files to be downloaded with anti-virus/spyware tools
- Disable the automatic execution of JavaScript, Word macros, or other executable code, which might be contained in an e-mail or attached to it

Avoid or limit your use of public computers

If a public computer is to be used out of necessity, use it for relatively low-risk activities such a reading e-mails. Do not use it for online banking or other activities where personal and confidential data needs to be entered. The reason is that the computer may be infected with monitoring software that can monitor your activities and record your keystrokes.

Avoid chat room and IM risks

All types of individuals and hackers patronize Internet chat rooms. At such locations, avoid clicking on hyperlinks or receiving file attachments from the chat room participants. Such actions are risky and can lead to the installation of a Trojan or some other type of malware. The same precautions should be taken when an instant message (IM) is received. During an IM session, do not click on an embedded hyperlink or open an attachment.

Use SSL connections for working securely

Whenever confidential, financial, and personal information is to be transmitted via the

Internet to a website, ensure that the data is being encrypted and transmitted securely. Secure websites, which use Secure Sockets Layer (SSL) for their transmission, can be identified via their URLs, which begin with https:// (instead of http://). They also display a secure padlock icon on the status bar. The newer version of SSL, called TLS, is an even better choice that is expected to be widely implemented in the next few years.

Limit the Internet connection

The Internet connection should be disconnected when online access is not required. Keeping the computer connected via a broadband line, such as cable or DSL, will keep it "visible" to hackers and crackers and consequently expose it to potential attacks and probes.

Prepare for the worst-case scenario

Despite a user's best efforts, malware can end up destroying the data stored on the hard drive. Therefore, always plan for the unexpected and take steps to ensure that the disruption, if and when it occurs, is minimized. The preparations include backing up the data on a regular basis and making a rescue disk, which provides an alternative method for starting the computer if it fails to boot. The procedure involves turning off the computer, inserting the rescue disk in the appropriate drive, and powering up the PC. For backing up, you can use a number of utilities available for this purpose, including the *Backup Utility for Windows*.

C O N C L U S I O N

After reading this book and becoming aware of the numerous potential problems, you might be overwhelmed and maybe even pessimistic. However, I encourage you to have a positive attitude and realize that you are more aware of the potential problems, *as well as how to prevent them,* than the overwhelming majority of computer and Internet users. You now have the knowledge and the tools that will provide you with a high level of protection. The key for implementing and maintaining security is to implement protective measures, continue to update your protection, and also continue to educate yourself. If you implement these steps, the probability of your security being breached will be very low.

A P P E N D I X   A

Malware Software Review Sites

- www.6StarReviews.com
- www.anti-spyware-review.com
- www.consumersearch.com
- www.defeatspyware.org
- www.pcworld.com
- www.cnet.com/
- www.snapfiles.com/
- www.stopbadware.org
- www.toptenreviews.com
- www.winplanet.com
- www.informationweek.com
- www.pcmag.com
- www.zdnet.com

A P P E N D I X   B

Useful malware resources

- www.anti-spyware-reviews.net/
- www.anti-trojan-software-reviews.com/
- www.bullguard.com/antivirus/comparison-chart-main.aspx
- www.cert.org
- www.cert.org/tech_tips/securing_browser/
- www.consumersearch.com/www/software/anti-spyware-reviews/reviews.html
- www.defeatspyware.org
- www.epic.org/privacy/tools.html
- www.intranetjournal.com/spyware/removal.html
- www.microsoft.com/athome/security/protect/windows2000/Default.mspx
- www.microsoft.com/athome/security/spyware/software/about/productcom-parisons.mspx
- www.pcpitstop.com/
- www.pcworld.com
- www.shopping.com/xPP-software-anti_adware-network_management_tools
- www.spykill.com/?nextweb
- www.spywareguide.com/
- www.spywareinfo.com/email2.php
- www.spywareremoversreview.com
- www.spywarewarrior.com
- www.stopbadware.org
- www.virusbtn.com
- www.webroot.com
- www.wilderssecurity.com/
- www3.ca.com/securityadvisor/pest/browse.aspx
- http://antivirus.about.com/od/antivirussoftwarereviews/ss/msscreens.htm

- http://csrc.nist.gov/virus/
- http://securityresponse.symantec.com/avcenter/vinfodb.html
- http://us.mcafee.com/root/catalog.asp
- http://virusall.com/wormlat.shtml

Characteristics of good software

Disclosures before application installation

A good software application must only be installed with the knowledge and consent of the user. An application must never be installed in drive-by download mode. In this mode, software or files are automatically downloaded onto a user's computer, without permission or notice, when a website is visited or an HTML-formatted e-mail is viewed.

Before an application is installed, it must clearly, completely, and accurately inform the end user of the name of the application, its main features and functions, and the name of the organization associated with the application. It must also obtain the user's consent to install the application.

Method of disclosure and consent

Good software should have a clearly stated disclosure and consent policy that is disseminated to its potential users. The information must be disclosed via the End User License Agreement and the Privacy Policy documents. The Privacy Policy should list the information that will be collected or transmitted, whether it is personally identifiable or not.

The application must conform to the statements and representations made in the EULA and Privacy Policy documents. They should be written in a format and language that is easily understood by the average user and must be readily accessible from within the software application.

Additionally, the disclosures should be made interactively during installation, via pop-up windows, etc., so that a novice user is able to read the disclosures, be informed, and provide consent. Wherever possible, besides covering the legal requirements, such documents must follow standard industry practices.

Transparency guidelines

A good software application should not be hidden either during operation or when it is lying dormant. A typical user should be easily able to determine the existence of an application and, also, if it is running. The features and functions disclosed to a user must be complete. No purpose or functionality of the application must be withheld from the users.

Collection and transmission of personal data

Before it collects or transmits any information, a good software application must accurately, completely, and clearly disclose the type of information it plans to collect or transmit. It must also disclose the data collection method as well as its privacy policy. After these have been disclosed, the application should obtain the user's consent to collect or transmit such data. For example, when an application like MS-Word crashes, the Microsoft error reporting tool pops-up a window which asks for the user's permission before sending the report.

Changing settings

It is possible, through the use of scripting tools, to modify the registry without the user's knowledge. Often, such changes will not take affect until the machine is rebooted. If an application changes any operating system or application settings, which have the potential to impact the user's experience or other applications, it should obtain the user's permission before implementing any changes. The application must accurately, completely, and clearly explain the planned change and its potential impact. Also, the user's consent must be obtained before the changes are implemented.

Bundling applications

Some applications are bundled with others, which is acceptable provided some good bundling practices are followed. Before a bundled application is installed, the user must be made aware of all the applications that will be installed. The user must be informed of any relationship between applications in the bundle. It should be clearly explained what the impact will be, on the installation and operation, if only selective bundle components are selected for downloading, i.e., the impact of rejecting some bundle components.

The user's consent should be obtained for installing the bundle and an option should be provided to pick and choose the individual applications contained in the bundle. All applications contained in the bundle must conform to good software practices. The application must also provide a mechanism, preferably with a master uninstaller, for easily removing all the applications contained in the bundle. The uninstall procedure of one application in the bundle must be independent of the removal of another application in the same bundle.

Application uninstall requirements

The deactivation process for an application must be easy and straightforward. An application should preferably enable users to uninstall it using the designated tool for applications removal, such as the *Add/Remove Programs* menu in the *Windows Control Panel*. The application should provide clear and easy-to-follow instructions for uninstalling the program. An application must not change any application or system setting that will impair the user's ability to uninstall an application.

After an application has been uninstalled, it must not re-install itself without obtaining the permission of the user. It should also reverse, as much as possible, the original settings before the application was installed.

Summary of actions good software will avoid

A good software application must avoid undesirable behavior such as:

- Deception
- Actions that can interfere with the user's ability to use the computer or browse the web, through the use of undesirable functionality such as pop-up windows
- Using of a computer for any purpose, such as transmittal of personal data or change browser settings, without the user's consent
- Unauthorized actions, such as transmitting confidential data to third-parties, that can cause financial and other losses to users
- Actions that can cause a computer to malfunction by intentionally creating/exploiting security vulnerabilities
- Repeatedly asking a user to accept something, such as changing the browser's home page or accept an offer, that has previously been declined
- Interference with the browser's default search functionality
- Changing the default home page or search engine without the user's permission
- Redirecting browsers away from valid website addresses

Internet Explorer 7
Security Zone Settings

Setting	Default Setting Per Zone (and recommendation if they vary from Microsoft's defaults)			
	Internet	Local intranet	Trusted sites	Restricted site
Default Security level	Medium-High	Medium-Low	Medium	High
.NET Framework-Loose XAML	Enable	Enable	Enable	Disable
.NET Framework-XAML browser applications	Enable	Enable	Enable	Disable
.NET Framework-XPS documents	Enable	Enable	Enable	Disable
.NET Framework-reliant components-Run components not signed with Authenticode	Enable (Disable)	Enable (Disable)	Enable (Disable)	Disable
.NET Framework-reliant components-Run components signed with Authenticode	Enable (Prompt)	Enable	Enable	Disable
ActiveX controls and plug-ins-Allow previously unused ActiveX controls to run without prompting	Disable	Enable	Enable	Disable
ActiveX controls and plug-ins-Allow Scriptlets	Disable	Enable	Disable	Disable
ActiveX controls and plug-ins-Automatic prompting for ActiveX controls	Disable	Enable	Disable	Disable
ActiveX controls and plug-ins-Binary and script behaviors	Enable (Disable)	Enable (Disable)	Enable (Disable)	Disable

ActiveX controls and plug-ins-Display video and animation on webpage that does not use external media player	Disable	Disable	Disable	Disable
ActiveX controls and plug-ins-Download signed ActiveX controls	Prompt	Prompt	Prompt	Disable
ActiveX controls and plug-ins-Download unsigned ActiveX controls	Disable	Disable	Disable	Disable
ActiveX controls and plug-ins-Initialize and script ActiveX controls not marked safe for scripting	Disable	Disable	Disable	Disable
ActiveX controls and plug-ins-Run ActiveX controls and plug-ins	Enable	Enable	Enable	Disable
ActiveX controls and plug-ins-Script ActiveX controls marked safe for scripting	Enable	Enable	Enable	Disable
Downloads-Automatic prompting for file downloads	Disable (Enable)	Enable	Disable (Enable)	Disable (Enable)
Downloads-File download	Enable	Enable	Enable	Disable
Downloads-Font download	Enable	Enable	Enable	Disable
Enable .NET Framework setup	Enable	Enable	Enable	Disable
Java VM-Java Permissions*	High safety	Medium	High safety	Disable Java
Miscellaneous-Access data sources across domains	Disable	Prompt	Disable	Disable
Miscellaneous-Allow META REFRESH	Enable	Enable	Enable	Disable
Miscellaneous-Allow scripting of Internet Explorer web browser control	Disable	Enable	Disable	Disable
Miscellaneous-Allow script-initiated windows with size or position constraints	Disable	Enable	Disable	Disable
Miscellaneous-Allow webpages to use restricted protocols for active content	Prompt	Prompt	Prompt	Disable
Miscellaneous-Allow websites to open windows without address or status bars	Disable	Enable	Enable	Disable

Miscellaneous-Display mixed content	Prompt	Prompt	Prompt	Prompt
Miscellaneous-Don't prompt for client certificate selection when no certificates or only one certificate exists	Disable	Enable	Disable	Disable
Miscellaneous-Drag and drop or copy and paste files	Enable	Enable	Enable	Prompt
Miscellaneous-Include local directory path when uploading files to a server	Enable	Enable	Enable	Disable
Miscellaneous-Installation of desktop items	Prompt	Prompt	Prompt	Disable
Miscellaneous-Launching applications and unsafe files	Prompt	Enable	Prompt	Disable
Miscellaneous-Launching programs and files in an IFRAME	Prompt	Prompt	Prompt	Disable
Miscellaneous-Navigate sub-frames across different domains	Disable (Prompt)	Enable	Disable	Disable
Miscellaneous-Open files based on content, not file extension	Enable	Enable	Disable	Disable
Miscellaneous-Software channel permissions	Medium safety	Medium safety	Medium safety	High safety
Miscellaneous-Submit non-encrypted form data	Enable	Enable	Enable	Prompt
Miscellaneous-Use Phishing Filter	Enable	Disable	Enable	Enable
Miscellaneous-Use Pop-up Blocker	Enable	Disable	Enable	Enable
Miscellaneous-Userdata persistence	Enable	Enable	Enable	Disable
Miscellaneous-Websites in less privileged web content zone can navigate into this zone	Enable (Disable)	Enable	Enable	Disable
Scripting-Active Scripting	Enable	Enable	Enable	Disable
Scripting-Allow Programmatic clipboard access	Prompt (Disable)	Enable (Disable)	Prompt (Disable)	Disable
Scripting-Allow status bar updates via script	Disable	Enable	Enable	Disable
Scripting-Allow websites to prompt for information using scripted window	Disable	Enable	Enable	Disaable

Scripting-Scripting of Java applets	Enable	Enable	Enable	Disable
User Authentication	Automatic logon only in Intranet zone			Prompt for username and pass-word

* Note: Java VM Permission only available to browsers with a Java VM installed.

This table has been provided through the courtesy of Roger A. Grimes.

APPENDIXE

Examples of different malware types

- Spyware: Spyware.ScreenView, Spectre, SpyClock, SecondSight, WatchDog, Watcher, NiceSpy
- Viruses: Adolph, W32. Welinf.A, Avone.A, Backdoor Agent, Sumtax, BAT.Brainsell, BAT.Jerm
- Worms: ACTS.Spaceflash, W32.Secefa.D, W32.Mular.A, Blaster Worm, Happy 99, Klez Worm, Lirva, Loveletter, myDoom, W32.Sobig
- Adware: Adware.Optserve, CoolSavings, Gator eWallet, AdBlaster, About Blank, Avone.2, BTGrab, Career12, CoolWebSearch
- Trojans: Trojan.Cinmeng, W32.Mediasups, Keylogger.Mose, Trojan.Emcodec, 2000Cracks, AcidBattery, Acropolis, Adverbot, AlexTrojan, Amitis, Beast, CIA
- Monitoring software: Spyware.XPSpy, Alexa, Webhancer, SafeScreen, BagKeys, Computer Spy, CQMA, Diablo Keys, DKS KeySpy, KeyTrap, Chat Watch, KeyKey, KeySpy, KeyTrap, ABCKeylogger, Active Keylogger
- Remote administration tools: Backdoor.Rat.Client, Indoctrination, Almaster, Digital Spy, EventHorizon, FeRAT, InCommand
- Remote access: MyShell, Surveil, SpyAnywhere, ABSystemSpy, RemoteAccess (source Symantec)
- Hacking tools: NetCat, Spytector, CyberSpy, Nibor, Vanquish, SpySharp, and Misoska (used for denial-of-service attacks)
- Dialers: Dialer.DialXS, MasterDialer, Webcont, Active-X Dialer, CrossKirk, Coulomb Dialer, Dataline Dialer, Dialer2004
- Joke programs: Joke.Apeldorn, AnnoyGreet, Bonus, Meltscreen, ScreenFlasher, Stupid
- Data Miners: MarketScore, Alexa Toolbar, DialupRipper, NavExcel
- Miscellaneous: A97M.Loaded, SafeandClean, EasySpywareKiller, SpyFalcon, WinFixer, World Anti-Spy, X-Con Spyware Destroyer, Advanced E-mail monitoring, AdwarePunisher, ErrorSafe

Additional protection tools

Anti-spyware applications

- a2 Software *(www.emsisoft.com/en/software/free/)*
- Aluria Anti-spyware *(www.aluriasoftware.com/)*
- AntiSpy *(www.softvers.com/)*
- Ashampoo AntiSpyware *(www.ashampoo.com)*
- Geek Superhero *(www.geeksuperhero.com/index.shtml)*
- HiJack This *(www.spywareinfo.com/~merijn/index.php)*
- InterMute's SpySubtract *(www.intermute.com/)*
- JavaCool SpywareBlaster *(www.javacoolsoftware.com/)*
- Keylogger Killer *(www.tooto.com/keyloggerkiller/)*
- Personal AntiSpy *(http://blazingtools.com/antispy.html)*
- Spy Detect *(www.spymode.com/spydetect.htm)*
- SpyCatcher *(www.tenebril.com)*
- SpyRemover *(www.itcompany.com/remover.htm)*
- Spyware Fighter Cleaner *(www.spyfighter.com)*
- Spyware Terminator *(www.spyterminator.com)*
- StartUpList *(www.spywareinfo.com/~merijn/index.php)*
- Sysinternals' Autorun utility *(http://www.microsoft.com/technet/sysinternals/default.mspx)*
- Trend Micro Anti-Spyware *(www.trendmicro.com/en/products/desktop/as/evaluate/over-view.htm)*
- Who's Watching Me *(www.trapware.com/)*
- Yahoo Anti-Spy Toolbar *(http://toolbar.yahoo.com/)*
- ZeroSpyware *(www.zerospyware.com)*

Commercial (Enterprise) anti-spyware products

- Acronis *(www.acronis.com/enterprise/products/privacyexpert/)*
- Aluria *(www.aluriasoftware.com/corporate/)*
- BlackHole DNS for Spyware *(www.bleedingsnort.com/article.php)*
- BlueCoat *(www.bluecoat.com/solutions/spyware.html)*
- DynaComm i:scan *(www.dciseries.com/products/iscan/)*
- EMCO Network Malware Cleaner *(www.emco.is/networkmalwarecleaner/features.html)*
- FaceTime *(www.facetime.com/)*
- Intermute *(www.intermute.com/products/corporations.html)*
- Lavasoft *(www.lavasoft.de/software/enterprise/)*
- McAfee *(www.mcafee.com)*
- Norman *(www.norman.com/Product/Home_Home_office/AntiSpyware/en)*
- Omniquad *(www.omniquad.com/antispyenterprise.htm)*
- Pest Patrol *(www.ca.com/smb/etrust/pestpatrol.htm)*
- SonicWall *(www.sonicwall.com/products/gav_ips_spyware.html)*
- Spybot S & D (Intranet Update Server) *(www.safer-networking.org/)*
- SpyEXPERT *(http://stbernard.com/products/spyexpert/products_spyexpert.asp)*
- Spyware Doctor *(www.pctools.com/spyware-doctor-enterprise/)*
- Sunbelt *(http://sunbeltsoftware.com/CounterSpyEnterprise.cfm)*
- SurfControl *(www.surfcontrol.com/Default.aspx?id=364&mnuid=1.3)*
- Tenebril *(www.tenebril.com/products/ghostsurf/spycatcher-enterprise.html)*
- TrendMicro Anti-Spyware for SMB *(www.trendmicro.com/en/products/desktop/as-smb/)*
- *TrendMicro (www.trendmicro.com/spyware/us.asp)*
- Webroot *(www.webroot.com/products/spysweeper/enterprise/)*
- Websense *(www.websense.com/products/about/Enterprise/)*
- Xblock *(www.xblocksystems.com/products.php)*

Personal firewalls

- 8Signs Firewall *(www.consealfirewall.com/ or www.8signs.com)*
- AlertWall *(www.alertwall.com/helptut.asp)*
- Armor2net Personal Firewall *(www.armor2net.com/products/products.htm)*
- BitGuard Personal Firewall *(www.tryus.dk/bitguard.asp)*
- Bullguard *(www.bullguard.com)*
- Demarc PureSecure *(www.demarc.com/products/puresecure/personal/)*
- eTrust EZ Firewall *(www.my-etrust.com/products/Firewall.cfm)*
- Filseclab Personal Firewall *(www.filseclab.com/eng/products/firewall.htm)*
- Firewall X-treme *(www.stompsoft.com/firewallx/)*

- InJoy Firewall (*www.fx.dk/firewall/*)
- ITShield Firewall (*www.itshield.com/*)
- Jetico Personal Firewall (*www.jetico.com/*)
- Kaspersky Labs Anti-Hacker (*www.kaspersky.com/antihacker-usa*)
- Lavasoft Personal Firewall (*www.lavasoft.com/software/firewall/*)
- Look'n'Stop (*www.soft4ever.com/LooknStop/En/firewall.htm*)
- NeT Firewall (*www.ntkernel.com/*)
- NetVeda Safety.Net Pro (*www.netveda.com/consumer/safetynet_pro.htm*)
- Norman Personal Firewall (*www.norman.com/products_npf.shtml*)
- Omniquad Personal Firewall (*www.omniquad.com/pfirewall.htm*)
- pcInternet Patrol (*www.pcinternetpatrol.com/downloads/pcip.php*)
- Personal Firewall Pro (*www.3bsoftware.com/products/mprod/firewall.html*)
- PktFilter (*www.hsc.fr/ressources/outils/pktfilter/*)
- PortsLock (*www.ntutility.com/pl/index.htm*)
- Primedius Firewall Pro (*www.primedius.com/*)
- Prisma Firewall (*www.prismafirewall.com/*)
- Privatefirewall (*www.privacyware.com*)
- SecureIIS Application Firewall (*www.eeye.com/html/Products/SecureIIS/index.html*)
- Securepoint Firewall (*www.securepoint.cc/en/products-firewall.html*)
- SecureUp Personal Firewall (*www.secureup.com/*)
- Sunbelt Kerio Personal Firewall 4 (*www.sunbelt-software.com/Kerio.cfm*)
- SurfSecret Personal Firewall (*www.surfsecret.com/products/product-SSFWL.html*)
- TheGreenBow Personal Firewall (*www.thegreenbow.com/bob.html*)
- Tiny Personal Firewall (*www.tinysoftware.com/*)
- Virus MD Personal Firewall (*www.virusmd.com/products/firewall.php*)
- VisNetic Firewall (*www.deerfield.com/products/visnetic-firewall/*)
- Webroot Desktop Firewall (*www.webroot.com/consumer/products/desktopfirewall/*)
- Wingate (*www.ccsoftware.ca/wingate/*)
- WinProxy (*www.winproxy.com/*)
- WinRoute Firewall (*www.kerio.com/kwf_home.html*)

Anti-virus applications
- Agnitum Outpost Firewall Pro (*www.agnitum.com*)
- Command AntiVirus (*www.authentium.com*)
- Dr.WEB (*www.drweb.com/*)
- eTrust EZ Antivirus (*www.antivirus.ca.com*)
- eXtendia AntiVirus (*www.extendia.com/extendiaantiviruspro.htm*)

- F-PROT AntiVirus for Windows *(www.f-prot.com)*
- Freedom Security & Privacy Suite *(www.freedom.net/index-nf.php)*
- Integrity Master *(www.stiller.com/)*
- MicroWorld eScan Antivirus *(www.mwti.net)*
- NOD32 *(www.nod32-anti-virus.com)*
- Norman Virus Control *(www.norman.com/)*
- Quick Heal *(www.quickheal.com)*
- RAV AntiVirus *(www.ravantivirus.com/)*
- Sophos Anti-Virus *(www.sophos.com/)*
- The Shield Pro 2007 *(www.pcsecurityshield.com)*
- V-Buster *(www.vbuster.net/)*
- Vet Anti-Virus *(www.vet.com.au/)*
- Vexira Antivirus for Windows *(www.centralcommand.com/windows_products.html)*

Scanners
Anti-virus scanners
- Command AntiVirus
- eSafe
- Invircible
- McAfee
- NOD32
- Norman
- Norton Anti-Virus
- Principal Anti-Virus
- Protector Plus
- QuickHeal
- Solo
- Sophos

Some of these products can be used for free for a trial period.

Other scanners
- Acronis Privacy Expert *(www.acronis.com/products/privacyexpert/)*
- Advanced System Optimizer *(www.systweak.com/asov2/spydetective.asp)*
- Aluria Spyware Eliminator *(www.aluriasoftware.com)*
- AOL Safety & Security Center *(http://downloads.channel.aol.com/windowsproducts)*
- Bazooka Adware & Spyware Scanner (free) *(www.kephyr.com/spywarescanner/index.html)*

- EarthLink Protection Control Center (free) *(www.earthlink.net/software/pcc/)*
- F-Secure AntiSpyware *(https://f-secure.com/products/fsas/)*
- Omniquad AntiSpy *(www.omniquad.com/antispy.htm)*
- PCdefense *(http://cms.laplink.com//pcdefense/index.html)*
- SpyBuster *(www.spy-buster.com/)*
- SpyRemover *(www.itcompany.com/remover.htm)*
- Spyware X-terminator *(www.stompsoft.com/)*
- Steganos AntiSpyware *(www.steganos.com/en/products/saspy2006/)*
- System Mechanic 6 *(www.iolo.com/sm/)*

Detection and removal tools
- BHODemon *(www.spywareinfo.com/downloads/bhod/)*
- CWShredder *(www.trendmicro.com/cwshredder/)*
- HijackThis *(www.hijackthis.de/)*
- Nitrous Online *(www.nitrousonline.com)*
- RapidBlaster Killer *(www.wilderssecurity.net/specialinfo/rapidblaster.html)*
- Scumware.com – Disinfect *(www.scumware.com/disinfect.html)*
- Spybot Search & Destroy *(http://spybot.safer-networking.de/en/)*
- Spybuster *(www.spy-buster.com)*
- SpyCop *(www.spycop.com)*
- SpySweeper *(www.webroot.com/consumer/products/spysweeper/)*
- Spyware Doctor *(www.pctools.com/spyware-doctor/)*
- Toolbar Cop *(http://windowsxp.mvps.org/toolbarcop.htm)*
- TopText Disabler *(www.thiefware.com/disabler/)*
- VX2 Finder *(www.pchell.com/downloads/vx2finder.exe)*

Malware prevention tools
- Browser Hijack Blaster
- CookieWall
- DNS Redirector
- IEGuardian
- IE-SPYAD
- Internet Spy Hunter
- preEmpt
- Registry Firewall
- RegRun
- Script Sentry

- Security Task Manager
- Settings Sentry
- SockLock
- Spy Chaser
- Spyblocker
- SpyWall
- Spyware Shield
- Spyware Inoculator
- SpywareStopper
- Start Page Guard
- WinPatrol
- WinTasks 5 Professional
- WMP Scripting Fix

Privacy and covering your tracks

- Ace Utilities
- CookieWall
- Eraser
- Evidence Terminator
- FileVac
- iClean
- IEClean
- Invisible Secrets
- MRU Blaster
- NSClean
- Panicware Pop-Up Stopper Companion
- Privacy Defender
- Privacy Inspector
- R-Wipe & Clean 6
- System Inspector

Anti-Trojan tools

- AntiScanner *(http://status3.i-r.co.uk/antiscanner.htm)*
- Anti-Trojan Shield *(www.atshield.com/)*
- CyberSight Pro & Lite *(www.cryptic.co.uk/)*
- Hacker Eliminator *(http://hacker-eliminator.com/)*
- Iparmor *(www.luosoft.com/)*

- Jammer *(www.agnitum.com/products/jammer/)*
- NoBackDoors *(http://home.swipnet.se/technotel/index.us.html)*
- PC DoorGuard *(www.astonsoft.com/products/pdg/)*
- Swat It *(http://swatit.org/download.html)*
- The Cleaner *(www.moosoft.com/)*
- Trojan Check *(www.windowsecurity.com/trojanscan/)*
- Trojan Guarder *(www.softpedia.com/get/Antivirus/Trojan-Guarder-Gold.shtml)*
- Trojan Remover *(www.simplysup.com)*
- TrojanShield *(www.trojanshield.com)*

Anti-popup products

- Free Surfer
- Pop-up Blocker Pro Rich Media Ads
- PoPup Terminator Lite 8
- RottSomeTime Toolbar 4.5.117
- Speereo Flash Killer
- sQusi Tracking Blcoker 1.04.0007
- Surf Clean Lite 8
- NoAds 2006.07.28
- VSPopUp 1.1
- Popup Free 1.54

APPENDIX G

Terminology

ActiveX: Set of Microsoft-developed technologies. It is a programming framework, not a programming language, which was developed to basically allow any other program written in nearly any other language to be distributed over the Internet using Internet Explorer (IE). ActiveX programs are called ActiveX controls.

Adware: An advertising-supported software application, the most common form of malware, which displays pop-up advertisements on a computer.

Application integrity: Refers to checking if there are any changes to an application, such as configuration changes or upgrades, implemented since it was last used. Any change, if it was not made by the user or the administrator, raises a flag as such a change could be the result of an action by a malware program.

Attachment: File that is attached to an e-mail message.

Auto-complete: Feature in browsers and other software applications which enable users to type in the required information quickly when entering data in fields.

Auto-update: Feature that enables a software application to be automatically updated with the latest virus and other malware definitions whenever the computer is connected to the Internet.

Bandwidth: Transmission capacity of a communication pathway such as a DSL or cable line, computer bus, network, etc.

Blacklist: A list of unwanted senders whose e-mail is filtered or blocked before it reaches a user. The list can include e-mail addresses (individuals or domains), IP addresses, known spammers, etc.

Boot disk: A diskette or CD containing the operating system which can be used by a computer to boot instead of the hard disk that it normally uses. It is typically used if the hard disk does not, or cannot, boot due to it being damaged or contaminated by malware.

Boot sector: When a computer boots, it searches for the master boot record of a disk's reserved sectors, for loading the operating system.

Broadband: High speed transmission that uses cable or DSL—which is significantly faster than dial-up service—for connecting to the Internet.

Browser Help Object (BHO): Library of Windows executable functions or data, which can be used for controlling or customizing Internet Explorer.

Browser hijacker: Malware program that takes control of a web browser.

Bundling: Practice of combining the sale and/or installation of multiple software programs as a single item. For example, the installation of many P2P programs is bundled with adware programs.

Configuration: Setup of a system's components or application settings. For example, an anti-spyware application can be configured so that it is launched at startup, scans the hard drive, and performs a full scan every Saturday at noon.

Content filtering: Feature that blocks or allows websites and/or content from being accessed or viewed by computer users.

Control Panel: A component of the Windows operating system where various settings can be made. The settings pertain to display, users and passwords, sounds and multimedia, folder options, printers, fonts, Internet options, etc.

Cookies: Text files, small data tags that are placed on a computer by websites that enables them to recognize and/or track the user's behavior and navigation, customize displays according to user preferences, pop-up ads, etc.

Cracker: An unauthorized intruder who breaks into a computer or network with malicious intent.

Cross-site scripting: A computer security vulnerability. In this method, a developer attaches a malicious script to a transmission to a website, which can be an element in an interactive form (a form that a user fills out on a web page, for example). When such a website responds to an Internet user's request, it transfers the script to the user's browser. Sources for such contamination can be e-mails, URL links and HTML tags, website forms, discussion group sites, etc.

Data miner: Software programs such as spyware and data mining applications, which are used to monitor and/or analyze a computer or its users. Any information collected is transmitted back to the program's installer, typically via the Internet.

DHCP: Dynamic Host Configuration Protocol (DHCP) is a protocol for assigning dynamic IP addresses to network components or devices. The IP number, which is assigned to a computer or device from a list of numbers that are configured for a specific network, can be different every time it connects to the network.

Denial-of-service (DoS): Involves initiating a simultaneous attack using thousands of hijacked computers (called zombies) in order to prevent the DoS target from functioning. The target is unable to handle the huge volume of data requests that it has to deal with in such cases and, consequently, is made ineffective and useless.

Download: To copy or transfer a file onto your own computer from another system such as another computer, an online source such as a website, or a peripheral device.

Drive-by downloading: A download that takes place, typically during visits to unscrupulous websites, without the knowledge or consent of the user. It is usually associated with the download of malware.

Dynamic IP address: A device requests an IP address every time it connects to the Internet. The address assigned to it may or may not be the same address it used during the previous connection.

Encryption: A technique for securing data so that it becomes unreadable by anyone except the user to whom the data is transmitted.

End User License Agreement (EULA): The EULA is a legally binding contract between the software developer/vendor and the user that specifies the parameters and conditions under which the application can be used.

Executable: A type of file which contains a program that can be executed or run. Such a file can be identified through its extension such as .exe or .com.

Executable file attachment: An attached file that contains a program which can be executed or run. If such a file attached to an e-mail is opened, the program will execute. Malware is often transmitted through this method.

File infector virus: A virus that infects files, such as .exe and .com programs, and subsequently spreads whenever the file is opened or executed.

Firewall: A piece of hardware or software application that resides between two different security domains, like a computer and the Internet. It supervises all inbound and outbound traffic and prevents unauthorized access to/from the computer.

First-party cookie: Is placed on the user's computer by the website being visited in order to store information such as user preferences, login IDs, passwords, etc.

Third-party cookie: Originates from a website other than that being currently visited by the user. Such a cookie could originate from the website's advertiser or partner.

Hacker: An intruder who breaks into a computer or network for non-malicious reasons. The most common reasons are the challenge of breaking into secure systems, demonstration of technical skills, bringing attention to vulnerabilities, and desire for fame.

Hardware firewall: A device that is installed between two security domains such as a PC or network and the Internet. In the case of a network, a hardware firewall is placed between the Internet and the network computers, typically using a hub so that the Internet connection can be shared.

Heuristics: Problem-solving technique that uses intelligent guesswork, rather than some pre-established formula or algorithmic programming, which enables newly developed threats to be identified.

HOSTS file: A database, like an address book, that contains a list of remote hosts' IP addresses.

HTML: HyperText Markup Language, an authoring language that is used to create web pages, which can be viewed using a web browser.

HTML tags: Are used to create the structure and layout of a web document. They specify how a document should be formatted.

In the wild: Viruses that have been not contained and continue to contaminate computers.

Inbound filtering: Firewall feature that refers to the filtering of data coming into a computer.

Interface: Common boundary between two independent systems that communicate with each other.

Internet Connection Firewall (ICF): A software firewall provided in Windows XP for protecting a computer while connected to the Internet.

Intrusion detection: Monitors the legitimacy of incoming data based on known penetration methods, comparison against known attack fingerprints, and behavior evaluation. If intrusion is detected, it notifies the user, who is made aware of the hacking method being employed.

IP address: Unique number assigned to each device connected to the Internet. The TCP/IP address uses this address to route data packets to the desired recipient.

ISP: Internet Service Provider (ISP), the company that provides access to the Internet, usually for a fee.

Java: Programming language that is used extensively for enabling feature-rich interactive web pages and functions.

JavaScript: Scripting language that enables interactive website features and functionality.

Keylogger: Type of malware that records a user's keystrokes and then transmits them to its installer over the Internet.

Lock down: To restrict the functions of a system so that limited operations and functions can be executed.

Log file: A file that maintains a record of actions, events, etc., executed on a computer or network.

MAC address: The Media Access Control (MAC) address is the physical address of a device connected to the Internet.

Macro: Saved sequence of commands, keystrokes, and/or actions. The macro can be recalled through a single character, word, command or keystroke, which causes all the recorded steps to be executed.

Macro virus: The most common type of virus, which is encoded as a macro and embedded in an MS-Office or other type of document.

Malware: Generic term for malicious software.

Mobile code: Refers to Java, JavaScript and ActiveX, which are programming languages/framework used by web developers.

Mobile virus: Type of malware that targets mobile devices such as personal digital assistants (PDAs), handheld PCs, cell phones, handheld devices, laptops, etc.

Online scanner: Tool for identifying malware installed on a computer, which can be run directly from a web browser.

Operating system (OS): Main software program that manages the overall control and operation of a computer.

Outbound filtering: Firewall feature that refers to the detection and filtering of data being transmitted from the computer.

P2P: Acronym for peer-to-peer, which is a type of network that is widely used for sharing files, music, videos, etc.

Parental controls: Software program feature which enables a parent to specify options that limit what a child can view or do on the Internet. This can include blocking of inappropriate websites, filtering of foul or other key words, time spent online, blocking of downloads, etc.

Passphrase: Sentence or collection of words that is more secure than a password.

Patch: Also called a service patch, it is a temporary solution, usually in the form of a code, issued by a vendor to fix a software program bug.

Phishing: A deceptive baiting technique designed to scam the user into providing personal and confidential information.

Plug-in: A software or hardware component that provides an enhanced feature to an existing program or system.

Port: A computer interface to which a device such as a printer or a monitor can be connected.

Port number: Identifies the type of port. A unique port number is associated with every TCP/IP application program. For example, port 80 is used for HTTP traffic.

Protocol: An agreed-upon format that is used to transmit data between two computers or devices For example, Internet communications are based on the TCP/IP protocol.

Proxy server: Server that acts as an intermediary between a user's computer and the Internet. Besides improving performance, a proxy server can filter requests which an organization can use to prevent employee access to undesirable websites.

Remote Access Trojan (RAT): Malicious software program that enables a computer to be accessed and controlled remotely by an unauthorized user or computer via an Internet connection.

Restore: To retrieve a file from a backup. If a file has been accidentally erased or corrupted, it can be restored if there is a backup system.

Replicate: To duplicate, copy or reproduce.

Rollback: Database feature that enables the last transaction to be reversed.

Rootkit: Malicious software that is used to hack into a PC and gain administrative level access, which allows it to modify operating system functions. It can be used to monitor traffic and keystrokes, attack other computers, modify log files, etc.

Router: A network device linking networks that forwards data packets from one network to another.

Safe mode: A Windows startup method in which the operating system and only a limited number of programs are loaded. This mode is used to troubleshoot when the computer has a serious problem, such as malware infection or the installation of a new application that conflicts with existing programs.

Scripting language: A high-level programming language such as JavaScript and Perl that is used to add functionality to web pages.

Spear phishing: Highly-targeted phishing attack. Spear phishers send an e-mail that targets employees or members of a particular organization, group, or government agency.

Spoofing: An impersonation technique with the aim of inducing a user to provide personal and confidential data.

Spyware: Covert software program that scans or monitors activities on a computer or system, online or offline, and then transmits the gathered information to other computers or locations on the Internet.

Spyware severity indicator: A code that indicates the level of risk associated with an identified malware.

SSID: Acronym for Service Set Identifier, which identified the network name, that is attached to a header of packets sent over a wireless network.

SSL: Acronym for Secure Sockets Layer, which is a protocol for transmitting, encrypted data over the Internet. URLs that support an SSL transmission start with https instead of http.

Static IP address: The same IP address used by a device every time it connects to the Internet.

Stealth mode: Firewall feature that enables a computer to remain hidden from other computers on the Internet.

System monitor: Tracking software, such as keyloggers, that monitor the activities of a computer.

TCP ports: Acronym for *Transmission Control Protocol,* a protocol used in TCP/IP networks that enables two hosts to connect and send/receive data.

TCP/IP: Internet protocol that enables communications between different computers and networks.

Temporary Internet files: Browser's cache files.

Trackware programs: Used to track the activities of a computer and/or a user.

Trojan Horse: Also called a Trojan, this is a non-replicating malicious computer program. To a user, such a program appears harmless and, in some cases, useful. However, when executed, such a program performs harmful actions.

UDP ports: Acronym for User Datagram Protocol, which is another Internet transport protocol.

URL: Acronym for Uniform Resource Locator, which is an Internet address. For example, Yahoo's URL is *www.yahoo.com.*

Virus: A program that spreads itself by infecting executable files and/or computer system areas and subsequently replicates without the permission of the user.

Virus definitions: List of viruses that an anti-virus program can detect.

Vista: The latest version of the Windows operating system.

VOIP: Acronym for Voice Over Internet Protocol, which is used for transmitting phone calls over the Internet.

VPN: Acronym for Virtual Private Network. It is used by enterprises to provide secure communications over the Internet between its employees and the corporate system(s).

WEP: Acronym for Wireless Equivalent Privacy, which is a protocol for wireless networks based on the 802.11 standard.

Whitelist: A list of senders whose e-mail will be accepted.

Wi-Fi: Acronym for Wireless Fidelity, which refers any type of 802.11network.

Windows registry: A Windows' database used for storing configuration information.

Wireless network: Network architecture that is based on the use of wireless components, which do not use a physical wired connection.

Wireless router: A network device that enables computers and peripherals to be connected without using any physical wiring.

Worm: Self-replicating computer program, similar to a virus, which replicates from system to system.

I N D E X

Symbols

802.11b 103, 105

A

ActiveX 21, 25, 26, 27, 68, 94, 95, 111, 112, 113, 114, 123, 124, 125, 126, 132, 133, 138, 139, 165, 166, 169, 172, 176, 177, 178, 191, 195, 206, 215, 218, 235, 236, 249, 254

Ad-Aware 171, 172, 173, 176, 193

Ad-Aware SE Personal 171, 172

Add-on 53

address 18, 19, 50, 58, 61, 72, 76, 80, 81, 82, 87, 90, 99, 103, 107, 108, 113, 136, 137, 141, 149, 166, 197, 200, 202, 220, 221, 236, 251, 253, 254, 257

advertising 24, 26, 67, 75, 202, 249

Adware 4, 22, 24, 67, 68, 69, 70, 222, 239, 244, 249

Agnitum 91, 177, 179, 180, 243

alerts 86, 88, 179, 180, 206

America Online 76

Anonymizer 220

anonymous 9, 79, 198, 220, 221

Anti-Hackers Toolkit 23

anti-malware 7, 9, 20, 23, 31, 33, 34, 49, 60, 66, 72, 73, 77, 86, 161, 162, 163, 164, 165, 167, 168, 169, 192, 214, 219, 222

Anti-spyware 3, 5, 39, 47, 55, 161, 164, 165, 214

Anti-virus 5, 42, 64, 65, 164, 165, 188, 194, 210

AOL browser 157, 158

Apple 89

application integrity 178, 179, 180

attachments 23, 31, 32, 36, 58, 61, 62, 63, 72, 73, 82, 87, 95, 180, 182, 184, 185, 201, 208, 216, 223

auto-complete 197

auto-update 55, 164

automatic cookie handling 146, 147

automatic installation 88

Avast 181, 184, 185, 186, 189

B

backdoor 28, 72, 94, 101, 104, 203, 206, 208

backup 47, 64, 176, 191, 206, 207, 211, 256

bait 187

bandwidth 17, 60, 67, 76, 102

Baseline Security Analyzer 90

behavior 14, 20, 23, 24, 25, 29, 31, 32, 37, 41, 42, 50, 57, 58, 62, 64, 67, 68, 70, 76, 77, 79, 86, 93, 111, 115, 163, 185, 193, 213, 216, 222, 233, 250, 253

benign 40, 57

best-of-breed 163, 164, 205

BHO 26, 172, 250

BitDefender 164, 165, 181, 182, 185, 189, 190, 192, 205, 210

BlackIce 91, 177, 180

blacklist 200, 201, 202

blacklisted 166

Bluetooth 99, 100

24.95   7/07

LONGWOOD PUBLIC LIBRARY
Middle Country Road
Middle Island, NY 11953
(631) 924-6400
LIBRARY HOURS

Monday-Friday	9:30 a.m. - 9:00 p.m.
Saturday	9:30 a.m. - 5:00 p.m.
Sunday (Sept-June)	1:00 p.m. - 5:00 p.m.